F 2

Riding Shotgun
Through a Hurricane

A Memoir of Addiction
and Radical Recovery

Matthew Kowalski

Radical Relief Productions

Copyright © 2013 by Matthew Kowalski

Book design by
Matthew Kowalski and Kathryn Sterbenc.
Graphic design and formatting by Daria Lacy.
Book editing by Kathryn Sterbenc.

Cover image © 2011 Matthew Kowalski,
POWER THROUGH DELEGATING,
airbrushed acrylics on paper, 23 x 35 inches.
See more Kowalski artwork at
www.MatthewKowalskiArt.com.

Library of Congress Cataloging-in-Publication Data
Kowalski, Matthew.
"Riding Shotgun Through a Hurricane:
A Memoir of Addiction and Radical Recovery"
p. cm.
ISBN 978-0-9848914-0-5

Radical Relief Publications, Oakland, Calif.

www.MatthewKowalski.com

Contents

Introduction

The Story!

Is any of it true?

It is almost impossible to accurately describe what a child remembers. Is it true that I can relate to others the eternal truths of our times as experiential remembrances to be passed on and learned from?

Disputing what is factual is not the point. The deepest and most profound truths of the human condition are more important. How we move past them is the key to a future where we do not repeat the past. Our future is bright and spotless, and by honoring the past, we move into the future with a beginner's mind – willing, honest, open, and flexible to change and not repeat what we know to be untrue.

In the truest sense, this is the only freedom worth standing up for: what it is to feel like you are in the wilderness of a military-industrial complex. What it is to hope for a promised life of belonging, feeling part of, success and abundance, not measured in material values. What it is to escape modern slavery, caste systems, the stigma of the have-nots.

This is an essential story because it gives up truths and shows honestly what can go wrong, how we can assess it, and how we can stop the historical oppression and generational dysfunction of our times. It is our duty to slowly move into the light and love of honoring each other within this timed event we have on the planet – to share and enjoy each other. If it were easy, everyone would be doing it. We do the work now that will be known in 500 years and ask not for the rewards – just for the chance.

You have all the answers within you. No matter how far you have fallen, it is more than enough to begin. Right now is the beginning of what happens next! What will you choose?

Matthew Kowalski

August 2013

* Not Their Real Names

This is a true and accurate accounting of the first
42 years of Matthew Kowalski's life, to the best of his
recollection. When a person's name is preceded by an
asterisk on first reference, the person's real name has been
changed to a pseudonym to maintain anonymity – first, to
do no harm, and second, so we don't get sued.

The Editor

– 1 –

A Ride to the Bus Station

I dug my fingernails into the dashboard of my father's car and hung on for dear life. Seat belts weren't that popular in 1972, and besides, I needed to be able to jump out of the car, in case he started swinging.

Dad stood on the accelerator and swerved all over the road, missing other cars by inches. He'd take a sudden left and I'd slide across the bench seat and slam into his shoulder; a sudden right, and I'd fly back across the seat, bouncing my head off the passenger window. The night streets of Dover, Del., were a blur through the windshield. It was already raining, and Dad was driving so fast, the windshield wipers could barely keep up. The windows were fogged up by sweat, cigarette smoke, adrenaline, and the familiar smell of alcohol.

My father had gotten as drunk that night as a human being can get. I was drunk, too – it was New Year's Eve, after all. In truth, he rarely drank in front of us kids. But he'd seen this moment coming like a slow-moving freight train for more than a year, and there was no more putting it off. He talked while he drove, as much to himself as to me. Under normal circumstances, his booming voice naturally carried, and he could silence a room in five seconds if he wanted to, without need of a microphone. On a night like this, distraught, crying and hammered, he achieved a volume that was overpowering. All I caught of this one-sided father-and-son chat was that he had tried to be a good father. I might have been able to listen better if we weren't constantly one swerve away from a fiery crash.

Then, Dad slammed on the brakes. The car screeched to a halt in front of our destination – the Greyhound Bus Station. We were both crying now. "You want to go? Well, just remember this!" he boomed. "I drove you to the station! I brought you here! I love you more than anything, but if you want to go, there is nothing I can do!"

My bag was in the back seat, waiting. I'd kept it packed for more than a year now: military sleeping bag, survival knife, mess kit, flannel shirts, sweatshirts, boots, hats, and my favorite pair of jeans, solidly armored with more than 150 patches I'd sewn on during the past two years. I probably had some homegrown weed in there, too. After a couple of practice runs, tonight I finally had what I needed: my father's permission to run away for keeps. He'd refused that permission for the past year, and in frustrated retaliation, I'd made my family's life even more hellish than it already was. Now he urged me to go, to make my move – to stop holding my family hostage with my anger and sullen behavior.

I was a week shy of 16. He was 40. Neither of us had a clue how we'd gotten to this point, but there was no turning back now. From what I would later learn, we were at least two generations, one suspected murder and about 300,000 beatings past the Point of No Return.

I got out of the car, crying as hard as he was, and grabbed my pack. Those same controlling, overpowering hands that had ruled my life with soul-numbing violence for 15 years were now, finally, setting me free. I had fought desperately to make the break from the dysfunctional, drinking, drugging, lost, violent chaos that was my family – but I could not walk away without my father's consent.

I turned my back and headed toward the station door, trying to make the last bus to New York City, the 100-pound pack bearing down on my wiry frame. I started my new year the same way as a million other runaways that night. I was capable of moving in one direction only – away.

When I was a kid, I asked my dad where I came from. His stock answer was that I started out as a candy bar in his front pocket. The real story of our nuclear-family holocaust actually began when my mother, Marie, married my father, Lester, in 1955 in Topeka, Kan. The details of their childhoods, let alone my own, are sketchy, since there wasn't much opportunity to sit around the proverbial campfire laying out the family history. My dad worked incredibly hard to support his family and was away from home for weeks at a time. Mom did the best she could to run the show in his absence, but she often worked two jobs herself in a futile attempt to keep up with her own compulsive spending. And even when they were home, it wasn't exactly a "Leave It to Beaver" situation. As much as both of them longed for a stable, fulfilling family life, neither received the tools to build one when they were kids.

The little I know of my mother's background begins and ends in Kansas. Her maternal great-grandparents were a Scottish-Irish immigrant man and a Blackfoot Indian woman, I'm told. Their daughter – my maternal grandmother – never traveled more than 50 miles from her birthplace. She was not a big fan of automobiles or airplanes. As a child, I visited her three times in Kansas and then saw her in her casket. Hers is the only funeral I have been to in my life. My mother made a videotape of a visit to her homeland, shortly before her own death in 1985. As she rode in a car, her voice softly lamented the fact that the town, Strawn, was about to be submerged forever beneath the soon-to-be-constructed dam that would eventually be named the John Redmond Reservoir. Mom got out of the car and walked down a long path, carrying the old video recorder. She explained how simple life used to be. You had nothing to provide entertainment other than your own creativity. A ride to the store for a stick of candy was a major event.

Mom came upon a few pieces of broken wood, then held the pieces up for the camera and began to cry. After a moment of silence, she said, "This right here is your heritage. This is the soil where we come from. This is the dirt from which we gained sustenance to barely live." I am proud to have come from such simple beginnings. I would never have known of this watery grave of a place if not for this videotaped message from my mother – the simple girl from the country.

The earliest tale from my father's side of the family involves World War I courage and intrigue. My great-great-grandfather was a trained guerrilla whose goal was to blow up a train in Germany. According to family legend, our guerrilla was fleeing the scene when German soldiers discovered him, shot him and chased him into the woods. He hobbled into a German town just as a funeral was taking place. When the soldiers burst onto the scene and began searching for him, the sympathetic townspeople acted fast. They shot the dead man in the coffin and then told the soldiers they were burying the wounded guerrilla who'd just staggered into town and died. My great-great-grandfather then took the dead man's name – Kowalski. We've heard many versions of his (and our) original surname, so no one is sure.

The next Kowalski generation spawned an architectural engineer who traveled to Beaver Falls, Pa., and began

making a fortune designing a steel mill. He sent all of
his money back to his wife, Helen, in Poland. A shrewd
woman, she began buying apartment houses, a hotel, and
other properties. Doubting his fidelity, she eventually came
to the United States herself, where she became pregnant
with my grandfather, William. She became extremely ill
after William's birth and stayed in the States for several
months before regaining her health and returning to Poland.

Life in Poland was not easy for William. First, he was
considered to be an American – a foreigner – because of his
birthplace, so he never felt he belonged in Poland. A bigger
problem was the growing conflict between William and
his often-absent, but strict and aristocratic father. William
was somewhat spoiled and accustomed to doing what he
pleased. When his father was home, he would try to impose
some parental authority, right down to clean-fingernail
inspections. William would have none of it. When he
was 15, he ran away from home. Eventually, William
decided to claim his American citizenship, and he bummed
around all over Europe to work his way to the States.
Once William made it to the U.S., he got a job putting on
car frames on an assembly line. He eventually met and
married my grandmother, a kind-hearted woman named
Rose Tylec. William and Rose soon had two children – a
daughter named Helen, and then, about 18 months later,
my father, Lester. Many years later, they had a third child,
my Uncle Ray, whom Dad calls a "war baby" because he
was conceived to keep William out of the war. Ray was the
apple of his big brother Les' eye.

Today, my father still uses a variety of expletives to
describe his old man, calling him an "S.O.B." and a "big
prick" and any number of other terms of non-endearment.
From the sound of it, the labels unfortunately were well-
deserved. William was an abusive alcoholic who made life
hell for his wife and children.

"We were always battling back and forth with wits to see

who could hurt the other one the most," Dad recalled. "Shit, when I was 13 years old, I thought 13 was a goddamn unlucky number. I got my ass beat every day. That's the way it went back in those days. Today, they'd put him in jail. ... Do I forgive him? Hell no, I don't forgive him. I just say that's the way it was. I look at it this way now: Who the hell am I to forgive him? He had his hard knocks, too. That's the way he understood life, and that's just the way it was. Everybody had their way of doing things."

Despite William's violent nature, Dad also describes my grandpa as a man blessed with many gifts. He spoke five languages – Polish, Yiddish, Italian, French and German – in addition to English. And he sang opera better than Mario Lanza. "He loved opera – and that son of a bitch could SING," Les said.

But he wasn't known for his musical talent. He eventually worked as a butcher, and that line of work seemed to represent his true nature more than opera. By all accounts, Grandpa was a hard-drinking, mean-spirited man who spent his life working in refrigerated places, cutting up meat with sharp objects. He was violent and hateful, notorious for having few parenting skills that did not involve his hand or belt, or worse. It seems likely that everything my father ever had to unlearn in the area of parenting skills was taught to him the hard way by this brutal patriarch.

– 2 –

From Kansas to Morocco

When my dad was 15 years old, he ran away from home and joined the Navy. Not long after that, Grandpa went after him. Dad remembers a dramatic, terrifying confrontation between his father and his superior officer, who refused to let Grandpa take his teen-age son home against his will. Grandpa left, defeated, and Dad stayed in the military – first the Navy, then the Air Force – for the next 20 years. After serving aboard the USS Allagash, young Les Kowalski was assigned to serve in Topeka. Dad enjoyed some success charming the ladies – and I do mean enjoyed. Then, along came pretty, vivacious Marie. After a quick courtship, Marie told my dad that she was pregnant, and Les did the honorable thing and married her. Some months later, on Jan. 7, 1956, there I was. Dad says they waited until I was born to name me either "Matthew" or "Dillon," both in honor of the TV show, "Gunsmoke."

I haven't heard many stories about my babyhood, but Dad recently told me that I sometimes would get so angry, I would hold my breath until I turned blue. This would scare the hell out my parents. Finally, they took me to the doctor, who advised them to plunge me into a tub of ice-cold water the next time I turned myself blue. The idea was I would jolt from the shock and be forced to inhale. Knowing my dad's belief in the character-building potential of water sports, I'm sure I got my nostrils cleaned out a few times this way.

A year after I was born, along came my brother, Mark, and a year after that, my sister Kathryn, whom we called Kat. I have no memories of life without them. In his baby years, my brother repeated the words "truck" and camel" so endlessly that he came to be called Mark "Camel Truck" Kowalski. My own first memories are simple and brief. I remember eating ice cream in the back seat of a slow-moving car until the door swung open and I fell out. I remember family gatherings in the trailer park where we lived, with robust partying by the elders and hot dogs and Coca-Cola for the kids under roll-out sunshades. As evening approached, it felt magical and mystical to stay up so late and witness all the excitement.

Before they knew it, my folks had three toddlers under age 4 – a challenge for the best-prepared parents. At this age, I remember having some responsibility as Big Brother and baby-sitter. The first time I got in trouble for baby-sitting negligence was when I allowed Mark and Kat to eat cigarette butts and gum wads off the pavement. Since I was never punished for allowing them to eat dried dog stool, I concluded that this must be OK.

During another 4-year-old baby-sitting episode, we decided we wanted the cookies on the top shelf of the kitchen counter. I got myself up on the counter all right, but I knocked down the big container of flour on the way. Flour went all over the floor. If that wasn't bad enough, someone decided it was the perfect time to break out our family collection of 8-millimeter movies of Mickey Mouse and his cartoon pals. Sad to say, within a few hours, we'd mixed soda with the flour, and the movies were unrolled the entire length of the trailer and "breaded" in the goo on the floor. Here and there, puddles of water showed our futile efforts to clean up the mess. Eventually, our folks got home, and my dad gave me the beating by which all future beatings would be measured.

Another time, the frigid Topeka winter inspired me to leave my cold bed, take my pillow and head for the warmest place I knew – the front grate of the furnace. I leaned my pillow there and enjoyed the nice, toasty warmth until someone snatched the burning, smoking pillow from under my unsuspecting head and beat it on the furnace to put the fire out. This is where adults and kids remember moments differently: My parents probably remember with horror the time their family almost burned to death. I, on the other hand, remember my little-boy fascination as sparks flew through the air like fireworks.

A visit to our cousins' Kansas farm had its own disfigurement thrills and opportunities. My sister got her arm caught in the wringer of an old Maytag and just narrowly missed having her arm pulled through the machine. Then, Kat and I had an encounter with an archaic contraption used to shuck hard, dried corn off the cob. I put in a cob, Kat turned the handle, and in went my finger into the rasping gears. I screamed a scream that seemed to last for hours. When we got my hand loose, the top segment of my third finger was dangling, and blood flowed freely. In the country, doctors are hard to find, and even a veterinarian comes at a premium. The doctor who came to treat me was a horse doctor with needles the size of pencils. Admitting that he'd never sewn something this small before, he pushed a giant needle meant for the hide of horses into my tiny finger and sewed me up. The tools he used were bigger than my finger or its wound! I lost feeling in this finger for many years, and only through diligent guitar-playing, drumming and finger exercises was I able to create a sensitive tip again.

These are my memories of my first four years on Planet Kansas. And then one day, our world expanded exponentially. It was time to get ready to follow Dad to his new assignment at Ben Guerir Air Base in Morocco. Off we went to the doctor's. This preparation involved getting a series of painful immunizations against the diseases that awaited us. My overly confident young doctor boasted that he was the "fastest shot in the West" and gave me the shots in rapid succession. Carried away, he got one of the needles stuck in the bone of my arm. He needed an assistant and a pair of pliers to finally pull the needle out. But that momentary pain soon faded, replaced with the bright, blinding sun and vast, expansive desert of Africa.

We lived on the edge of the desert. Squinting is what I recall of the daily blast of the sun's powerful rays. The heat was pervasive. You could see the Atlas Mountains 250 miles away, snow on their peaks. The adults would often talk about this snow thing, whatever it was, and say how they wished they were there right now.

I wanted to look just like the cool old caravan desert wanderers. Their skin was all wrinkly from the sun, and it had a leathery appearance. I remember the smell of people from the desert. They had no running water, and it rained for only a few short months of the year. I remember seeing them look at each other on the bus, and the musky fragrances were their signatures. It was a very palatable perfume that took on its own persona. It was a sort of calling card. You could smell the pheromones. The men known as "yard boys" wore four or five changes of clothing. It insulated them from the sun, and they always had a clean set of clothes for the next day under the set they were wearing.

I could not just sit inside all day. I was young, and there was a whole world out there. I remember having a Model T out in front of our house and trying to turn the crank. I was told by the adults that it would rip my arm off if it caught a revolution.

I'm not sure, but I believe my mom started her civil-service career with the government at this time, because we had a housemaid named Hadeesha. This woman spoke in a broken language I could not fathom. The communications we agreed on were a frown on her face for "no" and a smile for "yes," "OK" or "please do this!" I believe this woman cared for and loved us as her own. I have often felt this loving kindness from strangers who had no reason to be so kind; from my relationship with this woman, I was able to access a primal trust with people throughout my life.

Hadeesha would bring oranges in her scarf and tell us of her great adventure of stealing the king's fruit that lined the boulevards. She said you could lose your hands for taking this special fruit. This made the oranges taste better than anything I could remember. Pomegranates were another strange treat. I remember eating them one seed pouch by one as they squirted into my little mouth, then summarily spitting the seeds out onto the street. Our neighborhood was safe and welcoming. I remember walking around the blocks and experiencing the sights and smells of life in the military housing project.

Sooner or later, though, the brutality of our family dynamic had to rear its violent head. There was a kid with a brand-new bike that disappeared. The whole neighborhood was looking for it – everybody. As I watched this spectacle unfold, the fact that I had hidden the bike under my own bed didn't seem to bother me in the least. I can't remember exactly how this came to pass, but the consequences were as inevitable as a fist in my face.

Somehow, my dad looked under my bed and found the missing bicycle. He decided my punishment must be a public beating in front of all the neighbors. With one of my little arms held firmly above my head and my toes just barely touching the ground, I swayed back and forth like a rag doll as the blows took their toll on my innocence.

On some level, I understood even then that this flogging was less about teaching me the evils of theft than it was my punishment for humiliating my father. I wondered, would I be marked as a branded child from this moment? If we went this far with a beating in public, were there any limits on brutality in private? It all starts to make sense now – the absence of any memories of effective interaction with my parents. My mom was working, and my dad was flying around in airplanes. We kids were at home with a housemaid who spoke only a little broken English, and yet we managed to communicate with her better than we ever could with our folks.

In spite of the violent interludes, I have special memories of our life in Morocco. The days we visited the markets were always special. The smells of perfumes and incense – frankincense, myrrh, sandalwood – all graced the boulevards and bazaars. When we would go to the markets, we did learn of the brutal forms of justice exacted on those caught committing crimes. The mark on thieves was brutal – a finger cut off for the first crime, then another finger for the next crime, ending up with a whole hand lost for continuing these behaviors. Scar tissue was rampant in the crowded city plazas. Ears were cut off for hearing things that you were not privy to. Eyes were gouged out for seeing things. Tongues were cut out for saying things. I remember the carnage amongst the snake charmers with their flutes and baskets, the hawkers and sellers carrying their trade and stock under their robes with watches rolled all the way up their wrists. A man who stole a bicycle carried the bike around his shoulders with a sign that said he was a thief; this was his public humiliation in the marketplace. My dad made sure I saw and understood this.

Around this time, I recall the modest beginnings of my abiding love affair with alcohol. I had a toothache. In an effort to soothe my helpless crying, my dad gave me a shot of whiskey and made me hold it for a minute, then swallow. I tried to get out of this, but my dad was persuasive. Thus it was that alcohol "cured" the first of ohhhh so many ills.

Sometimes, our family would jump in the car and head like nomads into the unknown. You could drive for hundreds of miles in the desert without hitting a tree. I remember a story of a family with a drunken driver who hit a tree in the desert and killed the whole family. For some reason, we liked the idea that you couldn't find anything to hit in the vast expanse of flat, hot desert.

At any village we would drive through, throngs of kids would run up to the car and beg for candy and cigarettes. These were kids my age. I just couldn't understand how they were so motivated to run up to the car. Later, I recognized my place of privilege, and as I grew older in the United States, I understood better the ravages of poverty.

Once, we drove 150 miles to our yard boy's place out in the desert. It was a small village of eight or nine mud-brick huts out in the middle of nowhere. While the parental units made social chit-chat, some of us kids went off and started playing together. Kids are so easily contented; they can be happy with some sticks and a pile of dirt or dung, and we had plenty of both. I remember the dung beetles rolling big clumps to their hideaways.

My sister Kat and one of the little girls were playing, and my sister held out her hand and gave the girl her little red purse. For some reason, this exchange has followed me throughout my life. The purse was plastic and shining red in the evening sun of the colorless desert. What happened next was just as moving. The little girl went to show her mother and brought back three wonderful, brownish eggs laid by their hen. When my sister showed my mother, we kids were the stars of the show. Somehow, we had done something admirable. Parents all around were smiling and their eyes were twinkling about some act of unity that bonded us all together for that moment. Such simple acts of kindness have saved me innumerable times throughout my life.

As the evening sun waned, my brother Mark and I were getting crabby and anxious, so the adults gave us a pull on the hookah pipe. I don't know what kind of wacky weed was in that thing, but they put me between the humps on the back of a dromedary camel, and I was in a dream world going in circles around the well, as dusky redness turned to black.

– 3 –

My African Homeland

Life at home was marked by long, hot days of relentless sun. Often at the dinner table, my dad would tell us that Tinkerbell was flying around the room, and if we didn't eat our dinner we would have to go where the lost children went. Of course, that didn't work real well, but his firm hands succeeded where fairy tales failed. A peaceful meal would suddenly erupt in horrid Brussels-sprouts pandemonium, and then to bed without dinner was the order of the day.

One day, our dad placed two pairs of boxing gloves on the outdoor barbecue in the yard. In his view, it was a method to teach us courage and boxing skills at the same time. To us, they looked ominous. We put on the soft red and blue gloves and waited to see what came next. My dad encouraged us to spar with each other, so like dancing mannequins, we pirouetted and were puppeted around by the master puppeteer. Then, we were told to hit each other. Suddenly the fun drained out of this exercise, and it became

a competitive, mean-spirited joust. I believe that is one of
the first times my dad butted our heads together to make us
fight. If we didn't, we had to answer to his hands.

Trying to please Dad, we started hitting each other. We
both landed some minor blows. I think my dad was rooting
for Mark, and he was starting to feed off of my dad's
inspiration. Mark was on fire and suddenly landed a blow.
I landed on my back and was impaled on a pear cactus.
These barbed denizens of the desert pack a powerful prick
that is as hard as hell to remove. That ended Round One.
My mom attended to my back for a long time, trying to get
the needles out as they surfaced on my back during the next
few weeks.

During rainy season, the desert turns into mud and then
into life. The giant dirt clods and the cracked earth all meet
to create an oasis environment. Everything tries to grow
and blossom in the short time it's given. The rain rolls
through thunder, and lightning lights up the sky, creating a
show that can be seen from far away. I remember walking
through the new growth that appeared out of nowhere.
Plants grew as tall as I was, blooming and blossoming right
into my nose. Every heavenly fragrance you can imagine
was calling my nostrils to ignite with appreciation. To me,
this was bliss.

By now, I had been shown the long walk to kindergarten.
It was a labyrinth to remember. I remember crying and
crying the first times my mom took me to this strange
place. I wanted no part of it. I wasn't having it – no way!
Being told to play, to stop playing, to take a nap, to snack –
what kind of prison camp was this? Being taught the value
of behaviors, grades, reward pathways, competition and
punishment for not fitting in, or doing what this stranger
told me – this was hard work!

Moments I did like were when the Campbell's soup we
often had for lunch would be heated up. Ooh, the smells –
mmm, mmm, good! I also got accustomed to having to stop

moving my little body and take a nap in the hot afternoon.
I don't believe air conditioning had made it to Morocco
yet. Walking home, you could see all the African women
carrying baskets on their heads containing the food and
clothing they had gathered for their employers. I would try
to carry things on my head, but usually with no luck.

A typical day around the house started with checking
your clothes and shoes for spiders or scorpions. Then I
would eat toast with jelly and go out to see what the big
kids were doing – or what they were going to make me do.

A favorite event I remember happening 10 or 11 times
were rock fights. Living out in the desert, it got a bit
uncivilized at times. It was a brutal environment. The older
kids taught us this mode of battle. This is a country where
people were regularly stoned to death. Hey, what harm
could six or seven boys throwing big rocks at each others'
heads really do??

We would pick three or four vantage points, usually
behind the trash areas of our houses, and start lobbing
rocks at each other. We tried dirt clods, but they just didn't
have the bang of a rock. In the frenetic rush to find a rock,
dodge incoming ones, and not get stung by a scorpion
under or around the rocks, the damaging moments would
occur sometimes 10 minutes into the fray. Suddenly, a rock
would hit its target. Oh, just a body shot, he can take it,
don't be a crybaby now! Then the furious malaise would
begin in earnest, and real dedication was applied to the
inevitable laws of physics. Smack! A scream, bloodcurdling
crying, and everybody runs as a few mothers come out to
see what's up. As blood ran down someone's face near the
eyes, all fun drained out of the game. All seemed to calm
down for a few weeks until we forgot the dangers and pain
incurred, or until the older boys coerced us with dares.

We shared the desert with all sorts of insects. Praying
mantises would fly into the house. We heard about locusts,
although I'm not sure if we witnessed that 17-year

phenomenon. We also had a parakeet that had the run of the house. I loved that bird.

Speaking of birds, the older boys would have us set up a box and put food under the trap with a stick and string. This was very engaging, hard work and tricky for me in particular. Like fishing, you had to be patient and wait for the right moment to pull the string, or in a flash the birds flew off and were wary of our little game. After what seemed like an eternity, we would catch a bird. Then the older boys came running up with their high-tech, Dick Tracy tools. These included a wristwatch and a pocketknife. With calculated precision, one of the older boys would make us all get close for the spectacle that was about to begin. One boy would hold the bird, another boy would get the wristwatch ready, and a third boy with the knife would make a careful incision once the second hand reached 12.

The frightened timidity of the bird gained momentum as the chest was carved open and the ribs were spread to reveal the beating heart. It beat so fast. We would all get real close to see this amazing, moving red mass. One boy would count off the seconds: One minute fifty-five, one minute fifty-six. Then, the heart grew still. Aah! Didn't even make two minutes, the big boys would lament.

Stunned in silent reverence and abject fear, the younger kids processed this torture. I thought it would be like the lizards, where you break off a piece of their tail and they just grow a new one and go about their business. But this bird was killed and irreverently left on the ground. For the next couple of days, I would look down at the ground and remember as I walked by. The beating heart of this living thing was no more.

Scorpions were another story. They were everywhere, the sentinels of the desert, awaiting every move made by a careless person, it seemed. I've always liked the cool look of a scorpion, streamlined and deadly. My father taught us how to respect and deal with them without losing our cool.

They came in red, orange and black. You had to check your
bedding and clothing before bed and when you got up to
get dressed, just in case. We also had horny-toed lizards
and chameleons that would change to the color of whatever
they were sitting on. I really enjoyed playing with them,
as they were friendly and harmless and provided hours of
pleasure. I remember putting them on plaid and polka-dot
materials to see if they could reproduce that look with their
bodies.

Occasionally, my adventurous spirit took me far from
home. Once, a blue military bus stopped near me, so I just
got on, as if I knew where I was going. The driver asked
me if I knew what I was doing and where I was going. "Of
course I do," I said – yes, wouldn't any 5-year-old? He
drove the bus around the base. Then, he went off into the
surrounding desert area to the outer fringes of the civilized
area.

"Should I let you out here?" he said. I started getting
real honest, real fast, in frantic gibberish mixed with tears.
He laughed, calmed me down and sat me in the important
seat right by him. We had a great talk about anything I
wanted as we drove around the base. Finally he found an
area I recognized, and I went home. I don't think anyone
would have believed the stories of my adventures. But
since I never said anything for fear that I would get beaten,
I never found out.

One day, a yard boy rode by on his bicycle, and I called
him a new word I had just been taught by the older boys –
"zimmebuftizzla." He seemed displeased, to say the least.
The yard boy kicked me in the ass until I was running
scared and crying for my life. Only later was I able to find
out what it really meant. Thirty years later, I walked into
a corner store in San Francisco complaining about which
war I was supporting. In drunken anger, I quipped to the
store owner, "Iran, Iraq, and Ayatollah twice! Which war
am I supporting? And why do you keep raising the prices of

these beers? Zimmebuftizzla!"

The man backed away in alarm. "Ssh, sssh! The women, the children!" Then he asked slyly, "You like young boys?"

"Why, what does it mean?" I replied. Having sold to me at this store a hundred times, he knew me well, leaned close and confided, "My dick up your ass." We both laughed.

In the villages that were easily accessible from our base, meat hung out in the sun, flies all over it, dripping with blood after just being slaughtered. If you weren't careful, you would get rained on with redness. Some people favored a treat that I didn't care much for – "donkey ass doughnuts," they were called. The fat would drip from the slaughtered donkey's ass, and they would mix the fat with flour and make doughnuts out of it. They were a little rich for me.

Watching people make bricks out of straw and dirt was fascinating for a kid who liked to play in the mud. They would take milk cartons that were endlessly available from the air base and form bricks by the hundreds. They would dry them in the sun and then build traditional mud huts.

One day, we headed out toward the Atlas Mountains. My parents were excited at this prospect – some kind of cool experience they were after. We drove and drove, stopping now and then to pee in the desert, dozing off in the incredible heat and dust of the roads. The coolness was pervasive as we approached the hills, driving, stopping, the kids running up for candy, money or cigarettes. This scene played itself out over and over again through many mountain communities. We crept up the mountains on thin, one-lane roads that were precariously perched on what looked like future rockslide materials. We looked over the edge for what seemed like hours as we went up and up. I do not remember if we stayed anywhere for the night. I just remember my mom's fear that these roads were not safe.

On these forages into the unknown, my dad would always try to find the local leader or man of importance of

the area and impress on him how great it would be for them
to have dinner with these Americans. Imagine a dressed
table with all the Moroccan brasses and teapots. People
poured tea from 3 feet above and did not miss your cup.
Who knows what kind of meats and vegetables we were
eating or what the older folks were drinking. I believe my
father always brought some kind of tax-free liquors to
enhance the evening's revelry.

Once, the man of importance gave us firecrackers. We
exploded them without parental supervision all through the
dark alleys in the twilight, scaring ourselves, all the animals
and any innocent bystanders. We must have had an older
kid with us, because I still have all my fingers.

Around Thanksgiving, I remember huge birds being
corralled in a yard with families participating in this festive
occasion. I thought they were emus, but I now realize they
were turkeys – formidable-looking to a young child. A
few of us kids were in the yard when the adults, without
pretense, began to cut the heads off of these enormous
birds. Suddenly, pandemonium – headless birds as tall as
we were, with blood spurting everywhere, were running in
all directions. They plowed into us indiscriminately until
we ran for our parents in earnest.

One of my last and favorite memories of Morocco was
Christmastime. On Christmas Eve, my dad sent us to bed
early. He said St. Nick would be there soon. It was still
early, and we kids were not sleepy. He put on his best
loving face and pointed out the window to the North Star. It
was an unmistakably bright star – maybe the same star that
led the three wise men to the baby Jesus! Anyway, we were
definitely not sleepy. I don't know how he did it, but later
we discovered my dad built a whole train track on a piece
of plywood without us kids knowing.

Next thing we knew, we heard a loud, brash man come
in. Somehow, we were in the living room face to face with
Santa, the man himself. There before us was a large man

in a big red suit. "Ho ho ho, merry Christmas!" he chimed. Our Santa Claus was a jolly and happy black man, and we adored him. He wore Ray-Bans, smoked a cigar, ate cookies and drank a shot of whiskey with my dad. This was a true moment of joy. We gladly got on his lap, and he was more than accommodating. I loved Santa Claus. My brother and sister were mesmerized as well.

To my sad surprise, when we returned to the United States, I discovered some white imposter had taken the place of my beloved black Santa, and I was traumatized. Another important person I revered was Jesus. In Africa, he was a dark-skinned man of the desert. When we moved to America, he, too, was replaced by a white-skinned, blue-eyed imposter. Imagine my disappointment and confusion.

After World War II, the United States had air bases all over the world to ensure peace, democracy and crushing domination. For hundreds of years, the Moroccans had endured incursions through their country from every European nation to snatch up the wealth of Africa. The Moroccans were the first of all the peoples to say to the U.S., "Thank you very much for the protection; now, please leave us in peace." Abandon a whole air base? This was no easy task. We had an air base full of every form of protection imaginable to fight the communist terror. How could we leave this behind?

It would have cost too much to move it, and the spare parts and extra airplanes were modern technology that we would not leave behind. So our kindergarten class was allowed to watch fire drills that were quite a spectacle. Awestruck, we got to see old jets and C-131s being burned up. Even from a distance, the flames and explosions were mesmerizing.

This drew my African experience to an end.

– 4 –

Flight to Michigan

Boarding a jet amid the sweet smell of desert blossoms in the late afternoon, little did I know we were leaving for good. As we left Morocco, the water was an emerald green I will never forget. It glistened in the evening sun, taking up the whole horizon. Not yet old enough to know to be sad or wistful, I was leaving my homeland, where I had come to consider myself a light-skinned black person. This self-perception has followed me throughout my life.

We headed out on our 15-hour ride to Bermuda; from there, our destination was Michigan. The compelling thing I remember about that flight was that 10 or 11 hours into it, everyone passed out and was sleeping hard. I was transfixed and hypnotized by the atmosphere and clouds rolling over the wings of the plane. I was awake and very alive. I watched the wings, and I noticed a small fire. It grew, covering the engine behind the prop.

I jiggled my mom to wake up; no response. I desperately tried to wake someone up. This was like the "Outer Limits" episode in which William Shatner sees a little devilish gnome on his plane's engine, starting it on fire. Well, there was no gnome on this engine, but it was certainly on fire. I could almost reach out and touch it. I started screaming, and people woke up and wondered what this histrionic kid was babbling about. I was pointing and crying, and no one saw the disaster I was talking about. It had gone out, the fire vanquished. The smell of sweat and fear covered my body. No one believed me. I am not one to make up stories; I often was beaten senseless to ensure I was telling my father the truth.

My mom cradled me under her arm and fast went back to sleep, as did the rest of the passengers. I saw the fire again and screamed. This time I was put down, firmly and sternly cradled in a suffocating, vice-like grip. After all, I was keeping everyone awake. With my head forcibly turned away from the engine, I had to deal with whatever terror I imagined as a 6-year old. I eventually dozed off, and then I awoke to the startled panic of passengers looking out and seeing the engine on fire. Did I get the credit? Oh, no! Not me! Now who had the panic-stricken pandemonium?

Transfixed by the collective terror, with morning sun blindingly blazing through the windows, I heard someone say we were close to Bermuda. Did I imagine this hysteria and near-death experience? The engine kept flaming on and flaming off. Ahh, sweet mother of Jesus. Touchdown. We were stranded in Bermuda for a few days with engine trouble – imagine that!

We spent those stranded days mostly around a hotel pool. Bermuda lives in my memory as the smells of cigars and pool chlorine. My dad was king around a pool. One-and-a-half somersaults, gainers, back flips, cannonballs, preachermans – he was Aqua-Man. Naturally, he wanted his kids to be part-fish also. So the Flying Kowalskis would perform daring tricks for the crowd. If we didn't quite understand the trick, my dad would help. Holding me by my 6-year old ankles from the high dive, looking down 12 feet at what looked like eternity, he would say to me, "Don't move and hold your breath, and you won't get hurt."

It sounds easy. I guess anyone not scared out of his or her mind could easily do it. There was one small problem, though. As I was free-falling, I found I had plenty of time to scream my head off in terror. "AAAAAHHHHHHHH! AAAAAHHH! AAAAAHHHH! (SPLOOSH)"

The first four or five times that I forgot to hold my diving form, my dad was so obliging that he would repeat the trick until I got it. How convenient! Underwater for what seemed like forever, I arose coughing and choking to hear everyone ooh-ing and aah-ing; then, raucous applause. After that, my brother and sister performed smaller feats off the lower board. More applause. People were buying my dad drinks. We were instant celebrities through terrorist acts. This hardwired into my neural pathways the thrill-seeking, death-defying behaviors that followed me through my youth and into my adult life.

Eventually, a plane carried us away from this paradise and laid us down in an entirely different region of the planet: Kincheloe Air Force Base, in the Upper Peninsula of Michigan. It would be hard to find a climate more directly opposite from Morocco in the continental U.S. This northern land had birch trees and roadways lined with what seemed like sand. We moved into some kind of trailer park to await military housing. I have only one memory of that trailer, and it is my first real memory of Michigan.

Our first night there was extremely cold. Having just left the desert, this cold was unreal and frightening. A storm raged around us all night, with the wind screaming and blowing snow into drifts. A white substance filled the air. I was used to blackout sandstorms with bolts of lightning, but this was unnerving. It was quiet and eerie. The snow did not seem to stop. It covered the ground, and it was cold.

These were all things I was not happy with.

The next morning, we could see out of only one side of the trailer. The other side – the one with the door – was blocked. Now we were scared. This white stuff had covered the door – we're marooned! Being a wild man of steely strength, my dad pushed and pushed, bending the little trailer door until it seemed like it would break. He managed to use the door to make a 1½-foot gap in the snow. Exhausted and not wanting to break the door, my dad dressed me up and told me I was going to crawl upward from the top of the doorframe and tell him how high the drift was.

Covered from head to toe with too much clothing – hats and gloves, earmuffs and mufflers – I really missed the simple life of the desert with short pants and flip-flops. This boy of the desert was kicking, screaming, stammering and anything else I could do to prevent him from pushing me out into this alien white world that was cold and inhospitable. After two or three attempts at pushing my face and body into the frozen whiteness, I realized it was time to scratch, claw, cry and crawl my way upward into the abyss. As with all things in life, the fear and procrastination were far more debilitating than the actual feat. I broke into a glorious, white world lit with sunlight. Following my dad's instructions, I helped him get the door open. My "Welcome to Michigan" hazing party was complete.

Before too long, we moved into military housing. Here, my daily life consisted mostly of playing ball in the grassy areas around the buildings. The seagulls were almost as big as we were. They would curiously look and fly dangerously close to us little kids, all alone out in the field. Their 3½ - to 4-foot wingspans were massive. One of the older kids enlightened us with an urban legend that these birds were not chasing the balls in the air but were after an afternoon snack. They enjoyed pecking out children's eyes and then eating us when we could not see where we were going. This took throwing the ball to new dimensions. We knew Alfred Hitchcock's terror of birds before it was on celluloid.

I don't know if we had a television by then. 1963 was the age of Sputnik and Kennedy and "Camelot," whatever that meant. These were just a few of the words I heard but could not define. I remember once sitting on a trashcan, as all the little kids were made to do by the older kids, and being forced to learn even more words I did not understand. It was a strange language that caused great joy and laughter among the older kids, who said we were doing wonderfully with our linguistic studies. They encouraged us to use this new language right away, every day, everywhere we went.

These lessons fatefully coincided with a visit from my paternal grandfather – William the butcher. He and my dad got into a time-honored tradition of disrespecting each other and fighting about something. Inevitably, their visit erupted with the sounds of screaming, yelling, fists flying, and the cops being called. My family life had finally been revealed to the community. What I thought happened to all families was looked at with disdain and goose-necking, as fresh fodder for the neighbors' gossip.

During this tense summit, I found myself sitting in the middle of a long moment of awkward silence. So I tried to break the ice with the incredible new language I had laboriously learned. To my great dismay, it was not received with gratitude the way the older kids had forecast. Was I mispronouncing the word? With all the pent-up rage of the afternoon, my father silenced me in a way that was powerful and familiar. I now realized that this was a secret language that adults used freely and kids said sacredly and secretly.

One day in November, I remember looking through the Sears Christmas catalog and marking about a hundred toys I could not live without. I was already experiencing the grief of unrequited toys. My mom suddenly showed a look of horror. Crying, she turned on the TV or radio. Somebody had been shot and killed. All afternoon we spent trying to comfort my mother. She was sobbing uncontrollably. First, my little sister started crying with my mom; then, my brother and I chimed in without losing a beat.

All afternoon, listening to the same transmission over and over again, unfalteringly we bonded with our mom and learned how to cry and grieve for another person – not just from pain or failing to get our immediate-gratification needs met. Some great man had died. That didn't bother us in the least, but our mother weeping – that was a different story.

As the weeks progressed, our mom educated us about John F. Kennedy and how wonderful he was. When I got older, I saw compelling evidence that a lot of women enjoyed his good looks, and he was not too shabby as a politician, either. My mom was a poet, although we did not know the extent of it or appreciate the value of how she made sense out of the world she perceived until much later. Her poem about JFK was sent to the White House and published, I believe, in the Washington Post. The Post also published poems she wrote about Martin Luther King Jr. and Bobby Kennedy. It seems the good died young. This was my mom's quiet claim to fame.

We were a young family in the Baby Boom generation. It was the age of new music and sock hops, and Disney had really started to take off with "Bambi" and "The Sword in the Stone." Our baby-sitter worked nights at the theater, and I saw that movie more than once. It inspired me to start fantasizing and assigning magical properties to others. I fell in love with that baby-sitter, who inspired my very first poem: "Roses are red, violets are blue, only thing is I love you." This early puppy love eventually would morph into the idea that I needed girls and women to fix my problems … which would lead seamlessly to the era of free love in the '60s, and my sex and love addiction.

Our parents, like all hip and cool grownups, hosted

dances to enjoy and embrace the new music. We kids were told to go to bed while they chopped it up and partied. During one Christmas party, I remember staying over at a young man's housing unit. A friend and I were playing tent in the bedroom when the door opened. We were supposed to be asleep, so we quickly got under the bed, lying dead still in fear for our young lives for staying up and playing this late at night. We heard two quiet voices in the room with us and tried to breathe shallowly.

There was a famous song called, "I Saw Mommy Kissing Santa Claus." Well, what we experienced was a lot more than that. They were very drunk, and it was late. The bed started shaking, and their breathing got heavy. My friend and I were puzzled – what the heck was going on? We thought maybe they were trying to scare us. The event was quick, furious and suddenly over. The musty smell of adults permeated the air, and we had been privy for the first time to the strange goings-on of the secret, closed society of grownups. Very strange, the idea of shaking a bed and breathing heavy. I mean, what's the point? I later found out.

Winter in Michigan seemed to be available for a long time. My dad would drive on country roads in the hills and drag me on a snow disc tied with a rope behind the car. I was far enough behind for him to see if I was still there. Whenever the disc slid off the hill, Dad would stop the car and drag me back up again. What a blast. My whole life, I would love real-life thrill rides and the smell of car exhaust.

Duke's Lake was another winter wonderland. In the summer, it was a swimming hole. But in winter, I remember with great adoration seeing this vast expanse of water all hard and iced over. It was hard to believe that we would not fall in after sliding down the hill on our sleds. One day, Dad took the family for a drive up to the point where all the tobogganers launched to slide down the hill. It was a long, sloping hill that really got you up to speed, and then you rolled out onto the edge of the lake. It was getting dark, and all the tobogganers were gone. We wondered what we were still doing there. We looked through the car windows down the hill, the lake stretched before us, and enjoyed the end of a really fun day. My mom and dad were in front and we three kids looked over their shoulders for the view.

Suddenly, without a word, my dad rolled the car down the hill. We were off. The car went barreling down the hill, picking up speed and bouncing on all the rough surfaces under the snow, with the lake waiting below us. Everyone but my dad was screaming his or her lungs out in fear. We kids all wet our pants, bouncing around in the back. I'm not even sure if seat belts were around then. We slid down onto the glassy surface of the lake and finally slowed down.

Loaded with adrenaline, my dad decided to spin the car on the ice, and we did 15 or 20 quick rotations at unbelievable speeds. In shock, drained, wet, and delirious with fear, our family unit was stunned. My father, proud of his work, drove the car to the boat ramp and off the lake.

– 5 –

Dover Air Force Base

When I was 7, we moved again. We were military brats, and we would move almost annually throughout my childhood. This time, it was Dover Air Force Base in Delaware. We moved into an actual house off-base, which was a departure from our usual airbase housekeeping. For the first time, I had a back yard that went straight into the woods, with a river about two football fields away. What a place for a young person to have adventures.

The woods had a smell of the reclamation of nature's doing. There were fungi, mushrooms, molds, and mosses all over the place. Throngs of mosquitoes, flies, gnats, hornets, and bees flew through the air, as well as birds of every color. My favorite then was the red-breasted robin. The small squirrels, muskrats and snakes were great companions for the scary noises. All manner of deciduous trees were there; I remember sassafras the best because we made tea out of it when we kids went camping. Oaks, maples, and other giants provided great climbing adventures.

This was the time of Walt Disney's "Bambi," "Beauty and the Beast" and "Cinderella." Mark and I would stage sword-stick fights to determine who would get Cinderella. We would really swing those sticks: me to win the prize, and him to save his life. This began my sadly competitive style of living, when I really lost all hope or memory of traditional family ideals. It was a selfish place to live, looking to others to cater to my needs. More and more, my family became nothing more than the people from whom I would demand unreasonable things; then I would feel abandoned when my needs weren't met and turn to others, desperate for validation.

By now, my father had worked his way up to the level of chief engineer, flying for weeks at a time on all kinds of planes. He had a map with pins stuck into every country he had the pleasure to see. His pins circumnavigated the globe. He would often bring home strange and foreign objects, clothes, games, currency, and adventure stories. He also brought back the latest technological gadgets from Japan or West Germany, our major enemies from World War II.

With my father traveling and my mother now working in the Civil Service, we kids were often left with baby-sitters. After witnessing seven years of the troubled sexual dynamics between my mom and dad and other people around us, I already knew how to sexualize my feelings or seek attention through inappropriate behavior. One scheme I often played on my baby-sitters was to pretend the zipper was broken on my pants and ask them to fix it. These moments were confusing, but gratifying in a way that fed my increasingly insatiable hunger for the opposite sex. Already I was well-versed in the various sexual checkposts of manhood. And already, I would spend hours figuring out how I was going to reach those milestones myself – quite an undertaking for a second-grader!

My father, to his credit, could and still can fix anything.

You name it – if it broken, he could take it apart, look inside, and manipulate it until the object came back to life. Sometimes he even had spare parts left over – who needs these anyway! Often I was his indentured apprentice, willing or not. I would try to sit still and follow his instructions, while every fiber of my little body twitched to do something else and my three-minute attention span stretched to the limit. He would rebuild an entire engine, then ask me to repeat exactly what the parts were and describe each procedure – all while handing him tools that all had specific names.

During one of these lessons, I was distracted by some little girls nearby and wanted badly to go play. Dad cracked me in the head with a crescent wrench. "Do you want to be able to have a car and fix it, or do you want to waste your time and play with the girls?" he barked. The girls were my choice, and another wrench-shaped knot on my head was his reply.

At this time, my dad seemed to have a large vocabulary of 10 to 20 curse words that he could use to elaborate upon any situation with great gusto. He could discuss history, mathematics – even thoughts on religion and faith were expressed with off-color emphasis. If he got angry or frustrated, he used these words like swords to verbally eviscerate those on the receiving end of his wrath. And when he was expressing great affection and love, these verbal exclamations could not be left out. All his passion, happy or rageful, was expressed with these words. The powerful words I learned were: shit, goddamn, bitch, cocksucker, motherfucker, pussy, son of a bitch, bastard, fucking and dick. Hands were referred to with reverence as "dick skinners."

We lived near apple orchards and frequently went on gathering trips to get all different varieties of apples. We would find crates, climb trees and gather our edible treasure. Once, Mark climbed a tree while I stayed on the ground, and he dropped a crate on my head. This is typical of the violent pattern of abuse that by then was well-established between my brother, sister and me. Beyond the orchards lay the vast expanse of an industrial park that housed the nuts and bolts of the Department of Motor Vehicles. This held every kind of traffic light, sign and gadget the DMV needed to use along the roadways. We found the guts of a stop light one day, and Kat helped me attempt to drag, slide and carry this industrial booty home. It was way too heavy, so we finally abandoned it in the orchard.

Sometimes, the apple farmers would spray their trees with insecticide. The machines would move through the orchards, spraying the poisonous white mist on everything, including me. I enjoyed the aroma of this process as much as I loved smelling the exhaust from the tailpipe of my dad's car when he took me sled-skiing. How I still have working lungs, I'll never know.

Rehoboth Beach was renowned as the summer capital of the Washington, D.C., area. Our family would join countless other families and cram into a special part of the beach that had been used to guard the coastline during World War II. Tall, round lighthouses still stood there like sentinels. This beach was the scene of one my fondest and, simultaneously, most painful childhood memories. We were near a bonfire on the beach, and I accidentally stepped in it. As I screamed and panicked from the pain of the third-degree burn forming on my tender foot, my father picked me up and carried me down the beach. Somehow, my terror and pain brought out the best of his parenting skills this time. He carried me to a desolate part of the beach which was covered for about an eighth of a mile with tide pools. The wonder of this place, and the joy of receiving my father's loving, compassionate attention, made me forget all about my burned foot.

I saw hermit crabs living in shells, and I held them in

my hand. Eventually, they would come out and walk on my fingers. I saw and held kiwi's conch shells, shell gas shells and more crabs. This moment inspired my intense, lifelong appreciation of nature and led me to collect many curious, diverse objects through the years.

After this calming, spellbound moment in the tide pools, Dad lowered me down into the warm saltwater. As I screamed from the renewed burning, he calmed me with assurances that the saltwater was the best thing for my painful wound. We eventually returned to the other families on the beach, but I had seen something special and shared a moment with my dad that I will always cherish. When we got back, he broke the blister that had formed on my foot. I still have a thick scar on the bottom of my foot that bears testament to this experience.

One of our family vacations at this time began with a long drive across the country to return to Kansas – birthplace of Mom and us kids – to visit her side of the family. The trip consisted of torturous stretches of driving that seemed to go on for hours, punctuated with long-overdue stops at roadside restrooms. My brother and sister and I would sit in the back seat and pinch and annoy each other until things escalated enough for Dad to bellow, "Keep it down to a lion's roar!" or the classic parental threat, "Do I have to stop this car?" If we didn't react to this quickly enough, the car stopped, and quick and decisive punishment was administered to the perceived wrongdoer. Any time a child asked Dad, "Where are we going?" he would always answer sunnily in Polish, "Sta dupish be bach!" We found out years later that he meant, "Up a bird's ass singing."

Finally, we arrived at Aunt Lucille's rustic farmhouse. Lucille was my mother's older sister. She was a hard-working, no-nonsense, do-it-all woman who managed three sons and a husband in the middle of the vast plains of Kansas. Aunt Lucille was the only one of my mother's relatives we visited, and only three times in my childhood. Their life was austere, to say the least. Water was obtained from a pump in the yard. The toilet was located in an outhouse with an aroma that commanded your nostrils. Getting to the outhouse in the dark of night was a real adventure. Who knew what kind of wild animals you'd run into? I chose to hold tight until dawn and then run to do my business in the cold morning air.

Our Aunt Lucille's family lived off the land, which I deeply admired. She grew great vegetables in her garden and raised chickens, too. Foxes sometimes got into the chicken coop, but not all wild animals were considered enemies; the family also had a pet skunk. Surrounding the house, a fleet of machinery stood waiting to till the fields, harvest the wheat, and bale the hay. Our uncle kept every piece of machinery he bought and got an annual tax writeoff for each one.

Our cousins left the house early and returned late. This life required that everyone pull their weight. You had your chores, and that was that. Mark, Kat and I helped, if you could call it that. One day, we joined in the hay-baling. We threw hay into the baler and shoved any loose hay into the thunderous machine with pitchforks. The ominous beast consumed anything that was fed into it. The workers delighted in telling us tales of men who had lost fingers, arms and legs in such machines.

Once I got started on the next step of hay-baling, having a few of my limbs fed into the baler might have been a welcome relief. When we returned to the barn, we had to hurl giant bales up into the rafters to store for winter. The bale string sliced into the skin on my fingers as I tried to swing these cumbersome, heavy objects upward to my cousin above me. Bale hooks, like Capt. Hook's hand in "Peter Pan," were limited, and mine was taken away because I almost hit someone by accident. Hay was everywhere, and dirt clung to our skin. Our sweat dripped into our eyes, burning. Our reward for this hard labor was a tall glass of iced tea and a few hours off in the afternoon.

Our evenings were spent in the great outdoors. When it was time to clean up, we filled an old tub by the well, outside for God and all to see. Pots of water were heated on the stove, and one by one, we three kids got in the tub for a scrub-down. Sitting outside in the full embrace of billions of stars, for a few moments I was naked and by myself with the dim lights of the house in the distance. I was not afraid to be alone in the glorious dark. Mom came outside with a pail of water to rinse me off. She was loving and endearing, and the added splendor of the spectacular setting made it a memory I still cherish. Then it was up the stairs and off to bed, in simple, sparse rooms with old, creaky, musty beds. We were two or three kids to a bed, but we "city slickers" were so exhausted from a day's farm work, I didn't judge – I decided to "git in where I fit in" and quickly fell asleep.

Next morning, we were up bright and early and treated to a real farm breakfast. Our bacon was accompanied by the eggs we gathered ourselves in the chicken coop. This was the life. I even got a little cup of coffee with lots of cream and sugar. Life in Kansas seemed slow and easy, and the grown-ups had time to talk. My mom's relatives called Dad "Pollack" and "Ski" in conversation. These were meant as terms of endearment, and he took them that way. But I also listened to the adults talk about "wops," "chinks" and "niggers" casually, as if that were the thing to do. My mom didn't share their racist beliefs, but she chose a peaceful way to introduce new ideas into their point of view. She brought along a country record by Charley Pride and put it on. When she asked what color they thought the singer was, they said quickly, "White, of course!" Nope, guess again, she said. When she held up the album cover to show them a man of color, their tapping toes stopped in surprise. I always loved her for her efforts to help people feel safe while gently challenging their beliefs at the same time.

Kevin was the cousin closest to me in age, and we spent the most time together. As the Fourth of July was nearing, we went fireworks-shopping and loaded up on Roman candles, twirlers, M-80s, firecrackers and assorted other explosives. A few years earlier, Kevin had been bitten on the face while feeding the pigs. The crescent-shaped scar on his cheek fed constant fuel to his hatred for pigs, and he took every opportunity to punish the whole species for that one animal's indiscretion. Kevin took all of us kids and the box of fireworks out by the pigpen, which held about 22 pigs. Kevin staged a blazing assault on these innocent animals, blowing off round after round until he felt satisfied and they squealed in terror. We participated in this brutal assault by running any pigs that came our way in Kevin's direction.

Kevin and his brother, Terry, took similar delight in setting up their gullible "urbanite" cousins – namely, Mark and me – during a day in the country we would never forget. We were trusting and full of a desire to appear cool, so we went along with anything they said and questioned nothing. The first order of the day was calf riding. We gathered some calves into a makeshift pen on the side of a hill. I'd seen rodeos on TV; I was sure I could do it! Our cousins demonstrated a few times how easy it was to mount and dismount, showing us how to fall away from the animal so you didn't get caught under their hooves. I jumped onto my first calf, and the animal bucked wildly. The rough rope cut into the soft skin of my untrained hands, and I was thrown off immediately. Mark did a little better on his first try, getting bounced around like a rag doll until our cousins grabbed the rope and jerked him off the calf roughly before he fell off and was trampled. Our cousins took their turns again to show how easy it was, but I was learning quickly that this was a dangerous enterprise no matter how good you were. When it was my turn again, I was even more nervous and shaking than the first time, but I could not lose my cool. I had to try. They let me go sailing, and I clung to the calf's back. I was too close to his neck, so my face was getting smashed against this raging animal, but I was frozen and couldn't let go. Finally, I was flung off and landed in a heap. Now my cousins were satisfied that I had been humbled and punished enough, or so I thought. The next activity on their farm agenda was horseback riding.

I don't know what breed these farm horses were, but from my 10-year-old perspective, they were colossal behemoths who towered over me. Kevin, a farm superstar, rode a horse named Rock who would see Kevin approaching and lower his head toward the ground. Kevin would grasp the horse's mane, and Rock would raise his head and flip Kevin in a somersault over his head. Kevin would gracefully land facing forward and ready to ride. Rock was an ornery and cantankerous horse with real personality. I tried to win him over with apples and sugar, and he would take my treats and then give me a look that said, "Beat it, kid, or else." After my calf-riding experience, it took Kevin a while to talk me into trying this. Only after Mark tried it did I let Kevin boost me onto Rock's back. After several failed attempts in which I repeatedly fell the long distance from Rock's back to the hard ground, I finally found myself sitting on top of this commanding beast. I held onto both his mane and the leather reins for dear life.

We started off slowly, gently meandering in the hot noonday sun down dirt roads that crisscrossed and connected this expansive farm. Just as I was starting to get comfortable on the back of this old farm horse, the animals came to a muddy spot in the tall grass. Kevin casually said the horses liked to roll in the mud there to get the flies off of them. He dismounted and helped Mark down, but before I could dismount, my horse lay down in the mud. Suddenly I went from 8 feet in the air to having my legs crushed under his tremendous girth. The horse rolled toward me, and I was being pushed down in the mud by his full weight.

I gasped and tried to scream as the horse relaxed on top of me, putting tremendous pressure on my leg but leaving most of my torso exposed. Kevin pulled hard and the horse moved just enough for me to be dragged out, crying and covered with mud. This finally softened Kevin's tough exterior, and he kindly tried to calm me down. Finally, after I was able to get up and walk and realize I wasn't hurt, we were able to laugh at this painful episode.

Reluctantly, I went through the multiple attempts and hard landings and got myself back on that horse. I had no choice, since we were so far from the farmhouse. Riding in the brilliant morning sun, I felt like a mud-covered king who had defied all odds. Kevin promised a nice dip in a pond that was much closer than going all the way back to the farm. Even riding slow and easy, my nerves were shot, my false bravado gone. But as the ride wore on, adrenaline kicked in to ease my battered body, and I felt more comfortable and stable on Rock's back.

I was just getting into the Wild West fantasy of pretending I was in a Western looking for outlaws when the oasis of our swimming hole came into view. Kevin said, "Follow me!" It was then I should have hesitated. But no – he made everything look so easy. He casually walked his horse right into the water and skillfully maneuvered in a weightless "water dance" with his horse. When I guided Rock into the water, my experience felt nothing like Kevin's looked. I could feel Rock swimming in the deep water under me, and I slid backwards off of his giant haunch and into the churning waters. I was pulled underwater and struck by his legs and hooves. Now panicking and feeling a new kind of physical agony, I watched Rock swim away. Maybe it was the lack of oxygen that snapped me out of my shock, until I swam toward the surface and gulped precious breaths of air.

Once again, I was able to calm down and stay off the horse long enough that when the time came to ride back to the farm for supper, I was willing to climb aboard Rock and follow Kevin and his horse home. Right away, I noticed we were moving faster than we had before. Rock obviously was an alpha-male horse who would rather lead than follow, so he kept trying to pass Kevin's horse. Kevin, being an alpha male of another species, kept spurring his horse forward until they were galloping at full speed. I held on for dear life until at last, the farm came into distant view. This made Rock gallop even faster. When we got close, Rock realized that the barn door was closed, so he re-routed toward another familiar, smaller door. What did he care that the top half of that door was closed? As he passed through the door, I slammed into the door and was thrown backward onto the dirt. I stood up, dazed. It was the perfect end to a perfect day.

Inside the house, our parents were busy and unimpressed by any grandiose tales of our adventures of the day. My body was bruised beyond belief, but I was proud of my hard-won battle scars.

– 6 –

It's a Small World After All

When I was 10, I learned we were moving again – this time to New Jersey. By now I felt I would always be a wandering gypsy, never to belong anywhere or settle down in a community of my own. I was aware by this age of people who lived in the same neighborhood all their lives, went to the same school, knew the same people, and were able to develop in ways that only stability and security would allow – developing various skills, setting linear goals and aspirations, building lifelong friendships that enabled trust, intimacy and acceptance to grow. These were the things I felt couldn't be bought by chasing the wind. I sat on the corner in front of our house and cried, singing, "It's a Small World After All" over and over, feeling forlorn, broken, scared and disenfranchised. I knew I was soon to be forgotten by yet another group of people I'd hoped to build a life with.

This was the runaway mentality that would haunt my existence for the next 34 years of my life. I moved forward in this broken state in the only way I knew. I became gregarious, wearing a mask of confidence to hide the scared, repressed, lonely person inside. I began to seek massive amounts of validation, attention and escape. This high-maintenance "drama queen" lifestyle required constant feeding and came at a devastatingly high price.

Off we went to our next stop: Mansfield Township, N.J. "Bewildered" is the only word that comes close to describing my experience. New air base, massive new school, strange new kids, new house, new neighborhood, and I didn't know anybody.

My first shocking discovery was the school. It was a 40-minute ride to Northern Burlington County Regional Middle School and High School, an overwhelmingly large structure in the middle of the countryside. It was enough to handle starting at a new school, without the classes being football fields apart from each other. How would I remember all this new information?? With my fifth-grade mind stressed to the limit, I often would go to the school nurse and try to sound sick by swallowing huge gulps of air to produce loud belches. She soon caught on, though, so it was back to the hallways.

I believe it was the overwhelming corridors of Northern Burlington Middle School where I began to learn to live in fantasy. I would look down the long hallways at certain female students or teachers, and guess what they thought of me. There wasn't much point to these fantasies at the time, but they set the stage for the magical thinking of later years, when I believed I could almost read people's minds and then would act out in the extreme to see if I could get some action.

While I was wandering the school hallways and honing my superpower mind-control skills, my mother was building a destructive new skill set of her own. She had just bought a baby blue Dodge Charger and was revving up an unmanageable "look-good" lifestyle of working two jobs and maxing out her credit cards. Her rampant and irresponsible spending eventually broke the spirit of my father, who seemed to work endlessly in a futile attempt to keep up with his wife's spending. This was the financial behavior that was modeled for my brother and sister and me. The principles of responsible spending and financial planning were enigmas to us until much, much later in life.

My dad was on alert for the U.S. Air Force, traveling all over the world carrying supplies, bombs, and the bodies of young soldiers back from Vietnam. He also was part of the system that made sure the United States had nuclear bombs in the air at all times. He would be gone 14 days at a time and then home for three.

As you can imagine, by now my mom was unable to control her wild-eyed bunch of kids. The only weapon in her arsenal was the threat of "when your father gets home." When Dad would finally cross the threshold of his house after 14 days on duty, Mom would greet him at the door with his children's punishable offenses. We often would get beaten for some forgotten event that had happened two weeks before. Looking back, it seems that life offered my dad no real opportunity to have positive parenting experiences with us. He went from his own abusive childhood home straight into the Navy, and then into marriage and fatherhood. Now, his best, uninformed efforts to create a stable home seemed pointless, between the demands of his career and our mother's inability to maintain stability in his absence. That translated mostly into brutality for me, the firstborn son and ringleader of much of the mayhem. During those few days he spent at home, hell would be paid for this dad who did not have training or temperament to be a full-time father. Then, he was off again, defending our country against terrorism from afar – but bringing it on home with real style!

We lived in the classic cycle of domestic abuse. It started with the explosion of anger or frustration, erupting in beatings or name-calling. That was followed by the cold silence; then came the phase called, "I'm OK now, but be very afraid." When Dad went back to work, we had the honeymoon period between explosions. Then, he would return, and the next violent phase would begin. Oddly enough, this seemed to my 10-year-old mind to be the world in microcosm. We were living on a military base during the Vietnam War, and every day I met teen-age boys training to go off and join the body count. We watched the news, and I recognized that we were living in the belly of the beast.

I began to work and do odd jobs at this time to earn spending money, and the jobs always revolved around the soldiers. I sold seeds for the Burpee Seed Company, candy for the school, and newspapers at stoplights in busy morning traffic for sheer profit. The newspaper job landed me with a curious group of misfits who sold papers at Fort Dix, N.J. This Army base was a major training spot for the young men who went forth to exotic, foreign places to burn, pillage, maim and kill. The soldiers told me they were paid 13 cents for each hour they were alive, which comes out to $3.12 per day or only $93.60 per month of service. I couldn't believe what a great deal that was for the government. These guys were trained to be proficient in the use of countless deadly weapons, and yet they were too young to drink or buy Playboys. As I grew up and moved around the globe, I never could understand how the world could be so confused about drinking, drugs, sex, murder and morality in general.

After school, I would go and sell newspapers at Fort Dix. Somehow, we paperboys often got ahold of stacks of Playboys, which we sold to the soldiers for $5 apiece – a clear profit of $1.50 each. I would walk with pride, knowing that I was the reason these guys got to post some great views of Nancy Sinatra and her famous boots inside their lockers. I liked knowing that I was bringing some comfort to them.

The newspapers were my free pass to many different areas on base. I would walk freely anywhere I wanted and would often hear the drill sergeants pummeling recruits with their banter of unending abuse. It sounded eerily familiar – maybe this is where my father learned some of his parenting skills – from boot camp in the Navy? It fit in so naturally: He did a "white-glove test" after we cleaned our rooms, and I knew the recruits got the white-glove treatment, too. Sometimes Dad would pull our bunk beds away from the wall and touch the top of the floor trim under the bed with the glove – bad news! Or maybe the top of the door, which incidentally was about 2 feet above our reach, would get the glove. I grew to love and relate to the young men preparing to die for their country, and I learned to resent and distrust their authority figures as much as my own. These beliefs became deeply ingrained in my psyche.

One of my regular stops on the base was the sewing shop. The base seamstress was a major contributor to my impressive collection of medals, patches and ribbons from every military contingent I could find – the first of many collections I would assemble in my life. I displayed all of my finds on a big green Army blanket. Another frequent destination was the kitchens, where I had especially warm friendships with the cooks. One black dude, Cookie, would take me in, feed me, counsel me and warn me who to stay away from. I also would talk to the guys doing KP (Kitchen Patrol); this duty was usually administered to misfits or people who didn't really buy into the Army way of life. There, I often would get the real news about what was happening in Vietnam, how many were dying and why they didn't want to support the killing machine.

Eventually, these lessons combined with my resentment

of authority and led me to vent my anger and confusion
at the loudest targets within reach – the drill sergeants.
At first, I started with little jibes as they were doing their
business with their troops in line. I would hide and yell
obscenities until the sergeant said, "Who said that?" I
noticed some of the soldiers would suppress laughter,
and this just egged me on. I had it in for one sergeant in
particular, and one day from my hiding spot, I yelled at
him, "You cocksucking piece of shit!" This time, he spotted
me. Enraged, he yelled at his men to go after me (although
I noticed that the sarge was the only one who actually
started running in my direction). I panicked and bolted,
newspapers and all. I darted in here, ran over there, and
he was closing in. I hauled ass toward the familiar back
door of the Mess Hall, burst inside and begged Cookie to
hide me. Without a word, Cookie stuffed me into a giant
cooking pot and put on the lid. I was terrified, sweating,
and damning myself for doing something so stupid.

I don't know how long I stayed in the pot, but after
listening to a lot of nerve-wracking kitchen clangs and
smelling a lot of food, Cookie took the lid off and told
me the coast was clear. He warned me to stay invisible,
because if I was spotted by the wrong guy, all hell would
break loose. In the twilight, I picked the least visible path
back to the spot where all the newspaper boys gathered to
go home. Safe at last! Or so I thought. Suddenly, 12 angry
paperboys – all bigger and older than me – descended and
pummeled me into a fetal position on the ground. They
punched and kicked until the man who orchestrated the
beating – the guy who drove us onto the base every day –
pulled them off. I was told I had disgraced everyone on the
newspaper crew and jeopardized the whole operation on
the base. I was ordered never to show my face around there
again.

With my newspaper career abruptly ended, I was forced
to find new pastimes. I was a young man of 11 now –

mature enough to take on two American pastimes that involve some level of hand-eye coordination. I'm talking, of course, about baseball and masturbation.

I was a left-handed first baseman, which is a hot commodity in the baseball world. That was all well and good, but unfortunately, I also had long hair. No matter how well I played, the coach was all about the hair. He would berate me in front of the other players and often referred to me as "Miss Kowalski" during practice. This verbal derision was straight out of my father's parental playbook – very familiar to my ears. And yet, during one of my dad's brief stops at home, he caught wind of the coach's insults and decided to go have a talk with the gentleman.

From the sound of it, my dad showed about as much restraint with the coach as he did with me, because Dad lost one of his hard-earned sergeant stripes afterward. I think he slugged the guy, who was a lieutenant. I felt proud that Dad had stepped up to protect me, but I was heartsick that it came at such a high cost to his career and ego. Speaking of egos, the same day Dad went to talk to my coach, I found myself in a barber's chair, watching my long locks of hair tumble to the floor. I lost interest in baseball after that.

At that point, my sex life came alive at the hands (literally) of a curious child full of fervor and wonderment. One of the base kids set up his pup tent -- oh, the irony – in the middle of a field near the housing units. He invited me in one day, and we became friends. A couple of days later, he asked if I'd ever masturbated or had an orgasm.

"Yes!" I proudly lied.

"Oh, good," he replied. "I'll go get some magazines, and we'll do it later."

Later, the big moment arrived, and I followed him to his tent. He produced some magazines that had the most exciting body parts I'd ever seen, but my interest was mixed with anxiety and dread. I was determined to fit in, but I really had no idea what I was supposed to do next.

"OK, let's do it!" he said.

"Yeah!" I cheered – thinking, oh, God, now what??

He pulled out his penis, and every Catholic warning I'd ever heard was screaming in my head. His penis was bent at an obtuse right angle. I was convinced it was because he'd been jerking off so much that he broke it somehow. I prayed for mercy and pulled out Junior. I was completely lost, so I just copied what he did, and before my eyes in this sweaty tent of young, hedonistic endeavors, his crooked penis grew long and hard. I couldn't stop now, so on I went, knowing the Lord would punish me and give me the crooked brand of a heretic.

Suddenly, my friend moaned, so I moaned, too. Then, without warning, he started erupting and jerking back and forth, with white stuff shooting onto his stomach. Well, I couldn't match this trick, since I didn't even have a hard-on yet. I wanted to know how he did this, and why he felt so good. I wanted to feel that good, too. So I got clean and told him I'd never done it before.

"Do you want help?" he said. I said yes immediately, not knowing exactly how this help would be provided. I soon found out, though. He put his hand on my penis and said, "Look at the pictures," and gently demonstrated the proper technique for a few moments. Then he told me to try it. I worked diligently and vigilantly, but to no avail. Finally, he suggested we reconvene the next day and try again.

But I was on a mission. I masturbated until I fell asleep and was hard at work again the next day. No luck. When we finally get back in the tent later that day, my penis was raw and swollen. But that didn't hold me back. I tried and tried and was about to give up when finally I experienced my first orgasm. This was much different than the nocturnal emissions I'd experienced in the past, waking up with confused feelings and sticky underwear. I had a controlled orgasm! Now, what would I do with this powerful new skill and no magazines?

I often would look at women and girls and fantasize about what I'd seen in the nude magazines. I didn't have to imagine too much, though; this was the '60s, and the Age of Hot Pants, Motown and "free love" was in full swing. All of that was frequently mixed up on TV and poured directly into my pre-pubescent mind, which helped fuel my fantasies. I once was so horny I rubbed against my ever-patient dog, Duchess. Then I stepped it up a notch and had a tryst with our electric pad sander. I was determined to find a way to make this magic happen, but 20,000 vibrations per minute was a little too intense, even for me.

This was the beginning of my tireless pursuit of the universal cure-all I had found in sex. Who cared if my family lived in violence and chaos; if we moved so often I felt I was no one and belonged nowhere? This was something I could do to feel fantastic any time I wanted, free of charge! My pursuit of sexual attention sometimes took strange forms. Once, a German shepherd bit me right on the ass, and the neighborhood mothers made me pull down my pants so they could see if I needed medical attention. At first I was embarrassed, but afterward, I wanted to do it all again. Experiences like this led to the exploitative exhibitionism I would practice in the future.

My mother poured kerosene on my sexual curiosity when she invited all the neighborhood kids over to our house for sock hops. On the base, we lived with a culturally eclectic mix of all kinds of people – Asian, African-American, Filipino, Latino, you name it. Mom would play records and let us dance our booties off, and then she would orchestrate games for us. Some were innocent party games like Pin the Tail on the Donkey or whacking a piñata with a bat. But other games were different. Sometimes she would sit us kids in a circle and have us play Postman or Spin-the-Bottle. You'd spin the bottle and randomly have to kiss another kid, sometimes of a different race. Remember, this was a group of 11- and 12-year-old kids in the '60s. And yet, my mom was loving, caring and gentle, so despite the racially charged situation around us, it still boiled down to trying to make the bottle spin and point toward a girl you liked. Wow, what a rush.

After one of these Spin-the-Bottle parties, a man from Tennessee came to our house in a highly agitated state. He was upset that his young daughter had kissed a black boy under my mother's supervision. I noticed that my parents were much cooler about this whole race thing than other kids' parents.

Around this time I met a full-bodied "older woman" of about 13. We went to see "Gone with the Wind" together. Up in the balcony, "Scarlett" and I engaged in a three-hour marathon of kissing and groping. She had braces on her teeth, which didn't slow down my quest for French-kissing experience one bit. We kissed and kissed and kissed; the rubber bands snapped off of her braces, and my tongue was shredded to ribbons. I barely noticed, because her hands began their maiden voyage all over my body, over and under my clothes. I followed her example and introduced my hands to her training bra. I hit the sacred pay dirt of nubile boys, and it was grand. When the movie ended, I made my way home, confused and full of screaming hormones. I had picked up a couple more habits that would stay with me for the next few decades – being sexual in public places for a voyeuristic thrill, and allowing older women to take over and do what they wanted with me.

While I developed my sexual skills, I also worked on my keen fashion sense. My best friend at this time was Ben, an Indian who lived on the other side of the base. We wore Nehru shirts, moccasins, and all kinds of strange new clothes. His mom made us bell-bottoms out of Naugahyde, the vinyl-coated fabric usually used to make furniture. Ben and I also sometimes wore the Mexican-design ponchos my mom made for us. We looked so space-age. We were just about the coolest 12-year-olds around.

One evening at twilight, Ben and I, dressed to the hilt, were walking toward his house. The base was cut in two by a highway, and we had to cross a bridge to get to each other's houses. We were walking along minding our own business that night when a small group of older and much bigger kids drove up alongside us. They made idle conversation at first, then asked if we had a joint. At the time, we didn't even know what a joint was – but the question made us nervous. They asked us some other things we knew nothing about, and we anxiously kept up our pace. We had to cross the bridge; it was dark, and these guys were big. Suddenly, the guys leaped out of the car. They started with name-calling and quickly progressed to beating the hell out of us. The guys picked up Ben and threw him over the side of the bridge. The water below was shallow, and I thought Ben was dead for sure.

Then, it was my turn. They tried to hurl me over the side of the bridge, but my moccasin got caught on the chain-link fence. With blood covering my face and in my eyes, I yelled, "I can't see! I'm blind!" This slowed their roll and made them wonder if they'd actually blinded me. So I kept yelling, "I'm blind! I can't see!" over and over until they ran away, crammed themselves into their car and took off. In shock, I looked for Ben's body down below, but it was dark and I could see only shadows. "Ben! Ben! Bennnnnn!" Nothing. I walked toward the end of the bridge, and Ben emerged from down below, making us both jump out of our skin.

By now some passing cars had stopped, and the Military Police were on the scene. The guys apparently cut a blood vessel in my ear, which would not stop bleeding. The MPs wrapped my head in a turban of bandages and took Ben and me to the MP Station. Ben's parents were already there, but my dad was on the road and Mom was working at one of her customary two jobs. The police had already caught seven college kids who had been on a rampage, beating up people all over the base. The cops lined up these guys and brought us in to see if we could identify them as our assailants. They were mean-looking and bloodied. It had been dark and I was terrified during the attack, so I hadn't gotten a good look at anyone. Besides that, I didn't want anything to do with these monsters. So I said nothing.

With my first mugging behind us, Ben and I went home. This mugging put me in a defensive stance for the rest of my life, which probably saved me during the many near-death experiences that lay ahead.

– 7 –

Swamp-Tromping

Sixth grade, and time to move – back to Dover Air
Force Base in Delaware, the place we'd left to move to
New Jersey. By this time, my brother Mark and I were 11
and 12 years old, respectively, and old enough to hang out
together. This place was surrounded by a swamp, and we
often would go adventuring to the middle of nowhere on
the outskirts of the base. In some places, you could sit and
watch the planes take off right over your head, real low.
This was the best. Once, Dad told us what time his C-130
Hercules would fly over our school. He said we would
know it was him when he waved a white sheet out of the
open cargo door. Sure enough, his massive cargo plane flew
over right on time, and we saw a white something fluttering
out the back. That was quite a thrill.

The swamp around the base became my second home.
It was an unforgiving place, with mud up to my thighs,
voracious mosquitoes, and junk dumped all over the place.
As a result, my friends usually didn't want to go swamp-

tromping, which was fine by me. That meant I could have
the swamp to myself. I immersed myself in the wildlife,
watching the tadpoles, insects, muskrats, snakes and birds
pass through all the stages of life. I viewed nature like I
viewed the rest of the world – through two lenses, one of
curiosity and one of violence.

Sometimes, my brother and I would take our one and
only Stingray bike and go swamp-tromping together in
the area behind our school. We would find junk people
dumped – TV sets, fluorescent bulbs, anything that would
shatter and sink – and hurl it into the river. Or, we would
let something big and breakable drift into the current, then
take the Stingray downriver – me pedaling, Mark riding
on the handlebars – and follow the floating target, trying
to shatter it with rocks. These brotherly good times would
be punctuated, sooner or later, with the type of interaction
we were more familiar with – like the time I stopped to
take a dump in an abandoned building. Mark noticed a
hornet's nest hanging from the ceiling above me and started
kidding about making use of it. I knew he wouldn't dare
risk big-brother retribution, so I maintained my vulnerable
position with my ass up in the air. Next thing I knew,
he threw a bottle up at the hornet's nest and nailed it.
Laughing maniacally, he took off on the Stingray while I
ran screaming for my life. I don't remember what happened
next, but I'm sure with the amount of learned violence in
my family, it was not pretty.

On one of my most memorable tromping days, I found
a large snapping turtle in the swamp. He was about a foot
and a half wide -- irresistible. I chased him through the
reeds and cornered him. When he retreated into his shell,
I bombarded him with stones and then picked him up.
Apparently, this was no way to make friends with Mother
Nature, as he reached out and scratched the hell out of me.
Not the fastest learner, I dropped him on the ground and
reached inside both ends of his shell, trying to determine

which end was the head and which was the tail. He was
more than happy to solve that mystery for me when, fast as
lightning, his snapping jaws emerged and almost bit clear
through the tip of my forefinger. It dangled precariously,
neatly cut almost to the bone. I retreated, screaming in
pain, and he started to make a slow-motion run for it – but
oh, hell, no, now I was pissed and determined! I flipped
him upside-down and desperately searched for something
to tie him up. I found some nylon string, tied it to him,
and dragged him about 20 feet, until he slipped out. I
repeated the process over and over and until we reached the
pavement and people. Someone gave me a piece of rope,
and I dragged this poor turtle all the way home, no less than
25 blocks over blacktop and curbs, giving him the worst
case of turtle road rash. Once I had him safely in my yard
with no chance of escape, I found someone to take me to
the doctor to stitch my fingertip back on. Ego bruised and
finger scarred, I still had my prize turtle. I couldn't wait to
go to school and tell Mr. Wilson, my sixth-grade science
teacher.

Mr. Wilson was a tall, powerful-looking, fearless black
man with real panache. He had an imposing personality and
really knew how to keep 11-year-old boys in line. When
a boy misbehaved, he would send the kid to the restroom,
then pick up a gavel and walk toward the bathroom door
shouting, "Here come the judge!" – taking advantage of
Sammy Davis Jr.'s shtick that was popular on the TV show
"Laugh-In" at the time. He would leave the bathroom door
open, and everyone in the classroom would wait in hushed
silence until wailing screams of pain were heard. He didn't
have to tell kids twice when he wanted something done.
Finally, my turn came, and off to the bathroom I went. I
stood trembling by the urinal, waiting for the violence that
was so familiar. Mr. Wilson walked in and stood before
me, huge and menacing. He quietly made me promise that
I would never reveal to anyone what was about to occur, or

I would get a serious beating. I took the oath. Then he said, "Now, I want you to yell like I'm beatin' your butt when I say 'go.'" He gave me my cue, and I started hollering. I returned to class a changed man. The other kids looked at me with terror, and Mr. Wilson stole a smiling glance at me. Never would I act out in his class again.

This was one of the rare times in my distracted, interrupted academic career that a school activity inspired a lifelong interest in a subject. I brought my turtle prisoner to Mr. Wilson's class for Show and Tell. All the excitement over the turtle led Mr. Wilson to suggest that I make a volcano for the upcoming science fair. This was the first time I would compete for a scholastic prize. I was so thrilled with my new scientific venture, I let Mr. Wilson talk me into returning my turtle to the swamp.

I worked with my dad to create this volcano. We spent hours building the papier-mâché shell and then devising the recipe for the "lava" out of bicarbonate of soda and other secret fizzing ingredients. This type of project was like playtime for my father, with his almost mystical ability to build or repair anything. When the big day came, we added the chemicals and waited for the massive, explosive climax that would overshadow the displays built by the future Einstein kids and their super-achiever dads. Alas, what we got was a slow, bubbling froth oozing from the mouth of the volcano. Real-life scientists would have been excited by this kind of action, but this was not the small-scale drama I needed to wow the judges. I got an Honorable Mention. Deflated, I vowed to come back and win next year. But you know, next year never unfolded the way I thought it would.

My career with the Boy Scouts began around this time. Our Scout leader, Mr. Daniels*, had a problem that caused saliva to constantly drip from his mouth. That made him seem like the stereotypical "dirty old man," but in truth, he was a kind person, generous with his time and talents. My Scout pack included my friends and across-the-street neighbors, Johnny* and Rick*. I enjoyed true friendship with these two African-American brothers. We knew each other longer than most of the kids I'd met, and we got along great. My closeness and bond with them strengthened my lifelong affinity with black people and my self-identity as a light-skinned black person.

Our pack attended a state Scout Jamboree at a 20-acre campground with troops from all over Delaware. Our first brush with the crazy world of teen-age camping was a lot for our 12-year-old minds to take in. There were girls, for one thing. Then there were the older boys, who were just plain mean and enjoyed hazing new Scouts with all kinds of harrowing tortures. The older guys did come up with some fascinating innovations, though. My favorite was a compressed-air cannon made from PC plumbing tubes that could shoot a potato about 400 yards. As we moved through the campground, I noticed older kids partying in vans and drinking beer. This was a portent of my future, although I didn't know it at the time.

The jamboree kept us busy with hikes, activities, and the maintenance needed to support our pack's little corner of the campground. One afternoon, Rick and I were playing around the campfire, throwing pine needles on it to make the flames 4 or 5 feet high. We laughed hysterically as we played "Jack be nimble, Jack be quick" and jumped over the campfire. Suddenly, we were called to join a hike on a nature trail where we would build a pioneer bridge over a stream. Off we went, toting our building tools to where the action was, about a mile away from our campsite. We quickly became engrossed in the business of finding and cutting down the right kinds of trees to build a platform for our 15-foot rope bridge. One of our young teammates wanted to play with the ax his parents had given him. The scoutmasters tried to give him an on-the-spot lesson in how to use the ax safely and properly. Regardless, a short time later, a sharp scream echoed through the woods, and all activities ground to a halt. The ax blade had ricocheted off a tree trunk and chopped a chunk out of the boy's leg. Mr. Daniels and another scoutmaster rushed the boy to a hospital.

We hobbled along in our bridge-building effort, but it really never got off the ground. After a full day's work, tired and hungry, we headed back toward our camp and started picking up the buzz among the other Scouts that somebody had just put out a fire. We smelled smoke as we got closer to our own campsite, but still, it didn't hit home until we reached the perimeter of our tent circle and our exhausted Scoutmaster staggered out to meet us. "Now, boys, I've been sweatin' blood to get this fire out," he said. It turned out our "Jack be nimble" fire had spread around our camp, destroying two of our six tents, along with the plastic coolers that contained our food supply. I learned two valuable Scout lessons that day: Don't play with fire, and be careful with axes!

Back at school, the latest rage was putting "Fragile" stickers on your textbooks. I somehow acquired a fat roll of these red stickers with the image of a broken martini glass on them, and my career in sales took off once again. At 5 cents apiece, my stickers were selling like hotcakes. This kind of action got me some respect, and at 12, I was also quite the looker, so I got my first taste of being the guy people wanted to know. Then, I met the first love of my life. Her name was Patty. She was friendly, blonde and 11 years old. Talk about distracting! My attention for anything else became obscured. All the music of the '60s centered on love – getting love, looking for love, surviving lost love. This just egged me on.

My infatuation with Patty introduced me to the concept of class separation. I followed her home one day to see where she lived and found myself looking at Officers' Quarters. These people lived in nicer houses than we did and, as I was about to find out, their parents wanted nothing to do with the regulars in the service. But for now, I was living in heaven just walking Patty home from school, holding hands and talking. One day, during our after-school walk, a white kid called out, "Patty Swampwater." Outraged, I challenged him to a fight. I was full of adrenaline and ready to defend my femme fatale's honor. After I got in a few good hits, a bigger black kid stepped in and took his place. Apparently, this kid knew how to box. I tried and tried, but couldn't get a shot in. He kept punching me in the face and stomach while the other kid chanted, "Patty Swampwater! Patty Swampwater!" and the onlookers laughed. I was humiliated. After that, Patty's parents told her she should not hang out with me anymore. Reduced to loneliness, I would walk around her unfamiliar neighborhood, futilely hoping to catch a glimpse of her.

For kids with safe, supportive homes and stable relationships, the loss of puppy love can be a developmental stepping stone, or at least something to look back on later and laugh. But for me, a boy who changed schools and towns every year and who went home every night to the same-ole, same-ole, losing Patty's innocent kindness was devastating. I believe this is when my need for emotional validation skyrocketed out of control. The girls on the sixth-grade playground already chased me around and pulled my "fruit loops" – the loop you use to hang the shirt. I started acting out shamelessly for their attention with desperate and needy schemes. When I didn't get the action I wanted, feelings of abandonment and anguish overwhelmed me. I felt the only thing that would "make things all right" was finding another relationship like the one I had with Patty. It seemed to be the only kind of validation that would satisfy my incredible neediness. I began to treat anyone who wasn't a potential "Patty" as if they didn't exist. I was on such a desperate quest, I didn't have attention to waste on anything else.

I began to slip more and more deeply into a fantasy and

dream world. I assigned secret forms of communication to every conversation. I would slur their words into innuendoes that met my needs. There were always two conversations going on: the one we were actually having, and the one in which I fantasized their every word so they would meet my immediate desires. I also developed a secret body language, in which I re-interpreted their every glance, gesture, pursing of lips, you name it. All someone had to do was walk away, and I would study her and develop my own interpretation of these seemingly innocent motions to satisfy my stifled needs for intimacy.

The delusional quest was on.

– 8 –

Rock Star Dreams

By this time I still played children's games and, amazingly enough, had some shreds of innocence left. But somehow, most of the games would eventually get twisted around my desperate attempts to get what I thought I deserved, be it attention, love, validation or somebody else's stuff – no doubt somebody who didn't "deserve" it as much as I did. I learned to make a marble circle in the dirt and play marbles with other kids, and this became my new obsession. I wasn't particularly good at it, but I was drawn to the game. My desire to do well at marbles became more important than maintaining my already-shaky code of ethics. I was willing to lie, cheat and steal to improve my reputation and my inventory, when it came to marbles. Once I grabbed this big kid's favorite shooter; he caught me with it and beat me royally. This did nothing to extinguish my lust for the biggest and best marbles. I felt there was something wrong with a system in which the big and beautiful always got the prizes. What about the rest of us?

One kid who lived across the field from us owned two gallon jugs filled with marbles, which his mom would not let him bring into his house. My desire to own just one of his marble-filled jugs consumed me for weeks. I worked on a plot to get them. How would I sneak out and cross the field without getting caught by my parents, or his? After many nights of trying and failing to stay awake until after my parents went to sleep, the perfect moment finally arrived. I got up and got dressed without waking Mark, who was asleep in the other bunk. Then somehow, I got out of the house without waking Duchess, our dog. It was 3:30 in the morning, and I was outside in the scary, dark netherworld. I had never ventured outside this late by myself. I felt I had broken into a secret world of the darkness. I walked across the field boldly, coming to a halt at this kid's steps. I stared for what seemed like an eternity at that jug of marbles, and then, with adrenaline practically spraying out of my ears, I made my move. I sprinted up the steps and grabbed the jug of marbles, then took off as the neighborhood dogs started barking.

I hurried back across the field toward my house, freaking out at how much noise a bunch of marbles could make shaking around in a plastic gallon jug. I could not possibly have chosen a noisier item to steal. In the end, I got home and the marbles were mine …but not mine. I learned to live with the discomfort of doing something I'd previously sworn I would never do. I made it OK so I could live with myself.

Soon after the marble escapade, I learned of a darker pastime. One weekend, all the boys in my neighborhood were talking about a tent that had been set up in a field that conjoined all of the base's housing units. In the tent, they said, was a girl with her legs wide open. "All you have to do is go stick it in," they said. I'd seen and heard plenty of sex and nudity in my 12 years, but I still knew nothing about having sex. The idea of the girl in the tent terrified me but, not wanting to appear uncool, I decided after much frightened deliberation to go into the tent. I crawled inside and there, in the quasi-twilight, lay a naked young girl who appeared to be no older than I was. She lay there, the musty scent of male and female permeating the air. Any romantic notions I had about sex were shattered. I waited in the tent for a few minutes, not knowing what else to do and not wanting to give away that I was doing nothing at all. Sometime during those long minutes, our eyes met – a look I remember as one of infinite sadness that this world, at this moment, held nothing to meet either of our unrequited needs.

I climbed out of the tent and tried to leave quickly, pretending I did it and hoping the guys would be none the wiser. But as soon as I opened my mouth to describe what allegedly happened, I was easily found out. They laughed at my inability to even explain sex. I had no game – I had to get myself a new hustle! Looking back, I'm amazed I made it to age 12 with any kind of innocence intact.

At this point, my life changed again, and not for the better. I was playing at the base playground, walking on logs that had been arranged at various angles. I decided to jump from the logs onto a 4-foot-wide plastic turtle nearby. I made the jump but lost my footing on the sand that was scattered all over the turtle. I crashed down face-first with tragic force, breaking off both of my front teeth and pushing them through my lip and chin. In shock, I held my broken teeth in my hand. Rage overcame me, and I threw the teeth as hard as I could into the sand, lost forever. I ran home sobbing, a changed person. My father was home, and this was the first time I ever saw him cry for me. He was so upset, he didn't seem to know what to do. I wound up in the hands of ham-fisted military dentists who, lacking experience with children's mouths, experimented to find ways to put teeth back in the front of my mouth. I wound up with silver front teeth and a speech impediment. I worked hard to re-learn how to speak without a lisp.

In an instant, I had changed from a cute kid with a shot at some level of popularity to a self-conscious "weirdo" with silver teeth. The significance of this was not lost on me. I was devastated. On the sixth-grade playground, all the girls who used to chase me around and try to grab my shirt lost interest and gave me no more attention. My easygoing, attention-getting behavior with the young ladies no longer had any effect. I was really alone now, and I knew what it was like to be ostracized for being different. With the bitter new nickname of "Silver Tooth," I started to sort out the people who had discarded me as damaged goods from the ones who were real and liked me for me.

I buried myself in my newfound musical pursuits. Turned out I had the ability to pick up new instruments and learn them quickly. Of course, the coolness factor was paramount in my musical career at age 12, so the first thing I did after deciding to play an instrument was to assemble the proper coolness wardrobe. I got a pair of "Beatles shoes" – a highly painful style that came to a sharp point at the end. These permanently disfigured my feet Geisha-style. Then, I started shopping at places like Chess King with my mom and my sister Kat. Chess King was a mall store that sold unisex clothing we all would share. We shared other cool, lacy attire, too – stuff that "real men" might find questionable. But it was perfect for me, since I had no macho hangups.

My first intended instrument was the trumpet. But, having already seen Mickey Dolenz wailing on the drums on "The Monkees," I never really got behind the horn plan. One day, I let it fall down the stairs to make sure I couldn't play it ever again. Instead, I beat the hell out of my wooden snare drum and every pot, pan and piece of furniture in the house, until my dad finally relented and brought me home a set of Pearl Drums from Japan. Thrilled, I improved quickly and got my groove on. I finally had found a niche to express myself creatively. Our next-door neighbors had eight kids, and three of them played music well. This was my first opportunity to jam with others and be competitive.

Meanwhile, my dad was flying all over the globe and had a habit of bringing home the latest products of electronic genius. We always had the loudest stereo in the neighborhood, and we'd play it till it blew up and Dad brought home the next one. My mom belonged to every record club there was, so we had all the latest in vinyl grooves pounding out of speakers that would get bigger and bigger with each new stereo set. With all this musical inspiration, it wasn't long before I started playing my very first gigs. We played at OctoberFest on the base. People drank and had a great time in white tents as we played. I thought we flopped, but my dad was very supportive. We really started to bond for the first time over my musical pursuits.

Then we played at an Officers' Club. I, ever the glib frontman, introduced "Purple Haze" by saying, "This is the song we play to scare all the drunks away!" It was an innocent joke by a smart-alecky kid, but unfortunately, my friend's father ran this O Club, and he felt I had embarrassed him and everyone there. The man held me up by one arm and laid into my ass with a firmness that was real. I returned to the microphone, shaking, and apologized for my bad manners and bad taste. For a young and sensitive kid who had come to expect to be rejected and alienated in everything I did, this outcome set my negative expectation for decades to come when it came to audiences. It also set me apart from all the normal showmanship skills that were imperative to a blossoming career.

Around this time, our family took a trip to Michigan to visit my paternal grandfather, William – someone I knew only as an insanely violent man who abused the hell out of my dad and made his living as a butcher with a meat cleaver. However, before I could even start worrying about our destination, there was the journey itself to live through. We owned a camper we used for such family outings. My father was confident that his eldest son, at age 12, could drive the camper with no problem while he took breaks. So there I was, sitting on a bunch of pillows behind the wheel of a camper holding my entire family, driving through the Poconos Mountains while my father slept beside me in the front cab. I noticed the 1,000-foot dropoff signs as we continued to gain altitude. I gripped the wheel with my sweaty hands and did my best to stick to the narrow mountain road. The wind shears made me nervous, but I really dug the responsibility of being called upon to drive so my exhausted father could rest. This was a blast.

The heater in our old Ford camper efficiently pumped heat into the cab – and carbon monoxide fumes right along with it. As I drove, the white stripes in the middle of the long road became hypnotic, and I started getting sleepy. Feeling myself start to drift off, I opened the window and slapped my face a few times. With the cold air startling my dad from his sleep, he barked, "Shut that goddamn fucking window! What are you tryin' to do?" Not knowing that pulling over was a viable option, I stoically soldiered on until I drifted into a narcotic slumber.

With my mom, brother and sister sleeping in the camper; my dad konked out next to me, and me finally asleep at the wheel, the camper ran off the road. The rumbling of the shoulder strips woke us all, just as the truck went careening out of control in the darkness and rolled downhill. All of us bounced around like rag dolls. The camper rolled about 20 feet down into a ravine that was used for water runoff. The incline was slight enough that we rolled to the bottom and came to a stop. Dad got out to check and make sure everyone was all right. Miraculously, there were no injuries other than my wounded pride. Dad flagged down some truckers who called the State Police and got us towed back up to the road. I could hear my father explaining to the trooper that "those goddamn big rigs" and the wind shears had knocked us clean off the road. The trooper bought the story.

You might think that was the end of my early driving career, but no. The next day I was driving again. This time both Dad and my brother Mark were in the cab with me. Dad said he was going to take a nap, and he instituted a new safety precaution by telling my brother that if I so much as blinked my eyes too long, Mark was to punch me as hard as he could. My eyes stayed wide open for the whole drive.

Finally we arrived at the home of the legend, Grandpa Kowalski. Grandpa lived in a beautiful two-story house, but he seemed to do all of his living in the basement. He greeted us all in his thick Polish accent, and when my parents left us to go out to dinner with friends, Grandpa offered us kids a shot of vodka and the choice of the many fine meats in his possession. We ate heartily, only to find out later that our butcher patriarch had fed us things like "brain loaf," "tongue loaf," intestines and tripe. After that, he commanded us to tape dimes to a 1-by-1-foot piece of metal in the basement. Then he taught us to shoot targets with a .22-caliber rifle. With a rifle in our hands, and vodka and brain loaf coursing through our veins, this indoor shooting range was an exciting place to be. We enjoyed a less psychotic pursuit with Grandpa when he took us aboard a beautiful wooden boat for a gentle ride on the Great Lakes. It was an old family story that Grandpa had started building this boat in his precious basement. When the boat became too large to move out of the basement, Grandpa had to remove part of his foundation to get it out.

I also met my uncle and my older cousins then. My cousins enjoyed the free lifestyle of the '60s, which included experimenting with drugs. I was still a kid playing with Monster trading cards; these guys seemed all grown up. They took us to Cobo Hall, a famous rock mecca in

Detroit, to see Ted Nugent and the Amboy Dukes. Colored lights, weed smoke, no parents – and everyone there was so cool. I was given some kind of drug and warned to tell no one. Looking back, I believe it was MDA, or what is now called Angel Dust. Seeing Nugent wail on the guitar like a rock god, my life changed that night. Now I wanted to be a rock star. I would pour all of my energy into becoming the best drummer I could be.

I had another rare musical opportunity during this trip, when Dad introduced me to the great drummer Gene Krupa, who was a family friend. Somehow, he invited us over so I could play drums for him. I was nervous and played badly. He was kind and encouraging, but I could not hear a word of the confidence he tried to instill in me. My poor performance before this legendary musician helped to cement my low self-esteem and fear of success.

Back at school, the trauma of the "Silver Tooth" episode was mostly behind me now, and I made a few real friends. One of them, Donald, was a tall kid with a sweet disposition who wouldn't hurt a fly. One day, we encountered some kids who often berated us as we passed by them on our way home. This time, they started hitting Donald. I charged toward them, yelling for them to stop. Their attention quickly focused on me. I agreed to fight just one of them. As the most aggressive one rushed me, I said, "Stop! Just a minute!" I took off my shirt and shoes and rolled up the legs of my pants. Even in this heated moment, I knew if I ruined my clothes, the beating that awaited me at home would eclipse any beating this kid might give me. Now I was ready.

As the bully came toward me swinging, I had a moment of clarity. All the beatings I had received at the hands of my father flashed before my eyes. My dad had hit me my whole life – now this kid was going to hit me, and I got to hit back?? After taking a few hits, I focused. With all the rage of a lifetime of beatings roaring in my head, I swung once at his mouth and connected hard, breaking out his two front teeth. Suddenly all the life drained out of me. I felt terrible for doing to another person what had been so devastatingly painful in my own life. The bully turned out to be the son of the local police chief. I was escorted to the military police station. When you're a service brat and you go south of the law, it's your father who really suffers the consequences, because he is ultimately held responsible for the actions of his family. I was terrified of this intimidating place and of the punishment that my father might have to endure.

The officers sat me down and began questioning me about the fight. On the table in front of me, they spread out color photo after photo of victims who had been beaten and disfigured, with broken faces, arms and legs. They asked if I'd committed these beatings or knew who did. I began to cry. Then came the photos of break-ins and burglaries – picture after picture of the results of destructive energy that had violated and destroyed people's safety and property. They probably could tell by the bewildered look on my face that I had never seen this type of destruction. I stuck to the truth in telling the story over and over of how my own fight went down. Finally, they let me go. A week later, they called me back to remind me of how serious my violation was and that they were watching me. This fear kept me on the straight and narrow for quite a while.

I knew I could hurt and maim, and my revulsion of this ability made me seek new ways to deal with confrontation that would be just as ruinous, but to the mind and spirit only – leaving the body intact. Later in life, I came up with the adage, "It's not the crime; it's the mess it leaves behind."

Another friend I made lived a few doors down the street from us. His name was Trent*. He was two years older than me and turned me onto cool things like the comedy classic, "Firesign Theater." He and his family were short,

leprechaun-like, good-natured German people. We seemed
to bond when I almost electrocuted myself while playing
at their house one day. I had brought along my father's old
flight headset, which he'd given to me as a toy after the
protective padding came off. In Trent's living room, I put
the headset on and, with the raw metal pressing against my
ears, I naively plugged the headset into a wall socket. To
my surprise, I was jolted, frozen in place by the voltage.
Vaguely in the background, I could sort of hear Trent's
mother screaming. Finally, she took a broom and backed
me away from the wall, unplugging the headset. I was
tight with this family after that. I also was in love with
their daughter. For the short time I knew them, their home
was a safe haven for me. Eventually, they moved to Amish
country in Pennsylvania. Lured by the real estate in that
area, my father took our family to visit them.

Driving through Amish country was fascinating. Fancy
mandalas had been painted on all of the barns. We drove
past a slow-moving, horse-drawn buggy in which a young
couple listened to "ABC" by the Jackson Five on a portable
record player. My dad realized we were on the wrong road
and turned around. On our way back, we passed the couple
again – this time being punished by a man with a riding
crop, while the shattered pieces of the record player lay on
the side of the road.

Once we got to Trent's house, he and I went off to seek
outdoor adventure. He said he knew the coolest game on
the planet, but I probably was too chicken to try it. That's
all I needed to hear. He led me into the woods to a grove
of poplar trees, where he explained the rules of the game.
The idea was to climb 35 or 40 feet up to the top of one
of these trees. No problem! Anything you can do, I can
do better! Up we went. Once we reached the tops of our
respective trees, Trent started swinging his treetop toward
me and gestured, daring me to follow suit. I precariously
swung my tree toward his. Here came the next instruction:

Once our treetops got close enough to each other, we would
simply switch trees. The first time we got close enough to
attempt this outrageous feat, Trent caught my tree, held
on and yelled, "Grab my tree, quick!" I did. Swoosh – the
trees swung back into place. What an exhilarating brush
with danger. I was alive, and the tree didn't break. We
began swinging again and repeated this mid-air maneuver a
number of times.

I was getting good at it. Once more? No problem!
But as Trent's tree came toward me, I reached out and he
pulled back, not quite ready. My fingers grasped at the
quickly retreating branches and leaves and caught nothing.
Suddenly, I was falling. It seemed like it took forever to
finally hit the ground. I lay there blinking up through the
branches at the sky, wondering if I were alive or dead. I
had lucked out and landed on a deep pile of leaves covering
a bed of rotting vegetation. The soft bed had saved my
life, but I had the wind knocked out of me and couldn't
move. Lying there, I glanced to my left and saw that I'd
landed about 2 feet away from a giant roll of barbed-wire
fencing. I looked to my right and saw a 4-foot-wide tree
stump. My luck was unbelievable. And so was this story.
We didn't exactly want to go back and broadcast what we'd
been doing to our families anyway. So this little escapade
remained a secret between God, Trent and me.

Back in Dover, my pastimes were no less dangerous.
Sometimes a few of my friends and I would get together
to be "tunnel rats." This involved taking candles and
flashlights to the swamp and entering the labyrinthine
passages of Dover Air Force Base's sewage system.
We would go as deep as we could through the tunnels.
Sometimes it seemed we would walk for hours, only to
emerge where the gutter joined a street. We would strain to
see where we were. Other times, the candles would burn
out or the flashlights would die, leaving us to make our way
blindly through the tunnel water, past the smells of dead

things that occasionally bumped us in the dark. We were egged on by urban legends we heard, like alligators that had been flushed down toilets and had grown to 12 feet in length down in the tunnels. We knew we would be eaten alive in the dark.

Eventually, these hazards became familiar and comfortable. Then someone had the bright idea to liven things up by using lawn-mower gasoline to make a Molotov cocktail. We'd seen them in war movies on TV. We managed to play this dangerous game a few times before a near-tragedy occurred. One of the older kids held a candle and decided to terrorize us for fun. As he backed out of the tunnel, he lit one of the gasoline bombs and broke it on a tunnel wall, obscuring our path with a wall of fire. The fire quickly died down, which was a lot more luck than any of us probably deserved. We connected with our jokester friend on the outside, laughing that he really got us with that one. Our level of fearlessness was mind-boggling.

– 9 –

Bowers Beach

The year I turned 13, my father retired from the Air Force. The tension between my parents by now was suffocating. Even with his military pension, both he and my mother were working two jobs in an effort to keep up with Mom's insatiable, compulsive spending habits. She was always trying to fill the void inside with one spiritual pursuit after another, and when that didn't work, she'd fill in the gaps with large purchases and maxed-out credit cards. In addition to that strain, there was mutual infidelity. My father told me many years later that Mom had begun cheating on him back in the first year of their marriage, and after many years of pain, shame and frustration, he followed suit.

When the time finally came for Dad to retire and start a new career as a master electrician, my mom got her heart set on buying a particular house in Bowers Beach, Del. This was no ordinary house. It was a huge, wood-frame Victorian with about 16 rooms on 6 acres of land. The place had been neglected for about 25 years, so the worn wood had attained a silvery appearance. Besides the house, the property included other buildings that originally had served as slave quarters, a meat house, a chicken barn, and various other structures. We were told this house served as "the first house of abortion on the East Coast," where a Dr. Hubbard took care of the messy, complicated consequences of sex in the Victorian Age. For those mothers who didn't make it, there was a small graveyard in the back of the property with about 15 headstones that we could see. The graveyard had a particularly creepy look, since it had been overgrown for decades with trees whose massive root systems covered the stones. We got all the stories we could possibly handle from our neighbors, Mr. Nye and Mrs. Mandeville. They had the rich history of this small, strange, fishing town etched in their DNA.

All this history just increased the haunted-house feel of the place, which was spooky enough with all the overgrown vegetation and foreboding stained-glass windows. All of the windows were made of old rolled glass, which helped your eyes play tricks on you. Was that a ghostly apparition standing in the window? You couldn't be sure. The roofs on all the buildings were made of shiny black slate, and the main house had a widow's walk on top. Up there, the place afforded a grand view of the entire bay, as we were about a quarter-mile from the waterfront and the only house built on the hill. The front yard was lined with two rows of massive, 100-year-old trees. You definitely gained some serious altitude when you made it to the top of one of these 60-foot giants.

This property would have been a massive undertaking for a team of contractors simply to restore the old house. My dad faced the overwhelming task of reclaiming and rehabbing the entire property, armed only with his own formidable skills and workaholic endurance – and a work crew of two young sons. He slaved for 18 hours a day, holding down two jobs and using every spare moment to work on this ramshackle house. Our mom's dream house seemed like our dad's worst nightmare.

For us kids, the house was big, scary and dilapidated, but not without its fascinations. We lived in a trailer on the property while Dad tried to rehabilitate the interior. The trailer was cramped and uncomfortable, but the prospect of sleeping in such a menacing house wasn't that inviting anyway. In one of the house's many second-story rooms, I set up my Pearl Drums and practiced whenever I could. We explored the house in the relative safety of daytime. Mark and I discovered a glorious great white owl in the attic, but my brother shot the bird with a .22-caliber rifle. That was a sad day for me, and I mourned this giant bird with its massive wingspan.

Mom, usually an evangelist of universal peace and love, warned us to stay away from the neighbors, who were "bad seeds." I tried to avoid them, but it was inevitable that our paths would cross – which they did, right in front of our house. I encountered a group of about eight kids led by a bully named Clinton*. Clinton was a natural leader who later earned the nickname "Bullet Head" when someone fired a gun at his head during a residential robbery and the bullet seemed to bounce off his skull. Clinton approached me and said, "Who's playing the drums so loud you can hear them all the way down Three Mile Road?"

"My name is Matthew, and I'm a musician," I timidly replied. "The drums are upstairs, and it's hot, so I open the windows to get a cross-breeze."

Clinton explained the rules that governed his motley group of followers, which mostly involved swearing your undying allegiance, beating people up and raising mayhem. I said I would leave the beating and mayhem to them, but I could play music for them. Clinton extended a hand and said, "You should make your vow of commitment right now." As soon as I put my hand in his to shake it, I was pulled into a powerful, crushing death grip. He pulled me closer and then punched me in the eye with his other fist. Stunned and confused, I sobbed, "I'm a musician! I play music for people!" I ran inside. This event was inspiring for me musically – I was afraid to leave the house! So in the hours I used to spend exploring the outdoors, I would put on my headphones and play every record we owned over and over while I practiced.

My practice time was severely curtailed by my father's work schedule for Mark and me. He developed a system of deadlines, rewards and punishments for us, so things would get done on the house while he was at work. Mark and I tore down small buildings on the property, removed all the nails and saved any center-cut redwood, oak or maple beams that could be reused. We dug septic tanks and ponds. We got a tractor, cut down trees, and used chains to pull the roots out of the ground. Dad bought an old hydraulic dump truck, and each day I would have to earn the privilege of practicing my drums by filling that truck. That took hundreds of shovelfuls to accomplish.

We demolished the interior of room after room of plaster lathing, removing all the plaster and lathing and dumping it in a huge pile about an acre away from the house. This pile grew to incredible dimensions and later would be set on fire, creating an awesome blaze that attracted three fire battalions to come over and meet the Kowalskis. Mark and I removed three crumbling chimneys, with my brother getting on top of each one carrying a sledgehammer. He'd yell, "Look out!" then start swinging, and bricks would rain down. He worked his way down to each fire box that way, riding the chimney down brick by brick to the base of each fireplace. I removed the bricks one by one, which caused a variety of injuries. Both of us were coated inside and out with black soot from working on the chimneys.

All this work caused a great deal of consternation for my brother and me. We were kids doing men's work. We

worked like men, cussed like men, and threatened and
menaced each other like men. We worked as hard as we
could to outdo each other, always trying to be in Dad's
good graces. Once, Dad gave us a few days to dig a septic
tank. It was near a big tree whose root system had spread
throughout our digging site. We worked back to back
in close quarters with axes, shovels and picks, digging
downward in an exhausted frenzy. We kept kicking up
dirt on each other's backs and into each other's clothes
and underwear. It was a sweaty, uncomfortable, muddy
environment. Finally, we came to blows and crawled out
of the hole. Mark had a shovel, and he was pissed. He was
screaming, beyond his breaking point, and I egged him on,
calling him every insulting name in the book. He took a big
swing with the shovel and hit my wrist, causing my arm to
swell rapidly.

Just then, Dad showed up, angry that we were fighting.
"You want to fight? OK!" he said, grabbing us by our necks
and smashing our heads together two or three times. "OK,
let's fight! You like to fight! You want to beat each other's
asses? Let's go! The loser has to fight me, so you better
fight hard, 'cause I'm gonna kick your ass if you lose!"

Crying, pissed and nuts from the escalated violence
and unfairness, Mark and I went back at it. I tried to get
sympathy or at least attention for my injured wrist as blows
rained down on me. Then Dad yelled, "OK, now I'm gonna
kick the ass of who wins! You want to fight, let's go! Get
to it, come on!" We were dumbfounded. I wanted to quit
but kept fighting like a raging mad dog until Dad pulled
us apart. I was crying about my arm and asked Dad for a
ride to the hospital. He just walked away in disgust that
it had come to this. Mark was proud that he matched his
adversarial big brother in a one-on-one match. After a
lifetime of this competitiveness and violence, there was
nothing between Mark and me then but heartless, cold,
pitiless feelings. "You'll get yours later" was the order

of the day. The base hospital was about 15 miles away. I
hitched a ride and got home late.

This episode was one of the breaking points that
alienated me from my family. It was exceptional in its
madness and violence, but there were plenty of other
routine moments of abuse and insanity that drove me away
from the house every day as soon as my chores were done.
Violence was inevitable whenever we had to work with our
father. He was exhausted, miserable and pushed beyond
the breaking point on a daily basis, so he had no energy left
for coping with the emotional challenges of parenthood.
Once, Dad was trying to cut a stripped bolt off a wheel.
He made Mark hold the cold chisel while Dad slammed it
with a sledgehammer. Mark was terrified. I knew where
this was going. I told Mark to give me the chisel, so I was
holding it for the inevitable hand-smashing that came a few
strokes later. WHAM – the hammer smashed my knuckles.
But Dad wouldn't give up until his task was accomplished.
He'd react with banter like, "You should have held it
tighter," or "Why did you flinch? That's why you get hurt!"
Didn't make it hurt any less.

The gang kids in town started to look more and more
appealing as an alternative to my home environment. Every
day when my chores were finished, I would head for their
hangouts. This was a fishing town where people would
drive to the waterfront to charter boats for pleasure cruises,
get hammered and then drive home. To earn my place in the
gang, I agreed to help lure passing motorists into pulling
over. I did as I was told and lay down on the road as if I
were dead. When a driver would pull over and get out of
his car to see if I was OK, the older kids in the gang would
emerge from the surrounding woods, jump into the idling
car, and take off. When the driver chased after his car, I ran
and hid in the neighborhood. I did this about three times.

The younger kids in the neighborhood started camping
overnight on our property. We'd build a fire and bring

sleeping bags and cans of food. Our family's German shepherd, Shaft, would sit by the fire with us. This peaceful scene didn't last long, because the older kids eventually would drive up to entertain themselves at our expense. They told stories about horrible things that happened to campers, pushed us around and made fun of us. Once, they distracted our attention from the fire, and then threw our cans of food into the flames. Another guy had bullets, which he added to the fire. Then the older kids disappeared as quickly as they came. We composed ourselves and got back to the business of camping – just in time for all hell to break loose. Cans of food started exploding, spraying food everywhere. Can fragments flew through the air. Then came the explosive sounds of live ammunition. In the dark, we ran for our lives away from the campsite. A few more reports from the bullets rang out in the night sky, and an explosion sent the fire all over the campsite, embers everywhere. Finally, the blasts stopped. We approached each other and returned to the campsite, but Shaft was nowhere to be found. Eventually, we found Shaft skulking around the campsite like a coyote. For the rest of his life, Shaft never went near a fire again.

Some days, I would wake up, get together with my friends and go swamp-tromping in search of adventure. The swamp was capable of sucking you in up to your hips easily. We kept to the high ground, where we went in up to our knees at the worst parts.

Along the way, we would see the ecological disaster of DDT. We were taught that the way it contaminated the swamp and damaged the quality of life in Delaware should be equated with having the duPont family own and do whatever they wanted. As a tradeoff for the rampant polluting, after all, there were no tollways or state taxes, thanks to the duPonts. Nearly every anomaly of chemical warfare a peace-loving community could ever hope for was produced in Delaware. We were the Cancer Generation, with no place to hide. Better living through chemistry; it made us sick.

From the pesticides, chlorines, bleaches, detergents, oils, and petroleum products, you could see the reason birdlife had diminished. The waters were an oily rainbow of destruction, with white crusts and orange goop floating on the surface. We saw the remnants of a fragile ecosystem on the edge of extinction. I was aware of the ecological movement that was gaining speed around that time, and I enthusiastically participated in it by picking up beer cans that drunken fishermen left along the 3-mile road to the shore. We also would often go to the old boats rotting in the swamp and get all the brass screws and copper fittings off the rotting flesh of these old, forgotten maritime vessels.

So we walked, finding new and strange worlds for young people who could get lost, swept away and forgotten. We came upon many strange growths and unexplainable little places that looked like time had stood still. When the little kids in our gang inevitably got disoriented and started crying, the adventure would transform into a "Lord of the Flies" event of mean-spirited determination to keep focused and go on.

Once, in the midst of crying, we noticed a singular house, all alone. The little ones were momentarily fooled by the delusion of safety of something that looked like home. We meandered through a maze of swampy twists and turns and finally had to balance precariously on pieces of wood we tossed over canals to get to the house. Suddenly, in the middle of nowhere, miles and an eternity from the familiar hazards of our abusive home lives, stood the specter of this ominous house surrounded by the swamp.

It was creepy, with mud encrusted to the middle of the windows. It looked like the Wizard of Oz had transported this house and buffeted it to this spot. All the comforts of home, we realized, were not going to be found here. Fear replaced reassurance, but we were tired and worn out, and it was getting late. What to do? We were fascinated and scared. We dared each other to go toward the door, nervously darting our eyes around to see what horrific Creature of the Black Lagoon lived here. As I approached the door, we suddenly remembered the guy who walked unannounced into a beach cottage and was blown away by a shotgun rigged to the door. So then our plan changed from opening the door to propping a little kid on our heads to get a view inside. Were we really ready to trust the 6-year-old's opinion of safety? He was hungry!

Finally, out of desperation, we jimmied open the door. It opened surprisingly easily. There before us was a scary-looking, disheveled house that had suffered a violent removal from its foundations and been discharged into this God-forsaken place. Everything was covered in mud – rusty, musty, all the way up to the ceiling, about 6 to 8 feet high. Saddened that this was not "our happy home," we snapped back into reality and returned quickly to the swamp.

By this time we knew that we would be late for dinner and in big trouble. I now realized the value of marking a trail, especially through a swamp that twisted this way and that into endless, murky dead ends. Eventually, we focused on the setting sun and hurried in the direction of home. The terrain became more and more familiar and easily navigated until I heard the loud whistle of my father. Oh, shit. My dad could be heard miles away and if you could hear it, you might be able to run and avoid the inevitable beating. Running faster and faster as if driven by the wind, the others followed, not understanding that every fiber of my DNA was striving to avoid the feeling of his powerful retribution. Ah, back on solid ground, and it's our own property – the blessing of living so close to the swamp.

We appeared at the door, muddy and coated with every thistle or reed that was looking for a new home. Fortunately, my dad was in a great mood, working on a project in the garage. He wanted me to hold some greasy, oily thing underneath a jacked-up vehicle. What luck: I wasn't going to get beaten – just the usual life-threatening, under-the-vehicle danger. Life was good this day. I was blessed. Later, I ate like a wolf, showered and plopped into bed, my head brimming with the adventure of a lifetime. I had survived both Mother Nature and my father's wrath.

When the tide would flow into our beachfront town, the waves rolled by at about 15 to 20 miles an hour. If you tried to swim across this muddy quagmire, you took your life into your hands. My friends and I would often get up on the pilings 10 feet above the dock, dive into the murky blackness and play under the docks, getting cut up by the barnacles, mussels and other sea life clinging to the pilings. Once, we dared each other to try to go as far as we could underwater while carrying a 50-pound rock and walking on the bottom for ballast. You would sink up to your thighs in mud even underwater. It was one of the scariest things I remember being dared to do. When you could go no further, you would pop up to the surface, and the next person would try to outdo you. Stories of people drowning or being swept out to sea were common.

At night in the summer, the young kids were invited to hang with the older boys and go skinny-dipping. This was a form of hazing to scare us. They would say that the ghost of "Sandpaper Sally," who purportedly drowned there, would appear on the night of a full moon in August. The dare was to go swimming and get your freak on with Sandpaper Sally. The ritual, as you can imagine, scared the bejesus out of us kids. And with all the hysteria, you could almost see Sally drifting out with the powerful full-moon tide. We tried to be brave and hold on for dear life, fighting the tide, to be cool with the big boys, but a lot of youngsters got smart and braved all kinds of expletives as they ran for their lives back to shore.

Bowers Beach was famous for its horseshoe crabs. They

were about a foot in diameter with 12-inch rigid spikes for protection. Navigating barefoot along a beachful of these was dangerous, and the sight of thousands of these prehistoric beasts breeding was somewhat terrifying. When they were turned over, they had 18 to 20 wiggling crab-legs that were truly scary.

Our town offered some intriguing history, too. Back in the 15th century, America was being settled by newcomers. The Dutch chose Delaware and Maryland, for some reason. Usually in history you hear of brave battles, climates of negotiation, broken treaties, and indigenous peoples let down by abject misery. The Lenape Indians were a peace-loving, quiet and unassuming people who eked out a living on the marsh and coastline. They trapped and ate muskrats, caught fish and had a seafood, crab and shellfish diet rich in protein. The tubules of cattails provided a potato-like, starchy supplement. The Delmarva Peninsula has been an estuary of the Chesapeake Bay for millions of years, with the tide moving in and out, bringing nutrients and black, muddy silt in the marshlands. It grew the richest vegetables, apples, pears, and corn because of this black mud. The mud and the Indians combined to give me an experience that still awes me decades later.

As adventuresome, bored kids will often do, we had to make up games to play and create excitement. With no money and no rules and nobody watching, we did as we pleased. Along the river were numerous sunken boats — marooned, forgotten, storm-wrecked and in various states of decay. When we found one we knew nobody wanted, we spent an entire day scraping the black mud out of it. Our prize came out black, moldy, and half-sinking with no oars. We used a broom that was falling apart.

Somebody got the bright idea that we could drift down the six winding miles of swamp and get to some Indian burial grounds. The tide, once it really got going, would take about six hours to slow down. We did not count on the ebb tide where nothing moved, or the slow backwash out to sea, and we did not stop to wonder when or how long it would take to begin. We were a superstitious lot, and we believed in ghosts and spirits.

With curiosity as our compass, we put our leaky vessel in the water. It held one person – if that person continuously bailed it out, that is. So armed with a coffee can and the powerful pull of the river, we grabbed three inner tubes and filled them up. Daring each other to keep up the bravado to go through with this scheme, three of us slipped into the water.

It was a nice, sunny day. Gently drifting away from the 20 buildings on the docks, the boat disappeared around the bend. We were surrounded by murky reeds, black mud and a swift-moving current. Suddenly, we were alone. At that level of the water, you feel small and insignificant, at the mercy of the tide. Our childhood bravery quickly subsided, and an eerie silence transfixed the air. Where were we? What if we couldn't pull to the side when we found the place? How would we know where we were? There were no towns on this marshy nowhere land. Marsh and mud were all we saw.

We were getting squeamish. Jellyfish stung our legs. Now and then, the boat needed to be set back in the current, which required great effort, as it was full of water and we were in deep, scary, black mud. We realized after changing positions that the boat was more akin to driftwood than watercraft; it was water-logged from years stuck in the mud. Things were looking dismal.

Fear set in. Minutes of uncertainty seemed like hours. Drifting, drifting, we were crushed. Whose idea was this?? Why did we listen to this foolhardy madness to chase down the ghosts of angry Indians who had been unearthed like some Amityville House of Horrors?

Then, one of us noticed an odd sight at water level: a white, tarp-like tent near the shore. We made a mad dash in its direction, but the boat kept drifting. It would not easily move anywhere. We pushed and kicked with all we had and rammed it into the shore 100 yards past our stopping point.

Indians, shmindians – I was through! We angrily pulled our half-sunken boat to the reeds and hoped it would not drift away without us. We carried our inner tubes through the knee-deep mud and finally made it to the eerie-looking tent area. It suddenly occurred to us that no one was there. I wondered if we should dare to go near this place. How could we keep the spirit of the wronged Indians from killing us or cursing our lives like the mummies of the Egyptian tombs?

The excavation had just been started. There were 20 or so covered areas. With our inner tubes in hand, exhausted from the journey, we had no energy to be brave and look for the dead. No one had ever seen a skeleton other than fake ones on Halloween, and the real deal was scary. Too tired to quit, we made our way cautiously toward the closest excavation site. There, in a crunched-up fetal position, was a skeleton perched upon a bed of mud. We stood and stared for a long time. That incredible site energized and emboldened us. We went on a wild, exploring frenzy, yelling to each other to come look at our finds.

After scrutinizing our discoveries, we started looking for souvenirs. The peat-like condition of the swamp mud had virtually stopped time for these artifacts. We were acting like grave robbers. But even in our treasure-hunting frenzy, we kept an eye on the waning tide. The trip there had seemed like hours in the water, but traveling at 15 mph, the six miles had gone by quick. Now we had to wait a few hours before we could head back. Tired, thirsty, bored, and scared of getting back in the water, we rested and tried to scare each other with the worst ghost or Indian curses we could think of. Taking one more look at the skeletons, we felt like we were saying goodbye to important friends.

The tide was moving slow, but the water had an

unnatural glow. We hesitantly got in the water. No longer having immortal, unstoppable, undefeatable, kid-like powers, we moaned and complained, and the water seemed to take forever. It was more work to keep the boat going than it was worth. Every time our limbs were in the water, the fear of death was upon us, now that we had seen it firsthand. Mosquitoes, gnats and horseflies tormented us. Once we finally returned to familiar territory, we got our courage back and felt like world travelers. We started to drift back by the piers. We let that old wreck drift wherever it wanted to go and swam to the docks.

Of course, nobody believed us until a few years later, when the burial grounds became better known. We couldn't tell our parents, or we'd really get in trouble. It was the kind of secret that was only for people who were cool enough to tell.

– 10 –

Rebel Without Applause

One blistering July day, three boys with a lot of chores to do and no place to run decided to go cool off in a watering hole used by the largest farmer in the area – Mr. Andersen*. On the only road out of the God-forsaken, mosquito-ridden swamp, we walked – my brother Mark, our friend Eddie, and me.

To get to the irrigation hole, you had to walk two miles. After that, we were plum tired. Once we finally got near the watering hole, we had to trespass onto Mr. Andersen's large and abundant farm. He was the richest man in our county, as I recall. Sneaking past the house, quiet as we could be, we entered the heart of the farm where all the animals were housed.

We surrounded his chicken coop like wolves, went in and each grabbed six or seven eggs. Then we ran down the long road in the back of the farm, smashing the eggs into each other. Head hits, shoulder hits, smashes in the back, and a few road kills. Eddie was a smallish kid who often took the brunt of meanness, and this aerial assault was no exception. My dad also sometimes enjoyed a good round of kid torture at the expense of Eddie and any other children who might be hanging around. When he was working on an engine, he would hold a kid's hand, then touch the alternator on his running car. My dad would not get shocked, but the kid holding his hand would get a big jolt because he became the ground for the direct current electricity. Then, Dad would let the kid in on the secret, and they'd wait for the next sucker to get electrocuted. Don't try this at home.

But I digress. Mr. Andersen's pond was located strategically alongside the strawberry fields, so without haste, we gorged on strawberries. Then we smeared them all over each other's faces and bare backs. We were out of control. Covered in strawberries, we jumped into the water and roughhoused, trying to drown each other. We'd swim underwater, wait for the person to come up for air, and then push his head under. This degenerated into putting mud in our mouths from the pond's bottom, then spraying a struggling person with mud as he gasped for air.

Since we lived along the coast, it was no surprise that there was a regulation-size life boat in the pond. We played in it, dove off of it and tried to sink each other in it. We played all the lost-at-sea games we could think of. Then we acted like it was a sinking ship. We turned it upside down, got underneath and pretended we were stuck. After that, it was time to go needlessly tromp through more of Mr. Andersen's strawberries and smear them all over each other. Exhausted by all this vandalism, we lay back and snoozed in the warm noonday sun under a willow tree, satisfied with our day.

While we rested, we strategized our next debacle. We noticed the farmer's gasoline tank next to the pond. The tank held maybe 1,000 gallons of petrol. One of us suggested that we upgrade the sunken-ship game by turning it into a watery, fiery grave. Since the boat was overturned already, one of us got up the nerve to put the gasoline hose into the pond and let it rip. I don't remember being the one doing the act, but I remember going along with this crazy plan. The idea was to get two people under the boat, cover the top of the pond with gas, and light it up. The other person would then swim and join us underwater, getting under the boat where the flames could not reach. What a well-thought-out plan. After much debate, my brother and I decided to get under the boat, and Eddie lit the water on fire on the count of three.

At first, nothing out of the ordinary could be noticed, except the roar of a blazing fire and Eddie's panicked and terrified screams. Mark and I couldn't see anything from under the boat, so what's all the fuss about? I decided to swim deeper and look up to see the water's surface – and whatever Eddie was screaming about. Through the murky-green, algae-covered pond, I saw red flames on the water above me. It looked like fire was everywhere. I swam back under the boat and reported this to Mark, at which point we began to freak out more appropriately. We were in deep shit now. The temperature of the water's surface was increasing rapidly. It felt like a bath. As we considered the possibility that we were about to be boiled alive, Eddie started yelling at us to swim away from the main flow of the fire. Only problem was, we were blind underneath the boat and couldn't tell which direction he meant.

This seemed to go on for hours, but it must have just been five or six minutes. Eddie kept us posted, and the screams died down along with the gas-fed flames. The adrenaline pumped in our veins. We were exhausted, treading water and trying to hold onto the underside of the boat. Finally, with Eddie taunting us to come out, we yelled, "Here we come!" I went first and swam underwater as far as I could away from the boat. Finally, I had to surface. I looked up and hesitated as my face broke the surface of the water. I gasped for air, which was heavy with the smell of gas. Mark surfaced, and we headed to shore.

In our underwear in the sun, finally feeling safe, we laughed about our misplaced bravado. Then we heard the revving of a John Deere tractor barreling down the road toward us, leaving a trail of dust. Our sense of triumph vanished, and our faces went pale. We were briefly stunned and paralyzed, but then we sprang up and searched for cover. Our clothes were way over by the strawberry patch. We heard the explosive report of a shotgun blast – and a very pissed-off man screaming expletives.

Looking at each other and realizing we had seconds to make a decision, we ran barefoot and bare-assed toward the end of Mr. Andersen's farm, which straddled marsh and swamp for miles in every direction. Running out of paths and road and realizing that someone was riding shotgun for real on this tractor, we heard two more shots. We knew this was no game. If this was not bird shot, it was salt rock. At the edge of the swamp, the only way to get through was to run into 15-foot ravines of mud where the tide came in. Ignoring stickers and splinters that shredded our feet and mud that sucked up to our hips, we ran for our lives. I knew that this man shooting at me would be nothing compared to the beating my dad would give me if I got caught doing something this bad.

Behind us, the angry men yelled that they knew who we were, and we were going to get it. Their voices grew dimmer as we raced onward. Bruised, bleeding and cursing, we made our way through thickets, stickers, thistle, reeds, mosquitoes and two miles of living hell. Then we reached pavement. We couldn't run onto the road in our underwear. That would be a dead giveaway at worst, or would make us the brunt of jokes and humiliation at best. Mr. Andersen's farm was the only thing between town and the highway.

Finally, we picked our way back to civilization. Worn out, we ran to my house, which was one of the first places

along the road into town. With Mom and Dad both away
from home working, we were safe. Bruised and battered,
we showered and put on long sleeves and long pants in
the middle of summer to cover ourselves. Eddie borrowed
some clothes and went home. He lived right down the street
from where the rest of the Andersens lived in town. If he
didn't make it home, we knew we were in deep shit. He
called, and we finally exhaled in relief.

For weeks after that, I laid low, afraid to leave the house.
As far as the Andersen family was concerned, from that day
forward, I was branded. I felt deep shame for this.

The school year started, and I crossed the threshold
of yet another strange new school. This time it was W.T.
Chipman Junior High. Immediately, the staff went to work
on the speech defect caused by the loss of my front teeth, so
I could learn to speak without a lisp. In the meantime, I got
to know my sprawling new community, which had about
10 little towns and countless farms within walking distance.
Bowers Beach was Future Farmers of America country,
and status was attained by excelling at football, wrestling,
basketball, field hockey and baseball. Then, kids would
head home to do their farm chores. The people were stuffy,
straight-laced, and prejudiced against anyone who looked,
talked or thought different. I did all of the above, which
meant I spent some time developing survival strategies so I
didn't get my ass beat.

I was 13 years old and the presence of all the female
students reignited my flaming desire to build on my sexual
skills. One of the first friends I made was Darlene*, a quiet
girl with a ruffian boyfriend who had been held back a
few grades. That meant he was bigger and meaner than the
other kids in the class. We had several moments of tension
as he tried to establish a position of power over me. I got
threatened a lot, but I stood my ground. The up side of that
was that all the guys who'd watched me get picked on all
summer now stayed out of my way after seeing me stand

up to Darlene's boyfriend. Events took a shocking turn when her boyfriend went deer hunting and was shot with his own rifle. The story went that he climbed a tree and his rifle slipped out of his hands, struck a branch below him and discharged. He was hit by a "pumpkin ball," a large, round piece of lead designed to stop a deer in its tracks. He died instantly.

I felt bad that he was dead, but the disappearance of my bully undeniably made my daily life easier. Beyond that, I saw an opportunity to make a move on my newly available friend. However, the death of Darlene's big, intimidating boyfriend had painful consequences for her. It was common knowledge that Darlene and her boyfriend were doing the wild thing. Now that the menacing boyfriend was gone, everyone openly voiced their feelings that Darlene was a slut. She endured a lot of slander and innuendo, but of course, her 1969 choice of wardrobe – hot pants, mini-skirts and high heels – didn't earn her much support in this farm town, where most of the boys wore jeans and flannel shirts and the girls wore more modest clothes. Her choice of clothes drove me out of my mind, though, and my behavior became more and more outrageous. I would grab and grope her in the halls when I thought no one was looking.

All this sexual and social tension hit a breaking point one day when I grabbed her ass. In the middle of the school hallway, in front of everyone, Darlene raised one high-heeled foot and kicked me hard. The spike heel made a hole in the rear of my pants and gave me an instant colostomy. Limping, I was taken to the principal, who offered to let my parents know about my behavior. I finally got the point and promised to be the best, shining example of a good student they had ever seen.

This felt like a rare opportunity for me to prove that I could be good and actually be acknowledged for that by safe, mature adults. I dedicated myself to showing up for

school and started playing drums with the school band
at football and basketball games. I hooked up with some
brothers who played soul music, and we played for other
school events. By now, I wore all kinds of androgynous
clothing, and my playing attracted the attention of some
older musicians who took me on board. I started playing
steady gigs with the older guys at fire halls, base clubs
and the Airmen's Club. These guys smoked and drank and
looked terrible already. One guy was only 35 and he was
already toothless. I would jog and do pushups at gigs so I
didn't have to smoke or drink. I didn't want to wind up like
them.

Although I was only 13, these guys were brutal and
unforgiving with me. If I didn't play a song right, they'd
take me outside, hold me down, and hit my belly hard until
I cried. This was called "giving me a pink belly." It seemed
inevitable that the violence and dysfunction at home would
eventually erupt in every area of my life, so I wasn't
surprised that the old familiar pain was incorporated into
my music, too. Our band was invited to play a few songs on
the Jerry Lewis Muscular Dystrophy Telethon that year. We
went on at 2:30 in the morning. It was brutal for me to stay
up that late. As soon as we played our songs and headed for
home, I fell asleep in the car.

I gravitated toward all the strange, new music of the
day, but my older peers initially reacted to androgynous
musicians like David Bowie and Alice Cooper by calling
them faggots or worse. Then, before I knew it, we'd be
learning Bowie and Cooper songs. I never knew what drove
the fickle music machine; I was just eager to learn the
songs.

My dad was a master electrician who knew all the latest
grooves in strobe and black lights, and this was one way he
could communicate his love and support to me. Once, he
placed 4-foot-tall black lights behind my drum kit. Since
we were called the Medusas, from the Greek mythology, I

wore a shower cap with green fluorescent snakes coming out of it. I had rings of groovy colors on my sticks and lit my cymbals on fire. Between the tracers from the strobe lights, the flaming cymbals and the fluorescent snake lights swinging back and forth on my head, this was a fantastic spectacle, even for people who didn't happen to be on LSD!

For a couple of hours each day, I put on my headphones and diligently practiced my drums. I played along with the cool grooves on a pirate radio station that was on a ship past the 3-mile international line. This station played Savoy Brown, Motor City Five, Jefferson Airplane, Jimi Hendrix, Blind Faith, and dozens of other great groups. My dad encouraged me to learn the drum solos in Iron Butterfly's "In-A-Gadda-Da-Vida" and "Wipe Out" by the Ventures, and I willingly mastered them. I also played a lot of soul music, which was as much a part of me as breathing.

The race riots had just raged in Watts, Chicago and Detroit, and the violence was fresh in everyone's minds. But in Delaware, our community seemed to handle the racial tension with a little more willingness to try. Our school principal set a great example of community with seemingly small daily choices, like choosing three African-American musicians and me to play at the biggest school dance of the year. On the night of the dance, he introduced us to the student body as "Three Souls and a Pole!" The students roared with laughter. We could feel the tension, but the kids boogied peacefully until a black boy asked a white girl to dance. Quickly, the room changed from happy dancing to a dangerous, swirling melee. My white friends urged me to side with "my kind," but I grabbed our mike stands and stood firm. People cooled down and filed out of the dance, but that would not be the end of it.

Back in school on Monday morning, the threats and name-calling began: "nigger lover," "Polish nigger dog," "white nigger." Older students I didn't know accosted me.

Even my cool juvenile-delinquent friends asked me to choose sides. One positive thing I did learn from my family was the absolute rejection of racial discrimination, so there was no choice for me to make. It was a hellish year of facing down these threats and challenges on a daily basis, but slowly in the midst of all this tension, I felt myself start to become part of the community. I had friends in high and low places – some were ruffians, some were scholastic, some were religious, and then there were the girls, girls, girls.

I finally met the girl who initiated me into the world of real sexual experience. Her name was Maura*, and when she went on the fritz with her older boyfriend, I charmed my way into her good graces. She liked baseball, so I would go to games and jealously watch her get all excited about the guys on the field. She lived in a trailer court near the baseball field, and the day of opportunity finally arrived. There we were on her mom's bed, doing the wild thing with "Sesame Street" turned up loud on the TV. Her mom called, "Are you all right?" We both yelled out, "Fine!" This bliss lasted a few months until she reunited with her boyfriend. Then I was cut loose – abandoned, horny, and ready for more action.

I actively began practicing the selective, misogynistic treatment of women that would become second nature for the next 30 years. I lived different lives in different places and treated a woman I liked one way, while treating others the way I thought they wanted to be treated. That could get pretty ugly. I had been exposed to all sorts of confusing behaviors by then, so sometimes I acted like a superficial, sexist jerk toward women. Other times, I was so repelled by the abusive men I'd seen, I reacted by acting effeminate in some ways. Naturally, this just drew negative reactions that twisted me up even further. Needless to say, my 13-year-old understanding of the world was a big, confused mess.

Back at home, we began the Herculean task of jacking

our big house 8 feet off the ground. This was a massive undertaking, and Dad hired contractors for the task. We worked alongside them, cleaning up and excavating. Dad, Mark and I dug out 4 feet of the basement. We used center-cut redwood and jacked the house up quarter-inch by quarter-inch. I learned new skills and also came to understand how easy it was to be killed with one false move. It took a long time, but finally we got the immense house up in the air – just in time to save ourselves from a rainy season of biblical proportions. The whole community, from our house on the hill all the way to the beach, was flooded with black, smelly, muddy swamp water. The floods ruined hundreds of houses. Some people resented us for being the newcomers who avoided the devastation, while others accepted our offers of help and support.

I met many different types of people and made some friends. I discovered some common bonds among the diverse kids of the town. For example, it seemed that almost every last one of us had "the kissing disease" – also known as herpes – on our lips. Also, it seemed most people under 18 were or had recently been either pregnant or arrested. This was another community where the restless youths occupied themselves with sexual activity far beyond their years, and I willingly joined in. Once, I was walking by a local policeman's house when his teen-age daughter appeared at the window and called me over. I knew she had older boyfriends and I didn't want any trouble, but she kept beckoning and saying, "It's all right! Just come here!" Scared and nervous, I knew I shouldn't go, but the suspense was too much. When I got to the bathroom window, she opened the curtains, and I was face to face with a naked, fully formed 16-year-old girl. This was more than I could handle mentally, and before I even had a chance to try, her younger brothers and sister pushed open the bathroom door, yelling, "We're telling Daddy what you're doing!" I was out of there. In this town, things like this usually were settled with violence, and I knew no good could come from this.

That night, the policeman came to our house to get me. My dad intervened. "Wait a minute – let me talk to my son." After being beaten all my life as motivation to tell the truth, the facts slid easily off my tongue, and my father knew I was being honest. Dad stood up for me, and the officer finally left, failing to obtain justice for his "wronged daughter." I may have gotten off the hook that night, but I would have to stay down low from that man for some time to come. He had it out for me. Every time I saw his red lights approaching, I scrambled for cover.

My dad sometimes had his scuffles with the locals as well. One night, as we drove home down the 3-mile road from the highway, a driver swerved into our lane and tried to scare us. He bumped our car from behind. My dad went berserk – this driver had no idea who he was messing with. Dad turned off our car's lights and terrorized this man, chasing him, forcing him off the road, and hitting his car from behind until the perp-turned-victim finally pulled over. Dad went to his car and threatened his life. Our family went home, afraid that guys like this would pick us off later one by one.

Dad was working 60 to 70 hours a week, then coming home and working on the never-ending rehab of our property. He had lost some of his hearing from working near jet engines for so many years, and he also was deeply exhausted. An alarm clock just didn't cut it to wake him up in the mornings – he used a klaxon, the kind of deafening electric horn you hear at basketball games. That sound started the day for the five of us in the tiny trailer we shared while the house was being restored. Mom was working her Civil Service job and a waitressing job at the Village Inn (one of a hundred places she waited tables) on the side. Mom smoked Larks, and Dad smoked two packs of Pall Malls a day. In the winter mornings when they lit up, their smoke would get sucked into the trailer's ventilation system and choke us kids to death. This was a daily, torturous struggle for me, which may be why I have never smoked cigarettes and despise cigarette smoke. I couldn't get out of the trailer fast enough in the mornings. The more I got out and about, the more I noticed that other families seemed to deal with stress in ways that were less punishing and abusive. But the only other "families" I could find a place in were gangs, where the violence and brutal version of justice were all too familiar.

– 11 –

Sex, Drugs, and Ninth-Grade Politics

As I marked my 14th birthday, I continued to play music with seasoned musicians in their 20s and 30s. This took me to a lot of places where kids do not belong. When our band played at the local Bowers Beach dances, the gigs would often attract the attention of the Pagans, the East Coast equivalent of the Hell's Angels motorcycle gang. These guys would show up on their choppers and get down. After one gig, a Pagan called me over to his chopper and told me to get on. This dude had stuck a trident on the back of his chopper, so I climbed on right in front of it. He took off fast, trying to scare me. It worked. Then he did a wheelie, and all I could see was the trident and the long chrome "sissy bar" dragging on the road, making sparks fly everywhere. We stayed in that position for what seemed like an eternity. Finally, he put his front wheel back on the pavement and pulled up in front of the club, where he and his friends shared a laugh over my first ride. Somehow, I was being welcomed into the murky, criminal world of gang danger and drugs.

For a little podunk town, our community had a lot of drugs. As the son of an Air Force chief engineer who had flown C-141s into Dover Air Force Base, I later learned at least one source of those drugs. My father often would fly back from Vietnam with his huge cargo hold full of the remains of fallen soldiers. The story went that the mortuary techs who prepared the bodies for transport were part of a massive drug ring, and they would conceal drugs in the soldiers' armpits and other body cavities. The mortuary techs at the receiving end would unpack the drugs and send them on to their intended destinations. Some of these drugs wound up in the able hands of gangs like the Pagans, which had their own distribution systems. I found myself hanging out and trying to fit in with these older guys who, after club gigs, would gather at various houses to score weed, speed and heroin. One of the gathering places was right down the road from our house. One night, I shot heroin for the first time. I threw up violently, felt sick and went home to lie down until this horrible feeling passed. Heroin wasn't my idea of a fun party. I was 14; I drank beer.

We found out that a Catholic church in downtown Dover had kegs of beer, and we decided to relieve the churchgoers of this temptation. We piled into the rent-a-heap that belonged to one of the gang members and took the long journey to the church compound, which was overwhelming in its size and scope. By now, we'd worked ourselves into a beer-liberating frenzy, so we located the kitchen area and crept stealthily inside. There we discovered three large, aluminum kegs. That's where the stealth ended. We roll-bounced the big, cumbersome kegs out of the refrigerator, and they bounced on the floor against the stainless-steel tables nearby. Then we made a huge racket as we rolled them across the parking lot, saying, "Shhh! SSSHH!" the whole way. We stuffed the kegs and ourselves into the clunker and made our way back to Bowers Beach. We stashed one keg at my house, but we couldn't open or drink it. That is, not until I made a new friend, Dale*. Dale's grandmother owned the Heartbreak Hotel, a notorious destination for hard partying and drunken sex. Dale grabbed the keg hardware we needed at the hotel bar, and we were in business.

All the kids grabbed a cup and came to my house, where we proceeded to get completely pasted. One thing our dad always told us was if we were going to drink and do drugs, we should do it on our own property to avoid getting busted. He meant it, too. Of course, we then would have to answer to a higher calling – namely, his wrath. But until then, this was the life – staggering around, delirious, drunk and feeling so cool. I introduced our dog, Shaft, to the draught, so he was staggering around, too. This began a longtime habit of including my animals in my substance abuse, which I now regret. The next day, with the brew getting flat, we hobbled the keg up to the widow's walk on top of our Victorian house, and about 10 of us drank beer and smoked weed, delusional masters of all we surveyed. We could see for miles around, so no one could possibly sneak up and bust us. This was a phenomenal discovery, as it seemed that people were getting busted, disappearing and reappearing constantly in our community. We never knew if they went to juvenile hall or prison, and we didn't want to find out the hard way. I was hyper-aware and vigilantly observant – especially when the weed made me paranoid.

The change from innocent kid to hardened substance-user had begun.

I launched my career as a grower of marijuana. I would find places where no one would notice it – interspersed in corn fields or concealed in other areas I could access easily without attracting suspicion. Mostly, my life as a weed farmer was a farce. I would grow sprouts in milk cartons and then transplant them, and they would usually die. Sometimes, I would succeed in cultivating a large group of sprouts, but they would turn out to be "males" with no potency. I smoked it anyway, stems and all. Now and then, I'd successfully grow a "female," which I would smoke judiciously and milk for all it was worth.

My brother Mark, now about 13, was always nearby, and I regret that I turned him on to alcohol and weed. It still haunts me to this day. We were young, vulnerable and surrounded by role models showing us the worst kind of life.

Along with all of this substance abuse, my days were full: I did my schoolwork, completed the never-ending chores at home, and played music. I gradually became more comfortable wearing the masks that enabled me to fit in with anyone from the Pagans, to "normies," to different ethnicities, to the rich, religious and educated. I learned how to go to school high and not care about the looks I got. I began to live the continuing dilemma of getting a fix and justifying my actions.

I also spent a lot of time with my ass in the air, getting action from girls who became temporarily available between boyfriends or breakups. I became quite the junior womanizer, which helped establish my reputation as a legitimate man among the local guys. I let my hair grow long and began collecting patches to sew onto my favorite pair of jeans. Some kids still called me "nigger lover," so in an effort to help them pick me out of a crowd more easily, I embroidered a patch that said "Polishniggerdog" and sewed it onto the back of my jeans jacket.

As the end of eighth grade drew near, the students held elections to choose officers for our ninth-grade class at Lake Forest High School. Candidates were sought who could ably represent all the different subcultures that populated our school – rednecks, religious conservatives, African-Americans, just plain folk, and the rest of us

unclassifiables. I was asked to run for the offices of Student
Council Secretary and Ninth-Grade Class President. On
a platform of unwavering pride in my egalitarian beliefs,
I endured rampant racism and threats and was voted into
both offices. My dad, who dropped out of high school and
lied about his age to flee his abusive father and join the
Navy, didn't seem too impressed with this accomplishment.
He had a simpler goal for us that he often repeated: "All I
want from you is a good report card."

As I began to serve my term as a double-barreled
Secretary/President, I also developed my friendship with
Dale, grandson of the Heartbreak Hotel owner. Dale, who
also grew up without much parental supervision, was
a great companion for all sorts of activities. His older
brothers and sisters were always high, drunk, fighting and/
or fucking, and we tried to find a safe space from which to
observe all that fascinating action. But the Heartbreak Hotel
was not known as a safe haven. The Heartbreak's hotel
and bar attracted hard-working characters from all around
who would descend on the place nightly to smoke, drink,
play pool and pinball, drink some more, pump coins into
the jukebox, continue drinking, and then stumble into the
hotel rooms and hump like rabbits. Drunken rabbits. Twice
a month, Dale's grandmother would boil three barrels full
of Chesapeake Bay blue crabs, and the clientele would
brandish tiny wooden hammers to pound out all the crab
meat they could from these tasty creatures. When closing
time rolled around at 2 a.m., everyone drove home wasted.

Dale and I hung out around the Heartbreak and took
volumes of mental notes. We could climb up to the attic and
see into some of the hotel rooms, where we would watch
the strangely shaped creatures get down to the business
of intoxicated sex. This pastime never lasted long for us;
our screaming hormones always sent us on the hunt for
our own action soon enough. Dale also had access to the
money in the pool tables and jukeboxes, so he often would

liberate some cash for us to go have fun. We would drink beer straight from the tap (we hadn't yet developed a taste for the hard stuff), and then we'd buy candy and walk for miles.

Dale and I were mostly loners and were happy to hang out with just each other for company. We would climb trees in the woods or hike to remote swimming holes where we could skinnydip and relax in the sun without worrying about being accosted. I rediscovered the joys of relaxed nudity that I first enjoyed as a young boy in Morocco. When we arrived at one of our ponds, we discovered a bulldozer whose operator was hard at work at some project. We dared each other to climb into the bulldozer's scoop when it was fully extended to 35 feet in the air – and then dive. I took the dare and climbed up, failing to notice that as the dozer operator raised his scoop, he also backed it ever so slightly away from the shore of the pond. When I dove, I hit the water only a few shallow feet from shore. The silt of soft mud partially broke my fall. I sustained a concussion and a bruised, scabbed face and shoulders, but I was deeply grateful that I hadn't broken my neck. This was yet another of the countless near-death experiences I had in my life.

Oddly enough, I made another friend whose family owned and operated a roadside motel. Albert* lived with his widowed mother, and the hotel she ran had an odd, indefinable vibe that suggested the Bates Motel in Hitchcock's "Psycho." Dale and I soon recognized that Albert was one of us – a loner with family problems who liked to smoke weed, take LSD and talk about girls. We would go to parties at houses with beaded, tie-dyed rooms and try to be cool around the older people while the incense burned, the patchouli wafted, and Zeppelin and Chicago's "25 or 6 to 4" played in the background. We would usually be left in the common areas while the older cats would retire to shooting galleries, sharing needles and getting down with heroin and each other. Sooner or later, we would meet these people we thought were so cool in less flattering circumstances, like brandishing guns and freaking out during simple disagreements. They weren't the greatest role models. Inevitably, we would be summarily dismissed with, "Fuck off and get out of here, you little bastards." And we would.

While things went from bad to worse at home, I was going to concerts, playing drums at gigs, and having a social life at school that many (usually including me) might envy. One of my most enduring friendships was with a smart, friendly kid named Jimmy Hutchison. We ran track, played football and attended classes together. Jimmy and I had even run against each other in the race for ninth-grade Class President. On Sundays, his family's car would sometimes stop in front of my house to pick me up so we could go to church together. Jimmy was always encouraging and inviting, and the Hutchisons seemed like a kind-hearted, straight-laced family – startling evidence that such families actually existed.

In the ninth grade, I was invited to proms in two different school districts. I also became involved in the Christian movement, which welcomed a lot of social miscreants into the ranks of the "Jesus Freaks," as we were called. The church offered the saving grace of Jesus, which I sometimes sincerely sought. The Lord also seemed to have the finest women, and I enjoyed as many of them as I could. I was praising the Lord one way or the other. But one aspect of my Christian pursuits that I still regret was book-burning. Specifically, I would get on holy-roller tangents and burn my mother's books on topics she believed in, such as biorhythms, extrasensory perception, and the psychic abilities of Edgar Cayce, to name but a few. An open-minded and intelligent person, our mother had books on every kind of spiritual exploration and shared them willingly. I responded by burning her books not once, but twice.

By age 15, I had graduated from driving around our acreage in a 1959 Fiat convertible to plowing through 3 miles of surrounding cornfields in a classic station wagon. We emptied every can of spray paint my father owned onto the sides of that car. People would have been amazed at the crop circles we made while driving, drunk and confused, through these fields with our windows open, our outstretched arms thrashed by rough leaves on the passing cornstalks. If the farmer could have caught us, I'm sure he would have enjoyed killing us, and with good reason. Of course, with that paint job, you could see us coming for miles.

When I finally got my license at 16, the drinking age in Delaware was 21. However, Delaware is a thin state, so it took no time at all to drive across it to Maryland, where the drinking age was 18. I would saddle up an 18-year-old friend and drive him or her to buy beer for us. With the drinking math all worked out, I continued to attempt to make spiritual sense of my life experience by spending time with just about every organized religion in our area. I worked my way from Protestants to Pentecostals, Christians, Baptists, Southern Baptists who spoke in tongues, and Catholics.

Then I met a strange family of Seventh-Day Adventists who lived down the street. The family included three daughters, all of whom I eventually tried to have sex with. The eldest daughter was married to the lead singer of a Delaware rock band called Colours. The band was about as close to famous as you could get in that area. The marriage of Mr. and Mrs. "Colours" was on the rocks, and she was on the hunt for some "chicken." She was in her mid-20s, and I was 15, just the age she was looking for. She taught me a lot of my sexual prowess. On some levels, I thought that was a fantastic stroke of luck. On the other hand, it was what it was – statutory rape and molestation. Aspects of this experience scarred me for decades.

At home, my sex education was every bit as appropriate as you might expect. When I was 13, Dad handed me a rubber and said, "When it gets hard, it does all the thinking." The rest of his guidance was delivered throughout my childhood via his constant banter about women – "Look at that piece of meat! What an ass! Look at those knockers!" He could go on for hours. Mom, on the other hand, did her best to communicate what she felt was most important for a man to know. "Honey, don't grow up to be like all these men that just seek their pleasure and then pull out of a woman. Wait till she comes, and then pull out so you don't get her pregnant." At least this advice helped me avoid adding unplanned pregnancies to the accumulation of messes I created during the next 30 years.

I decided around this time that the best long-term plan was to have two or three relationships at the same time. All of the women would know each other and buy into the system, or else I would say a sincere "thank you" and leave. The obsessive-compulsive dances I had to perform to make "smooth" transitions from one relationship to another helped strengthen my unfortunate talents in people-pleasing, codependency, emotional enmeshment, validation and abandonment. I would endure my bleakest depressions at those times when there were no relationships, leaving me alone with the cavernous "God Hole" in the middle of my soul. The hopelessness was vast, expansive and overwhelming.

Without realizing it, I was emulating my parents, and with the same self-destructive results. My mother continued to have frequent extramarital affairs, and all of her friends seemed to be loose single women. She started hanging out at the Dover Downs International Speedway, and then she got a second job as a waitress at a nearby restaurant. There, she would meet some of the drivers after the races. She would sometimes have a whole table of drivers sign their paper placemats, and she'd bring the placemats home to her kids. Dad also continued to have affairs, partly to spite our mother and partly because it was the only way to get his needs met without abandoning his family.

Our dad had endured many years of living with his wife's infidelity, as well as her constant overspending, which forced him to work 20-hour workdays and keep multiple jobs and, worst of all, left him with no chance of spending quality time with his children or developing a family life. By now, Dad dragged himself through each day with sleep-deprived, bone-deep fatigue and emotional exhaustion. If he'd ever wanted a chance to be a different type of parent than his own violent father had been, he seemed to be living in the worst trailer in the world to reach that goal.

Mom bought herself a gold Dodge Charger with a 440 Magnum engine. This was one of the biggest muscle cars you could get. It was a fast, good-looking car that attracted attention. Dad seemed to be going out of his mind from the pressures of work, his marriage, his kids, his wife's friends. Not long after, the frustration level between Mom and Dad escalated to the point that Dad drove the Charger into a swamp.

The dynamic between my father and me wasn't much better. One thing I learned from all the young people I met was that other kids didn't seem to be abused as much as I was. As much as I loved him, I felt I was never able to please him with my grades, music or social success. It was never enough to get past the criticism, the questioning, the intimidation. He would hold my face tight in his hands and stand nose to nose, demanding that I repeat what he was telling me to make sure I got it. And that was the non-violent communication. His way of communicating was as devastating to him as it was to me, although neither of us realized it at the time.

– 12 –

Runaways in New York

By now, I had many ways to get gone from my home life, whether through drugs, drinking, school, music, or traveling to surrounding communities with my Christian friends. I would spend weekends out and about as a traveling Christian, newly saved but still pursuing drugs, sex and alcohol. You can't stop a lifetime of messages with one sermon; I needed to do a little more "research." Even with all these escape routes, Dale, Albert and I started making plans to hit the road for real. New York City was our ultimate destination. We accumulated clothing and camping supplies from the Army/Navy Surplus and other sources, and started walking everywhere to get our bodies used to traveling long distances. Finally, Albert suggested that we try a dry run.

We loaded up all of our gear and hiked a few miles on that cold November day. Then we found a suitable place to camp for the night and started a crackling fire. We spread tarps and opened our waterproof sleeping bags on them.

Near midnight, we hung our clothes over a branch in the trees above us, climbed into our bags and fell asleep. We were awakened by a torrential downpour that threatened to soak absolutely everything, but miraculously the sleeping bags stayed waterproof. We pulled the ends of the sleeping bags over our heads and returned to a glorious slumber. The glory lasted only until dawn, when Dale's shouting woke us up. I stuck my head out of my sleeping bag to see that a heavy layer of snow had covered everything around us. We slid out of our sleeping bags and, wet and freezing, had no choice but to pull on the clothes that had soaked and then frozen solid over our heads. Talk about cold balls! In great discomfort, we hobbled back to the safety of my family trailer, trying not to wake everyone with our packs and squishy hiking boots. It would be the last time we had an easy out from the perils of road life.

News of the Vietnam War on TV was unavoidable, and we'd heard how older guys were going to Philadelphia for induction physicals to join the military. We figured if we could get through the induction process, the military would give us bus tickets back home; we could then trade those tickets and travel as far toward New York City as possible. Dale and Albert looked older and could pass for 18. I couldn't lie to save my ass, but the guys liked my enthusiasm for the plan, so we schemed to figure out how to make this lie happen at the recruitment center. We figured we wouldn't have to try too hard. The military machine was hungry for bodies and didn't seem to care where it got them.

The time had finally come. We got ready to roll with our packs and sleeping bags and headed for the Greyhound bus station. My school life always hung by a thread, so to hell with my responsibilities as Class President and Student Council Secretary. We climbed on the bus in Dover and, victorious and excited, we stepped off hours later in Philadelphia. Immediately, the big city was overwhelming with its bustling noise, fast-moving traffic, and the smell of exhaust that would become so familiar. I noticed the homeless dregs milling around the bus station. Stunned, I realized, "There are too many of us!" And I thought running away was such a bold and innovative idea. We found the recruitment center in a faceless building and were surrounded by the messages of indoctrination. Do this, do that, put that down, move over here! We were herded like cattle toward the slaughter. Standing in our underwear and socks, we were guided through lines for complete physical examinations, as they sought any deformity or mental impairment that might inhibit our ability to kill strangers in exotic lands. I began to wonder if we already had passed the point of no return but, hours later, we returned to the streets and the freedom of running away. Leaving the recruitment center was like saying goodbye to the mother ship; with all tethers now severed, we walked into the new world. Back at the Greyhound station, we got on a bus and told the agent that the destination printed on our tickets must be some sort of mistake – we actually lived at an address in New Jersey. That was as far toward NYC as we figured our fares would take us. It worked, and the bus rolled to a stop and dumped us out in New Jersey.

The three of us trudged down the New Jersey highway with our thumbs out, trying to hitchhike our way toward New York. With no idea of where to stand or how to present ourselves in a way that would persuade strangers to pull over, we spent a few miserable days sleeping near endless freeway ramps, waiting painfully long periods for drivers to pick us up.

We quickly consumed what food we'd packed, and we panhandled along the way for food money. Coffee was our main food group. The choking smell of diesel exhaust was our accompaniment to the numbing, hypnotic sight of car after car whooshing past us with blank faces behind the windshields. We were half-frozen, hungry and dehydrated, and misery gripped our soft hides as we relieved ourselves along the road and wiped our asses with newspaper. The physical comforts of home were replaced with incomprehensible demoralization. This was just the beginning of the societal compromise.

A pickup driver let us climb into his truck bed and carried us through the Lincoln Tunnel. We inhaled deeply of the exhaust and freezing cold winds of our new temporary home: New York City. It was not the oasis or accommodating destination we had deluded ourselves into expecting. We wandered for days with no goals or plans, panhandling and trying to avoid scary neighborhoods and people. One day, we sat to rest at a corner, dejected and wrecked from the latest overstimulating experience, when along came a nice, gentle-looking guy who said, "You guys look lost."

Amazed that someone had even noticed us, we all started talking at once, a nervous bundle of stilted conversation. He told us his name was Rick, and he was a voiceover artist for a record company at a building nearby. "Sure you are, dude!" we replied. "Riiiiiight, uh-huh, OK." He bought us some cheap hot dogs and took us into a giant office building. Suddenly, we found ourselves sitting on the floor of a room with 3-inch-deep shag carpet and giant speakers. Rick played us different kinds of music that his company was producing at the time. He told us he was involved in recording the Lucky Charms commercials that we knew well; the three of us were raised on that stuff. Then he took us on a mini-tour of the recording studio. We peered in the studio windows to see the All-Star Jazz Band recording right onto a vinyl record in one room; in the next, Dionne Warwick was singing. We were stunned and mesmerized at all this big-city wizardry.

Finally, Rick gave me a phone number in case we wanted to reach him, and we went back to the streets. The days wore on in much the same way for us, and the resolve of our hardy little band of travelers quickly eroded. Albert met a woman and spent more and more time with her, breaking away from our little trio. He was in love. Yeah, right, we said. Meanwhile, Dale was missing his girlfriend, and I could see the writing on the wall. Someone back home wired Dale bus money via Western Union, and then he was gone.

Alone, I spent my days in Central Park, panhandling and sleeping. Panhandling was never easy for me, and I wasn't good at it. I would rather work for my money or create equity somehow. But I did the best I could to survive. One day I crawled out of a resting place in the bushes to find myself right in the path of an older couple. I must have looked like a wild man, hungry, filthy and desperate. This couple sat me down and talked my head off for at least an hour, listing all the reasons I should go back to my home and the comforts it offered.

Here I was, alone in New York in 1971, surrounded by a million other runaways who crowded the streets and parks. Maybe some of them used the resources that I didn't even know existed until decades later. But at the time, it was just me … and this guy's phone number. Desperate, I picked up the phone and called Rick. He was happy to hear from me and took me out for my first macrobiotic dinner. There was a buffet of every kind of vegetarian dish. I kept my chopsticks, and from that night on, I would eat only with chopsticks. They made a great weapon.

Rick and I got drunk, and then he took me back to his loft in Greenwich Village. He shared it with seven or eight other people, and with an equal number of hangers-on, it was a crowded mess. The shower and toilet were surrounded with a curtain. You were basically exposed to any voyeurs who cared to have a look while you did your business. I was wasted, smoking weed and drinking cheap alcohol. Rick beckoned to me to lie down in bed with him. Only a sheet separated us from the rest of the room, where people were partying. He talked real sweet and positioned himself awkwardly around me, telling me everything would be all right. I was as frightened as any cornered animal, but I had no alternatives that were better than this.

Rick went down on me, and I tried to relax. It was late, and I was beyond exhausted. It was all so distracting and unsettling – his male odor and rough breathing, the scratching of his unshaven face on my soft flesh, people looking in and giggling at us. Unable to get an erection, I finally snapped, grabbed my stuff and ran out of there. Shame, guilt and internalized homophobia welled up in me for the first time. I had never been with a man, and the cacophony of judgments I'd heard from society growing up played in my head. My mom always worked with gay men at her Civil Service jobs, so I'd met a lot of them and felt comfortable with them. But processing my Catholic guilt was another story.

Back out on my own, I grew more accustomed to life on the streets of the city that truly never sleeps. The city really came alive at night, with people filling the streets and bustling past each other. The Weathermen handed out literature detailing ways to disrupt the government. I met hippy women who took me in and gave me all kinds of big, strange pills that they claimed were vitamins. Down the hatch. On my back, I carried the weight of everything I owned: my pack, sleeping bag, clothes, and Abby Hoffman's "Steal This Book." I would walk for hours. Once, I walked all the way around the Twin Towers, which covered many city blocks. The Towers were so massive, my neck was wrecked from looking straight up for so long while wearing my pack.

Then, I walked through Harlem. People I passed would say, "Boy, you in the wrong neighborhood. Do you know where you are?" I'd just shrug and nod, and they'd let me go on my way. Yet, I felt safe as I walked by the houses, churches and bustling restaurants. I was becoming street-smart enough to know that I was invisible to most people. I was just another long-haired hippy runaway. I also walked through Hell's Kitchen at the time that the working-class people were being systematically forced out, in an effort to gentrify the neighborhood.

I eventually returned to Greenwich Village and started to dig the neighborhood. In a secondhand store, I found a giant, beat-up, old fur coat like guys wore to football games in the '20s. I looked like a bear, wearing that coat and my pack, but boy, was I warm, and it was cold outside. Living outside is a never-ending quest to find your serendipity and lose your previous reality. But usually, all you find is exhaustion and cold. When the time came that I once again was too exhausted and hungry to continue on my own, I pulled out Rick's number again. I knew what that meant: my ass served up on a platter.

Rick was excited to hear from me, and we started hanging out. Our agreement was simple: He would try to give me head, and I would try to relax. He took me out to gay clubs, and everyone flocked around this piece of fresh underage chicken. Rick beat them off, telling the bartender I was 18. We started using eyeliner pencil to give me fake mustaches and overgrowth. I dug the attention. These bars were smoky and dimly lit, and no one was complaining. One thing was for sure: It gave a whole new and unexpected meaning to the familiar tagline, "They're always after me Lucky Charms!"

At the time, I was spending my days outside and my nights in Central Park. To re-earn the right to spend the night at Rick's, he gave me an assignment. Across the alley in another building, someone was growing a pot garden on a fire escape. If I went and got some weed, I could stay the night. Sounded easy enough. I took off my shoes, and away I went. The buildings were all connected, so you just had to jump a few times to get to the other side of the alley. Ten stories up, I glanced at the people who were watching at

Rick's. Noting the look of terror in their eyes, I screwed up my courage, ran and jumped.

I landed safely, and then I remembered Rick's warning that the keeper of this pot garden was big and mean-looking. I walked until I was looking straight down at the pot plants, and then I began my descent down the fire escape. I grabbed two plants, and a ceramic planter fell off of one of the root balls and hit the fire escape, loudly giving me away. A window flew open, and out came an arm waving a chrome .38-caliber revolver. "I'm gonna get you!" he shouted, pointing the gun upward at me. I ran like hell and completed my James Bond-style getaway.

Back at Rick's, I proudly presented my prize of three skinny pot plants. My euphoria over winning a safe, warm place to spend the night was short-lived – I had stolen male plants. We dried them in the oven and smoked them anyway, but it didn't do much to earn me long-term standing in the zoo atmosphere of Rick's place.

Life on the streets was harsh and full of hardships, and I was beginning to deteriorate from constant exposure, sleep deprivation and hunger. I hit an emotional low point when I walked into St. Patrick's Cathedral looking for some kind of help or just a handout. I will never forget the feelings that welled up in me when the rich, impeccably dressed people in the cathedral pretended they didn't see me and I didn't exist. I was escorted out of the church by some "goons of God" and told not to come back.

The rage and infinite sadness I felt began to get hard-wired into my genes. The thoughts, "Why bother? Who cares? Give up, don't even try. Fuck it!" filled my head and became my trusted friends and constant companions. I was an angry, jaded young man, full of rage against my family and our society. My emotional armor was hardening by the day. I knew one thing for sure – it was time to get the hell out of New York.

I wanted to head north, but to my surprise, New York

City was a hard place to escape on foot. I finally walked across the George Washington Bridge and was on the road to Boston. From there, I hitched a series of rides that were a blur of endless towns, strange encounters and dangerous gun-brandishing moments. Sometimes I would successfully talk my way out of the car and onto the side of a highway, where I would have to hide for hours to make sure these freak demons of the road wouldn't come back and kill me. If I caught them early in their twisted dialogue and acted dangerous myself, they would let me right out of the car. By now, I knew how to find safety in people's eyes. But if I spotted danger before it began, I would scream, "Stop the fucking car and let me out now!" After being beaten so many times at home, I could read people's faces, thoughts and pheromones like a cheap novel.

Before I knew it, I was headed toward the Canadian border. The legal implications of getting caught trying to cross the border terrified me. All I could imagine was being caught and sent back home. I reversed course and started hitching west. I had heard a while back of a commune somewhere on Route 101 in California. I didn't know if it really existed, but that's where I decided to head, and nothing was going to stop me.

The weather was freezing. Numbing, biting cold pierced my clothes. Traveling in winter meant long, lonely periods of standing alone and freezing alongside endless highways, waiting for the kindness of strangers that was nowhere to be found. A sense of hopelessness engulfed my spirit as I spent nights shivering, squirming and breathing into my military mummy sleeping bag. If I somehow managed to survive this journey, I knew I would never travel and panhandle in winter again.

I made it to a truck stop somewhere in Ohio, where about 20 or so big rigs had lined up and unhooked from their trailers, so they could travel light for the evening. Delirious from exhaustion and hunger, I concluded that since there were no cabs hooked up to these trailers, they weren't going anywhere in the near future. That made this a safe place for me to sack out. I unrolled my sleeping bag under one of the trailers and fell into a much-needed, heavy sleep. The next thing I knew, I opened my eyes to see wheels moving right in front of my face. It took one quick glance to realize that several of these 18 wheels were on course to roll right over my bag. I rolled as fast as I could with all my might to get out of the way. Stuck in the mummy bag, I wiggled, wormed, and bunched up into fetal positions until I was out of the truck's path. Then, just as suddenly as it started, it was over, and I was alone in the icy parking lot, struggling to free myself from the bag. I was scared to death and my heart was pounding. This had used the last of my adrenaline, and I was tired beyond belief.

I had a phone number for my cousins in Detroit, and I decided to head in that direction. This meant a brief interruption in my march toward the California commune, but I just couldn't take anymore. I had to regroup. My cousins hid me in the tiny attic of their house for a week. I slept and slept and ate anything they could sneak away from dinner without arousing the suspicion of their father, who worked for the government. I found out I was on the runaway list in three states, including Michigan. If I didn't want to get caught, I needed to hit the road.

On my way out of Michigan, I stopped in Ann Arbor, a college town that I grew to really like. I was able to hang out with friendly students and hip, cool people. I also found a place for runaways called Ozone House. This was the first time on my trip that I found other young people like me in a place that was completely safe. Nice people at Ozone House offered me food and a safe place to stay. I tried to panhandle, but one of the shortcomings of a college town is that it's full of students who are short on cash. As nice as it was there, I had to thumb my way out of Ann Arbor.

I made it as far as Elkhart, Ind., before trouble found me

along the shoulder of a highway. I saw an Indiana Highway Patrol car approaching and tried to look as old and sophisticated as possible in my Army/Navy Surplus attire. I was glad I'd recently painted a mustache on myself with an eyeliner pencil, although it was without the aid of a mirror. No time to worry about that now as the patrol car skidded to a stop in the middle of the road. The trooper got out and strode toward me.

"Stop! Don't move!" Move? Where the hell in this God-forsaken place was I going to go? "Don't you know where you are, boy?" he shouted. No, sir, I replied. He proceeded to fill me in on his fine municipality and then began interrogating me. He took my pack and set it on the hood of his car. "Do you have anything in here that is illegal?" he barked. No, sir, I said again, blithely believing my own misperception of "illegal." He displayed the entire contents of my pack on the car hood and rifled through my clothes and survival gear, searching for any type of contraband. He found none, to my immense relief.

Just as he was ready to stuff my things back into my pack, all of the propaganda I'd collected from the Weathermen on the streets of New York City caught his eye. After he finished browsing all of the materials instructing people to blow up government facilities and so forth, he turned his attention to my copy of "Steal This Book." In addition to Abby's pearls of wisdom about how to get what you need to survive and rebel, the trooper also came across the marijuana leaves I'd pressed between the pages in New York. Bingo! It was the State of Indiana's lucky day. He made me hand over the ammo bag I wore around my neck and used as a purse, and then, while I held my hands behind my back as ordered, he went through the rest of my personals. He found a medicine bottle with no label full of the giant pills I was given by the hippy women in Greenwich Village. "Mm-mm-mm, you've really got some explaining to do," he said.

"Those are vitamins!" I insisted.

His fact-finding mission was interrupted by a call coming through on his police radio. He opened the driver's side door and reached in to grab his radio, telling HQ that he was on his way in with an undesirable. He left his door open and started questioning me twice as hard. "How old are you, boy?"

"Eighteen," I said, spouting the answer I'd rehearsed a thousand times as I walked along the side of the highway.

"You ain't no 18!" he said, laughing. "What year were you born?"

I guessed wrong twice, which made him laugh even harder. "You're lying to me, young man," he said, pointing to the pot, pills and revolutionary literature on the hood of his squad car. "Now you're in big trouble. If you don't want to get truthful, I'm taking you in, and you're goin' to jail with the men."

I started crying. Just then, a truck pulling a doublewide mobile home on a trailer bed rolled down the road toward us. With the trooper's car still in the roadway, the trucker did the best he could, but the trooper and I both jumped clear as we heard the unmistakable sound of crunching metal. The truck tore the open driver's-side door off of the patrol car. Shouting, "Goddamn it, you fucking asshole!" the trooper ran to move his car to the side of the road, while the trucker slowed down as quickly as he safely could and pulled over. As the trooper turned to run up the road and tear the trucker a new asshole, he yelled at me, "Don't you say a goddamn word, and don't you move an inch!"

Emboldened by this turn of events, I replied, "I'm tellin' on you!" What the hell – I had nothing to lose. Distracted and enraged, he turned and ran toward the truck, but I knew he'd heard me loud and clear.

Other patrol cars arrived on the scene, and I was packed into the back of one and taken to the station. As I was being processed, my old familiar trooper walked in and pulled me aside. With a conversation that consisted mostly of nods and uh-huhs, we came to an uneasy truce that he would say nothing about my drugs if I said nothing about how his car door was sheered off. His last piece of advice, offered surprisingly gently, was "Don't lie about your age."

I did, though, insisting to the obviously unconvinced booking officer that I was a legal adult. He finally gave up and said, "OK, it's out of my hands," then led me into the men's jail. I was elated to be treated like a man for a change – until the jeering started. "Give me that pussy! Let me cock that punk! Gimme that chicken! That boy's mine! Put him in here, boss!" We stopped at a cell with the keys clanging, and I cracked. "I'm not this old!" I pleaded. Back we went to the booking officer, where I told the truth about my age but provided one of my many false names. I also got a look at myself in a mirror and regretted how foolish my fake eyeliner mustache looked.

I was taken to the juvenile jail, where I was thrown in with the cream of the underage criminal crop. I was shaken down, pushed around, and slapped a few times. It was like they had been educated and hard-wired to replicate the behavior from which they came. But they were still relatively harmless. After dinner, I was given a bed where I spent most of the next two days, getting up only for meals. Once I was up and around, the inmates gave me the lay of the land. Most of them had been locked up for long periods of time, forgotten by anyone who might have cared. The only way they had found to get out for a few hours or a few days was by cutting themselves and being sent to the infirmary; from there, they'd go to the psychiatric ward for a brief period of observation. The challenge was to find something sharp enough to cut skin.

Toward that end, I was asked to scrape pennies against the rusty metal floor to make their edges sharp enough to cut. I worked on my first penny until my fingers were raw, and one guy succeeded in cutting himself and getting transferred. Unfortunately, he wasn't smart enough to get rid of the penny, so the staff discovered it. That was the end of our supply of coins, as well as the penny I'd shredded my fingers on. We deliberated for days to come up with another sharp edge. The only one in our vicinity was the 100-watt light bulb in the hall outside our door, and that was covered with a plastic dome.

To reach our goal, we applied the kind of teamwork and ingenuity we never used to solve any other problems in our young lives. First, I unraveled my rough wool blanket, which yielded a thick, rope-like twine. We tied that securely around a bar of soap, and our tool was ready for action. For hours each night, we would put our hands outside the bars of the door and swing the bar of soap, trying to knock the cover off of the bulb. This had become such a team event that now everyone wanted to cut himself and get out of there. The nightly target practice took on a frenzied momentum. We each took our turns swinging. We even lost the soap a few times, but the guards would walk by and nonchalantly toss it back into our cell. Finally, someone hit the target just right, and the plastic cover flew off. Now it was all about timing. The two guys who were serious about cutting themselves waited until the next day.

Time continued to drag on in jail. We had only two books available. One was a Gideon Bible, which started to give me strange feelings about God and life after a few readings. The other "book" was actually only two chapters about a baseball player. After reading those three times, I had enough. I walked up to a guard and told him my real name and how to contact my mother.

This was one time I truly felt my parents' love. As I was later told, Mom and Dad started out together in Mom's Charger to get me out of jail. But they got in a fight, so Dad got out of the car and Mom continued alone. Mom said she was escorted by three helicopters along the way, and cops kept trying to get her to pull over so they could talk some sense into her. But she drove as fast as the Dodger would go until she got to the jail and bailed me out. We had a tearful reunion, and our relationship grew from the experience. Mom and I were able to have real conversations after that, and I stopped treating her as an adversary. At least now, I felt like she could really hear me when I talked. Unfortunately, the painful dynamic between my dad and me continued, with peaceful phases interrupted by stormy arguments and physical altercations.

– 13 –

Jaded at 16

Life as I knew it resumed at home. I was back in school – in trouble after missing so many days – and back to music, drugs, alcohol and sex. I was accorded the respect that I could and would leave at the drop of a hat. My attitude was, "Don't fuck with me," but mostly I tried to stay away from home as much as possible, especially if I knew my father was home. This was the beginning of my long-lived couch-surfing era. Any mornings that I woke up at home, I would eat and run. Otherwise, I would sleep anywhere to keep from going home. My father gave me chores to do, and I did them. There was an old trailer on our property that was some distance away from the trailer where the family lived, and I crashed there as much as possible. There also was a camper on our property that I would sleep in as needed. I was smoking weed and drinking to excess daily.

One day, my mom and I had a talk about my runaway journey. I told her that on the road, few people fucked with me, slapped me around, swore at me, called me names or threatened me – and when they did, I had the option to engage or run. I encouraged her to make a change, set herself free from the miserable life she was living. Not long after that, she left my dad. I don't know if our talk had any influence on her decision, since their marriage had been a struggle as long as I could remember. But I felt personally responsible for breaking up our family. In the trauma of separation, our parents bled and we kids polarized. Mark stayed with Dad, while Kat moved with Mom into a trailer in town. I floated in between and stayed mostly elsewhere. I made sure I got to school just enough to not get kicked out. I really enjoyed the music classes and marching band. This saved my life and gave me at least one reason to strive to move forward.

Dad worked as a master electrician at a chicken factory called Shorgood Poultry in Milford, Del. The factory employed about 300 black workers and about 30 white workers. The black workers had unionized and gone on strike seeking better working conditions and a living wage. Huge picket lines surrounded the plant, with relatives and supporters of the striking workers joining in. It was a tough line to cross, but my father needed to work, and he crossed it. He asked Mark and me if we wanted temporary jobs there, too. We wanted cash, and more than that, we wanted to try to measure up as good, trustworthy sons – to know what that felt like for once. So we said yes. He assured us that it was a big factory, and we wouldn't be working for him.

When we arrived for our first day, we faced an angry crowd of picketers. They treated us like the scabs we were – threatening, shaking fists, gesturing at us, and calling out, "Scabs go home! Kill the scabs!" I was ill-equipped to deal with these desperate, determined people and their quandary. I was in their way; that much was clear. I feared for my life those first few weeks.

By the time Mark and I showed up, the strike was already 3 weeks old. The foreman brought us to the place where many thousands of dead chickens lay in different stages of putrification. Flies and maggots were swimming in this soup of every chicken part imaginable. The smell was indescribable, and we struggled not to gag. As a garbage truck pulled up, we were handed aluminum snow shovels and paper masks and told that this was our chance to prove ourselves to management. If we did well with this unbelievably sickening assignment, we might be able to stay on and work. The foreman and the truck driver made a hasty exit, gasping for air.

Mark and I looked at each other, cursing, and started shoveling swollen, rotted chicken bodies into the back of the truck. We both simultaneously vomited. The paper masks became soaked with our vomit. It didn't matter. We gagged after every shovelful. Our shoes slipped in the carnage. Through sheer determination, we got our rhythm going and finished the deed. The reward was a dubious one: Oh, boy, we get to come back to THIS place tomorrow? It was a payoff we weren't too excited about by the end of the day.

The next day, I began to learn the ropes at Shorgood Poultry. The chickens arrived in wooden coops on flatbed trucks. We would grab them by their legs and unload them as quickly as possible to minimize the pecking wounds to our hands. The birds would be hung upside down by their feet from hooks. The room where the birds began their death journey was kept dark and lit by black lights; someone believed this calmed the birds and stunned their senses. They would fight this until, exhausted, they would hang limply and move toward the killing blade: two opposing bicycle tires that came together at the birds' necks and slit their throats with a razor. From there, the birds would enter the 20-by-20-foot Blood Room, so named because the birds hung and bled out there. The blood stood several feet deep by the end of a typical workday. Once, my father came in to do electrical work and slipped. He had to swim in the blood to get out. This provided great comic relief for his son, of course.

From the Blood Room, the chickens were deposited into what looked like a washing machine the size of a cement truck. This boiling-hot washer would spin the chickens and loosen up the feathers. Then they went into a freezing-cold vat where the feathers were removed. After that began the gory and systematic separation of chicken parts, guts and waste, all of which had its own special destination. Hundreds of birds rolled by on an assembly line. First, the heads and beaks were removed, and then the guts would be vacuumed into pneumatic tubes that sucked them away to be used for animal feed. I would stand along with 20 or 30 other people, knives in hand, and wait to cut off whatever body part had been assigned to me. The idea was that every other bird was yours. Wings, legs, thighs, breasts, everyone had a part. Each of us was given an Old Hickory knife to ply our trade. I eventually learned to make quick cuts through cartilage, tendons and meat and to avoid dulling my blade on bone. Once you had the misfortune of dulling your blade, you were screwed. A dull blade does not cut, and the line can't stop.

The African-American men and women around me had been doing this line work for years. They teased me, but they seemed to respect that I was honestly doing the best I could. As soon as I learned to stop dulling my blade, I was put in charge of a boning crew. I now was "supervising" a crew of men and women of color, some of whom were 20 or 30 years my senior and had worked on the line since before I was born. My mercurial "promotion" to the pinnacle of the boning empire was a joke – I knew it, and the crew knew it. Fortunately, somehow, they didn't hold it against me. Instead, the elders showed their new 16-year-old supervisor the right way to de-bone a chicken

breast, and we bonded and became a tight team. After my
multicultural experiences in Morocco and the powerful race
riots I'd just gone through in school, I identified strongly
with their struggle for equality. Shorgood Poultry provided
one of the many mixed messages I would receive about
who I was as a white man and how I identified myself
in our multi-ethnic culture of haves and have-nots. This
also was the first of countless times throughout my life
that I would lead volatile teams of workers in hectic and
unpredictable environments.

The strike ended, and as trust grew again between
management and crew, the workers began to resume the
positions and stature they'd had before the strike. As
workers shifted around the factory, I was given a new
assignment at the controls of a machine that turned chicken
parts into ground patties. This elaborate machine used six
types of grinding dyes to transform bone and cartilage
into paste, with the rest of the byproduct formed into
patties. Any job you had in a chicken factory involved
guts and gore, and like many of the workers, I coped with
this by smoking weed and drinking beer. I was constantly
high and working 60 hours a week. This was the start
of my workaholic style, designed to help me fit in and
overachieve, usually at others' expense. This always led
me to rise to the top of whatever job I was doing, where I
would promptly self-destruct. That, in turn, fed my need for
drugs and addictive behaviors. I had an unquenchable thirst
to belong somewhere or to something, but I never could
relax long enough to let that happen.

Eventually, I worked my way through many of the
duties until I got a job in the Box Room. Another worker
and I would staple waxed-cardboard freezer boxes at a
frenzied pace in a room at the top of the factory. The pace
of this assembly was brutal; the idea of two people meeting
the boxing needs for the whole factory was ludicrous. After
loading boxes onto the moving conveyor hooks for the

whole production line, I sometimes had time to perfect a skill that would serve me well later in life: throwing knives. I would spend hours throwing knives at targets. I got good – really good – at throwing blades.

Toward the end of my brief tenure at Shorgood Poultry, something happened that crystallized my racial affiliation. Late one night, as I walked out, I passed a black man who was standing over a broken, motionless white man lying on the ground. The black man puffed wildly on a cigar, getting it red-hot. I noticed the charred, blackened hole where one of the white man's eyes used to be. As I passed by, the black man made eye contact with me, then bent down and, with rage and fierce determination, burned out the white man's remaining eye. Then he bellowed down at him, "Can't tell which nigger did this to you now, bitch! Can't pick me out of a line! Who's your nigger now, bitch??"

Racial tension was always in the air, with whites feeling entitled to be abusive as well as sensing the threat of the civil rights movement. These were hard times, and I felt affinity with the hardship of the black person. I went home and didn't say a word about what I'd witnessed. I'm not a stool pigeon and I'm not a victim, but I didn't feel safe working there anymore.

Back at home, Dad was enduring the early days of his separation. The marriage had made him miserable, but he'd done everything he possibly could to keep his family together. Now he contemplated the enormous amount of credit debt that Mom had left him with, as well as the albatross of a Victorian house that still needed more rehab than one master fix-it man could handle in a lifetime. He still started each day with the deafening klaxon as his alarm clock, worked 20 hours, and ended the day in his trailer.

One night, he dragged in the door after another long workday. I happened to be there that night – his long-haired, smart-mouthed, drinking, smoking, acid-dropping, 16-year-old, firstborn son. We started drinking and wound up at the kitchen table. Dad poured out his troubles, talking about the deep sadness and pain he was feeling. I minimized everything he said and put it all back on him. I was a smartass who had all the answers, a quick fix for every misstep anyone made (except myself, of course). In other words, I was a smart-alecky teen-ager who knew the "right" way to do everything.

This was too much for Dad to take. Saying he wanted me to understand just how desperate he was, he pulled out a handgun, opened the chamber and dumped out the bullets. He put one bullet back in the chamber, rolled it, and stood, crying, pointing the gun at my head. "How do you feel now?" he bellowed, and pulled the trigger.

Then he opened the chamber, put in a second bullet, rolled the chamber, and aimed it at his own head. Click. We were both sobbing. I was in shock. My father had made his point. I really felt for the first time just how much pain he was feeling. I also felt the excruciating loss of the last shred of trust that there was any sacred line my family would not cross and shatter in its dysfunction.

As powerfully, perfectly devastating as this experience was, it also made me fearless. My father had pointed a gun at my head and pulled the trigger, and I had survived. No one would ever top that pinnacle of shock and trauma again. I now felt I could live anywhere and face down anyone who might come after me. They were looking for a victim, someone to chase, someone who would cower. This would not be me. For most of my life, most predators would sense that fearlessness and look elsewhere. Several years later, when "The Deer Hunter" was released, the Russian roulette scenes awakened the trauma of that night all over again. In my 20s by then, I realized how much that event had damaged me, and it emotionally thrust me deeper into my addiction.

After that night, I gave my father a wide berth. My family had become a dangerous place to call home. I was

smart enough to know I could get away from it, somehow.
As soon as I could get my supplies together, I ran away
again. The next several months became a cycle of running
away; enduring life on the road until I couldn't take any
more; then coming back home to couch-surf, recover and
regroup until I could try again. While I was home, I showed
up for school and music as much as I could – and got my
hands on as much alcohol and drugs as possible.

Once, on my way home from a concert at the Armory,
tripping on LSD, I passed a troop transportation vehicle.
An older woman was sitting on the long front seat, and she
called me over. She told me she was a witch. Long story
short, I wound up on the front seat, having sex with her,
when we heard someone run by and drop something. We
didn't think much of it until police officers surrounded the
vehicle and yanked open the door to find us half-naked.
That's when we saw the 2 kilos of marijuana on the ground
next to the vehicle. I was grateful I was in the throes of
hot sex and hadn't noticed that tantalizing dope, because I
might have gone up on my first drug charges. As it was, the
cops believed the bewildered looks on our faces and let us
go.

Such encounters with bizarre older women seemed to
be a package deal with all the gigs I was playing at the
time, and they set the stage for the extroverted, drunken
debauchery that would become my daily routine. I would
be propositioned routinely after gigs, and my responses
generally varied somewhere between "anything goes"
and "say yes to everything" – no matter how disturbing
or repulsive the offer might turn out to be. This was how
I found myself, for example, in the back of my station
wagon, getting head from an unwashed older woman
who had become toothless and haggard from drug use.
Revolted, I said, "Stop, I can't do this," and she insisted
on continuing. I had to piss like a racehorse and begged
her to let me go, and she pleaded with me to urinate in her

mouth. The idea disgusted me, but finally it was either let loose or get violent to free myself from her. So I let loose. She accepted it gratefully and finally set me free, satisfied that she had given me a new experience. Looking back, this type of bizarre episode helps me understand how I turned out so jaded. I was a dirty old man before I turned 17.

I remember another extraordinary post-gig event of a totally different kind. Tripping on acid, I was taking a meandering path toward my neighborhood late at night, seeing trails and lights and hearing distant sounds. I heard the sweet sounds of music and singing coming from a church, so I walked in, my open switchblade in my hand. It was a black church, and the preacher at the pulpit boomed, "Thank God for bringing this white boy into our service!" The worshippers made room in the middle pews where they had corralled all the young people. Stunned and overwhelmed by the ushers and elderly ladies who rose to greet me, I found myself suddenly seated in the middle of this crowded church, trying to maintain my tripping composure – and also touched at this welcome.

I was wearing an oversize military coat, so I pulled my hand into the sleeve and tried to close my switchblade before anyone saw it. The kids seated around me didn't necessarily want to be seen in this spiritual setting, but they were giggling because I was so high and twisted while their bad asses were all lovey-dovey for the Lord. Heads and hands swayed around me and voices boomed, and I rode this gentle wave of praise until the service ended. I left that church feeling a sense of connection and belonging with this community.

Another act of kindness occurred right next door through the kindness of our longtime neighbor, Mrs. Mandeville. In an effort to distract me from the bad influences I obviously was succumbing to, she invited me in one evening and placed six postage stamps on the table. One of them, she said, was worth $600, and if I could use the multi-volume

stamp catalog to figure out which one it was, she would
let me keep it. This motivation to open the catalog was all
I needed to get hooked on stamp-collecting for life. The
history, the artwork, the details – I loved all of it. From that
point on, no matter how poor I was, I kept an eye out for
stamps.

My mother started dating a black singer whom I didn't
really know much about, except that he seemed to show up
only when he wanted sex. I didn't trust him, so this kept
me from visiting her often during this time. My dad, on the
other hand, had developed a relationship with a powerful
woman in the local black community. This was the only
time in my childhood that I remember seeing Dad in a
relationship that seemed to give him something solid and
positive. I would join them at barbecues, and I admired the
way a simple look from her could stop any trouble in its
tracks before it even got started. I grew to trust and respect
her.

This woman had a daughter my age, and Dad invited me
to attend a prestigious Black Ball as the daughter's guest.
We didn't know each other well, but we went along and
behaved like good, obedient kids. The event took place
in a giant, dimly lit banquet hall full of cigarette smoke
and cheap wines. After enjoying the entertainment and
the comfort of the company, I slipped out back with some
brothers and nervously smoked a joint, making sure to
return before our absence was noticed.

At one point, I looked around and realized that Dad and
I were the only white people in attendance. This seemed
to attract no notice until midnight approached and people
started gathering outside to smoke and prepare to leave. I
wandered around and sensed some tension from the young
black men, some of whom eventually surrounded me and
began asking angry questions about who I was and what
I was doing at their event. Suddenly, the crowd parted
like the Red Sea, and I heard the booming voice of Dad's

girlfriend. She made it clear that if any harm came to me, they would answer to her. That was the end of the trouble.

The four of us returned to Dad's girlfriend's place, where he and his date went upstairs and, from the sound of it, wasted no time getting busy. Although we both were nervous, the daughter and I began our own explorations. I was experienced, and it seemed that she was not, so I was careful not to do anything without her invitation. We were heavy into it when I heard my dad's booming voice from upstairs. "Son, are you all right?"

Sheepish and embarrassed, I replied, "Yes, Dad."

"Don't worry, son," he replied. "Once you get in, it's all pink on the inside."

This was the kind of experience I had to suffer through – so crass, so overbearing, so wrong!

Despite that, it turned out to be one of the few intimate, innocent and affectionate sexual experiences I had as a teen, and it deepened my bond with African-American people.

– 14 –

Stealing Mr. Martin

Around the time I turned 17, I started spending more time at my mom's place. She lived in a trailer on a dirt road, and I would frequent her home when I exhausted all other options. Across the road from her place was a farm field planted with corn. I planted marijuana in the corn rows. Mom's cat had kittens, which provided me with a great cover story in case anyone asked me why I had to go wandering among the corn stalks every day. I was looking for the kittens! I would stick two kittens in my shirt before I checked my crop, just in case I needed to provide proof to any cops or farmers who might come along. I thinned out all the male plants so only the females would prosper, and before I knew it, I had unlimited access to so much weed, I was bonging away like there was no tomorrow. I had dope left over to sell to my friends, and I earned enough money to take a trip to Pensacola, Fla., where my old friends, the three Seventh Day Adventist sisters, now lived.

Once I arrived in Florida and looked up the sisters, I

realized I was living in a time warp. It had been a while since I had enjoyed the privilege of sexual relations with each of them, and they, of course, had moved on with their lives. Only the youngest sister still would entertain me, but she didn't have the same fervor as before. During my visit, Hurricane Camille hit the coast, and the three of us went to a 600-foot pier where we could see 18-foot swells. I left the women on the beach and went to the end of the pier with the surfers. The pier was moving back and forth violently, weakening the stability of its pylons. A few brave surfers jumped in the water and quickly got on top of their surfboards, riding the 18-inch-high white foam that choked the water between the swells. I didn't really notice the foam until I jumped in the water myself, probably because I was blinded by my desire to impress my companions.

Once I was in the water, I couldn't catch my breath through the foam. I was already choking hard when the next 18-foot wave hit and swept me toward the crossbeams under the pier. I struggled to stay as high in the water as I could and rolled over a few waves, swimming as far from the pier as I could. Choking and losing visibility in the whitewash of the suffocating foam, I knew I was in danger of losing consciousness. Another wave crashed into me, tossing me like a rag doll through the pylons and the walkway under the pier itself. Helpless to resist the water's force, I desperately tried to gulp a mouthful of air as my body was tumbled and pummeled in the surf. The giant poles and supports under the pier seemed to whiz past me in a blur. Suddenly, I was jolted awake when I crashed into hard ground near the shore. I stumbled toward the dunes where the women waited. They knew me well enough to forgive my ego's intention. Life was precious, and I was humbled. My visit to Florida was over, but the place had left an indelible impression on me, and someday I planned to return.

When I got back to Delaware, I made the usual excuses

at school about why I wasn't there for the millionth time. Then, my mom told me that while I was gone, there was a real ruckus in the corn field across the road, with police and helicopters looking for some guy who was growing marijuana and transporting it. Did I know anything about it? I was furious – the nerve of those people, stealing my cash crop!

As I grieved for the loss of my "comfort crop," I noticed how relaxed my mother and 14-year-old sister, Kat, seemed to be. They would hang out in the bedroom, bonding, massaging and nurturing each other. This struck me as quite odd, after a lifetime of watching Mom torture herself in her endless quest to be the beautiful person she thought she never was. She went through a hundred diet plans and dyed her hair so many times, it finally turned a strange chemical shade of orangey green. She would plaster her face with mud packs and try everything to get rid of the varicose veins on her legs – everything except limiting her spending so she could quit her constant second job as a waitress and get off her feet.

I had to know how this restless woman had finally found inner peace. I relentlessly interrogated Kat, who finally took me to Mom's medicine cabinet and revealed the source of their bliss – Valium and diet pills. I was appalled. My sister was so young – and she wasn't sharing the good stuff with me! I wasted no time starting my own diet. When her kids' demand for her pills exceeded her supply, Mom hid her drugs from me, so I started buying it on the street.

Our dysfunctional family history was still very evident during my visits with Mom, and she put up with a lot. At this point, now 17 years old, I was already hooked on speed, weed, alcohol and LSD and dabbling in downers. My favorite kinds of speed were known as Christmas Trees and Cross-Tops. These pharmaceuticals were hard to beat during my 30 years of speed use. They were clean and powerful. By now, I also was well-versed in getting

my sexual needs met by men and women up to age 35.
No one could ever fill the void, least of all me. I had been
beaten much of my life to tell the truth. This turned me
into a rageful young man who lashed out even at innocent
strangers and transferred my violent imagery like wildfire.
I was a loner, a rogue, a desperate and needy person with
boundary issues and attachment disorders. I had gotten
a good grip on the beginnings of my double-psychotic,
paranoid schizophrenic armor. When I was in a religious-
zealot phase, I would burn Mom's books. I would steal her
drugs, verbally and mentally abuse her and call her names.
I would suck out of her spirit every bit of life I felt was
owed to me. It was the prototype of every relationship I
would have, twisted by codependency and substance abuse.

As the season cooled and turned to autumn, the kittens,
now almost 6 months old, developed the bad habit of
sleeping under the hood of Mom's Dodge Charger. One
evening, she left home in a hurry and started the car,
then burst back into the trailer crying. I lifted the hood to
discover that five of the kittens had been gruesomely killed
in the engine. Badly shaken, I did the best I could to clean
the kittens' remains out of the motor so Mom would not
be re-traumatized every time she drove her car. Our lives
seemed so tragic and empty already that to lose the kittens
in this brutal way was hard to take.

After this, I drifted again from friend to friend, house
to house, band to band, one after another. The days strung
together in a blur of drug dens, lost souls, and struggling
people trying to cope in the only self-destructive ways we
knew. More than anything, I wished I had one more chance
to do life right – to change my ways and live differently. I
drifted back into my mom's life and learned that she'd met
a military man she was serious about. They were getting
married, and she was moving with him to England. I began
an aggressive campaign to convince my mother to take
me with them, swearing up and down that I would change

all my evil ways and be good. Her new man, Ron, wanted nothing to do with the trouble I brought to my family, and he was adamant about wanting me to keep my distance. I used every begging, sniveling, sickening, annoying technique I knew to break my mother's resistance. After two months of this, she relented and said I could go. Strict conditions were established for me: I could go only if I guaranteed that I would blah, blah, blah. Yeah, sure, absolutely, I would do all that and more. I would attend a prep boarding school for my 12th year, living away from home all week. I was looking for a quick fix, and this fit this bill. I begged, schemed, promised, and even started believing my own bullshit.

As part of my preparations for my brand-new, clean and good life, I had some unfinished business to attend to. Having been constantly exposed to people doing various illegal, immoral and unethical things, I started routinely stealing for my needs when I was a runaway on the road. I would steal food because I was starving, and the institutions that were supposed to help often would kick me out like I was some kind of undeserving person. It affected my view of this capitalistic world of the Haves and the Have-Nots, or the Nazis and the Have-Notzi's, as I called them. Before I turned 18, I desperately wanted to do something illegal, so that if I did get caught, I would be treated as a juvenile and avoid adult prison. I couldn't get enough of anything, no matter what it was. I had an unrealistic view of what the world owed me and my kind. Having read Abby Hoffman's views, I felt strongly that the world owed me some kind of compensation.

There was a store called B&B Music. All the schools bought their musical instruments there. I became afraid to even go in there, having been treated badly on previous visits. In my hippy hey day, I probably bore too much of a resemblance to Charles Manson, which didn't seem to fill retailers with a lot of trust. My uniform at the time consisted of pants that were a patchwork quilt of patches and leather dragging on the ground. These were always worn with a smelly shirt; long hair that hung down to my chest, and a wild look in my eyes that said, "I'm on the prowl, and you're the target." Now, with my trip to England in place, I started working diligently on my plan to commit the Juvenile Crime of the Century.

I had the music store as my target, but how to get in? The State Police station was just across the field from the store, with nothing around for a half-mile except that obstacle. I noticed that the street had lights with big glass covers, then a plastic cover over the light, and then the bulb. I bought a rocket slingshot and started practicing. Hitting my own hand many times, I wondered how I could ever master this technique.

The store had brand-new alarms – window alarms, door alarms, and red beams that covered the hallways and the instruments. They were revealed with smoke. This was 1973. Thank you, James Bond. I decided that to get past the doors, I would use an electric carving knife, as this seemed a good way to cut through the interior hollow-panel doors. I would hold the door shut and cut the bottom without setting the alarm off. Then I would crawl through the bottom of the door. Yeah, that sounded cool. I would break the bottoms of the outside windows to avoid setting off the alarms. All right, far out, man. If there was one thing I had proven in my criminal attempts so far in life, it was that I could effortlessly find and execute the plan that made the most noise and blazed the biggest trail.

I obsessed over how to get past the sensitive sound alarm until one stormy day, when I surmised that an electrical storm like this would cause the store's employees to turn off the alarm so it wouldn't be triggered by thunder and lightning. I took a few more hits of speed and made up my mind. I had my plan. I was going to do the deed, and then throw the clothes and boots I was wearing off a bridge to get rid of the evidence. Off I went.

The wind was relentless, and the thunder was deafening. I believed the sound alarm was off, so I hid the car as well as I could and cautiously approached the building. Using my slingshot, I began trying to break out the street lights. It took some time, but I broke through the layers of one light and then began on the next. Nervous, sweating, wet and worried, I broke through the outside window of the store without setting off the alarm. I broke out all the small pieces of wood and crawled in below the alarm contact points. With my mind screaming as the wind and rain blew outside, I realized I had forgotten my flashlight. My eyes slowly adjusted to the dark interior, with neon signs outside illuminating the store. Someone left the door open from the office into the instrument area. What luck.

I was on my knees on the floor. Suddenly, before I could catch my breath, I saw the police station through the window and heard sirens. Police cars screeched out of the parking lot. I wondered why they didn't just walk across the field to get me. They zoomed by and kept going. It was then that I realized I pissed myself. I had wet my pants, which were already soaked from the rain.

I took another pill for fortitude and lay frozen for a few moments till I thought the coast was clear. Then I began the business at hand. The red beam alarms were my only real threat. They were just straight line beams. I found the three places they started and where they connected, and I crawled under and stayed clear. I started trying to find objects to steal that were small, which I could sell once I got to England. Again, I heard the screeching of tires and bloodcurdling sirens. As I looked through the window in abject terror, once again they whisked by. This time I managed to urinate on the floor.

Impulsively, I grabbed two flutes, an Ovation guitar and a Martin guitar. I'm sure I grabbed a lot more, but my mind has blanked on further details of this terrifying episode.

Sweating profusely, I started putting the objects outside the window till I knew I could not fit any more loot in my getaway Toyota. I stuffed the car until stolen equipment stuck out of its windows. I felt like the Grinch who stole Christmas. Then, I jumped in the car and barreled down the back road that led into the woods. This was my escape route. I went through the mud and rain on the dirt road until it narrowed, and I couldn't see beyond 50 feet ahead of me. I skidded to a stop. Suddenly, dogs jumped up on the side of the car and barked deafeningly through the open window on the other side. Bright house lights came on. Before I knew what was happening, someone yelled, "What are you doing here!" I was trespassing, and they were going to call the cops!

I yelled back, "Is this Jimmy's house? My band is playing a party at Jimmy's!"

"Jimmy don't live here!" the voice shouted through the rain.

I hastily maneuvered out of there. That meant I had to drive past the State Police station one more time. I was sweating blood and bullets, but I made it. I changed my clothes and threw my criminal ensemble into the St. Jones River. I don't remember how or if I went to sleep that night. The next day, on the front page of the local newspaper, there was a report that the mob had hit the Dover area, and three major break-ins had occurred the night before. I could not believe my luck. But that did not save me from the guilt I felt for many years afterward.

I asked my mom for an address in England to which I could ship ahead some of my belongings. I boxed up my musical loot, and that's where I shipped it. When I got there, I would have to go to the customs office and claim the value of the instruments, how I got them and what I planned to do with them. It was all too easy.

Now it was a mad rush to get our passports, so I could make the move and Mark could come visit. Mark and I got drunk and smoked some powerful weed before we went to the Military Police Headquarters to get our passport photos. I was freaking out with paranoia but somehow managed to go inside and get my picture taken without getting busted. Mom took one look at our photos and went nuts. My long hair was uncombed and sticking out all over like a homeless person; my eyelids were heavy and my pupils blown out. She was mortified.

On our very last day in the States, Mark and I visited some longtime friends in a rugged, hilly area where they rode their bicycles and mini-bikes over hills of various sizes. This was the perfect opportunity to maximize the hyper-manic mood I was in and take some real chances. I borrowed a kid's mini-bike and floored it toward the biggest and most dangerous drop-offs I could find. I was going to go for the biggest jump available, and I made sure all the kids were watching. It turned out to be not so much a jump as a 20-foot fall. It felt great, like flying – until the bike and I splattered into the ground. I got up, twisted and sprained. My face was badly scratched, I was bruised everywhere, and my ribs were cracked. My friends carried me back to their house.

I never let my mother know how badly I was hurt, because there was no way in hell I was going to endanger my brand-new start in England. The 15-hour flight to Europe was excruciating. My stepfather, Ron, greeted us at the airport and seemed to enjoy seeing me in so much pain. He had driven a military blue Air Force station wagon to pick us up, and I lay in the back for the 60-mile ride to Ramsey, the English country village where he and Mom would live.

– 15 –

School in England

My first ride on the country roads of England was punctuated by the thump of the rabbits Ron hit every mile or so. Confused or otherwise hypnotized by the approaching headlights, the rabbits could be seen frozen in the roadway until Ron bah-bumped over their bodies. Ron finally pulled up in front of his three-bedroom house. The area was experiencing oil shortages, so the electricity was off for periods throughout the day and night, he said. Something that looked like yams or sweet potatoes were piled high in the fields out back, awaiting winter storage.

During the day, Mom and Ron would go to RAF Alconbury, the Royal Air Force Base where Ron worked and where Mom found a Civil Service job. In three weeks, I would head for RAF Lakenheath, a base about 150 miles away where I would attend Lakenheath American High School in Brandon, Suffolk. But until then, I was alone all day, a stranger in a strange land. I adopted my usual practice of walking for miles and found that the town's streets were full of outdoor markets by day. People would crowd the markets to buy their daily produce. Most of them rode bicycles to get around. All of the elderly residents I saw seemed to be robustly healthy.

I learned that the town of Ramsey was celebrating its 1,000th birthday. I visited a 1,000-year-old abbey with ceilings suitable for much shorter people than us. At 5-foot-9, my head grazed the tops of its doorways. The yards of Ramsey were well-kept, each with a beautiful garden. I counted hundreds of flowering plants in the fields and alongside the roads. Alone and penniless with nothing else to do, I began to collect flowers and press them. I bought a book that identified the wildflowers and became quite knowledgeable. This collecting habit succeeded in keeping me out of trouble during my first few weeks in England. The townspeople were proper and polite and considered me a curiosity. We struggled to understand each other through our respective accents. For the first time I could remember, I had to stand still, move slowly, be mindful and observe with curiosity.

A phone call from the Customs Office reminded me of a cash source I could tap. The musical instruments I sent over from my music-store heist had arrived in England. The Customs Office asked me to come in to answer some questions. Nervous as hell, I showed up, and a clerk began to ask me all sorts of things. Guilt-ridden and paranoid, I thought his questions were designed to trip me up, and I stammered my way through some non-answers until the clerk finally gave me the instruments.

I took the instruments home and hid them, feeling like a worthless, unclean, common thief. The guilt dogged me for a long time. I didn't need a lot of money, but I needed some, so I took one of the instruments to the biggest nearby town and sold it. I made the cash last as long as I could. As a form of atonement, I promised God that I would make my stolen Martin D-28 guitar available to any poor person, bum, wino, freak, thief or otherwise untrusted servant of the Powers That Be who ever wanted to play it. So began "Mr. Martin's" battle-scarred journey.

By now, I was really ready for something to drink, since I had no connections to get drugs and wouldn't risk getting caught trying. I got into drinking wine with dinner, but it was hard to stop at one glass. Finally, I worked up the nerve to walk into a pub and discovered the "queen's pint" of ale. Oh, salvation never tasted so sweet. They offered every kind of great beer a connoisseur could demand, and after a few pints, I was quite demanding. At last, I'd found a familiar, safe niche in England, lubricated with liquid courage. Before I could get too comfortable, though, it was time to head to school.

Lakenheath American High School was the college prep boarding school where the Americans stationed in the area showcased their talented children. Students stayed in the six dormitories all week, and most went home on weekends. I packed enough clothes to last a week and was shown to my room in a two-story dorm. Boys were on the first floor, and girls were up above, with counselors guarding entrances and exits. I was introduced to my roommate, Dean, a strange, nerdy character. I was just starting to worry about his level of nerdiness when he put up a poster of a butler holding a silver tray full of shit. This changed my opinion of Dean, and we began a comfortable companionship.

My mother's house was about a three-hour drive away, and for the first month or so, I spent weekends at home. However, things between Ron and me escalated quickly. Ever the rebel, especially when Ron wasn't within earshot, I would walk around the house and even come to dinner in my BVDs. If that wasn't enough to annoy Ron, I was verbally abusive and disrespectful to my mother out of sheer habit. One night at dinner, I sat there in my underwear and used foul language toward my mother, and Ron couldn't take anymore. He left the table without a word and walked out of the house. Ron returned to the table a moment later carrying huge wire cutters.

"I'm gonna cut your balls off," he said, "so you can talk to your mom like a woman instead of like a man."

He lunged at me, and I bolted from the table and ran upstairs to put some clothes on. I would have run straight out the front door, but it was a blustery October night – not great streaking weather. However, Ron came upstairs after me and repeated his plan to separate me from my balls, so I detoured back down the stairs and out the door. It happened to be the night of a Sadie Hawkins Dance, when the girls in town asked the boys to a dance, so there were couples walking all over town. Here I was, darting from yard to yard in my underwear and hiding in people's bushes. I headed for the Old Abbey, because it had lots of trees and places to hide.

So cold that my toes were turning numb, I kept calling out to passing couples. Guys would leave their dates and approach the bushes, only to find an apparently crazy American in his underwear. They would chuckle nervously and back away. Finally, someone took me seriously and called the constable. Cold and tired, I was taken back to Mom's house, but I told the police I would not go in unless someone gave me a large kitchen knife to defend myself against the wire-cutter-wielding man inside. I made a loud scene in front of the house, yelling all kinds of obscenities and threatening Ron if he ever came near me again. It was an embarrassing spectacle for my mother. Finally, I agreed to go inside, but I did get a knife from the kitchen, and I kept it nearby in case Ron approached me again. Needless to say, I didn't feel welcome at Mom's house anymore, so I quickly made friends at school and began spending weekends at the homes of others.

Although I sincerely wanted to make a fresh start in England, the truth is I didn't know any other way to live. I wanted to excel in school, but I had never learned how to form trusting relationships or believe in my own ability to succeed. I didn't want all the trouble that usually came with constant drinking, but by age 18, I was certainly already an alcoholic and drug addict. And, even though stealing was a source of constant, painful shame for me, I once again turned to petty theft. I didn't have a job in England, and I spent my school allowance (frugally, mind you) on pubs and hash. I stole for cash.

I justified my lawlessness by observing the common umbrella-swapping that occurred in British shops and pubs. It seemed to rain constantly there, and everyone carried an umbrella. They would leave their umbrellas in stands by the front doors, and I noticed that many people would grab umbrellas that were not their own on the way out. Somehow, that phenomenon helped me feel OK as I started to steal small, expensive items from fine antique stores. I looked for belt buckles, Wedgwood pottery, Royal Doulton china, tiles from castle walls and Meerschaum pipes. These items were easily re-sold with no questions asked. I saw no alternative to stealing for cash; without stealing, I would be a poor person, sitting in shame in a freezing room.

My other source of income was hash. There was no weed in England, but the hash was cheap – $35 an ounce. You could find the scorpion, elephant or snake stamped on these bricks of hash. These were the real thing, and I needed only a little to stay medicated, since I was used to depending on the kindness of strangers. This was another old habit I couldn't break – keeping myself constantly "medicated." The rest of the hash I sold at school to make my drinking money for the weekends.

No one knew what I did or how I got my money. I was gone a lot of weekends, spending time with students and their families who had the money to travel all over England. I met a South African girl named Raven*, and she became my girlfriend for a time. Her father attended auctions and bought antiques, which he would ship to

America for a profit. I would go home with Raven for the weekend every two or three weeks and spend quality time with her family. I would spend the night in a guest room and then log three or four hours on the slow transit system back to school.

My mom decided to have a Harris Tweed suit made for me. I selected a Sherlock Holmes long coat with the button-on cape; waist coat, and stove pants with foot-wide legs. With that warm suit on and my Meerschaum pipe filled with hash, I could go anywhere in England and blend in with the landscape. That is, until I started adding LSD to my weekend excursions. My friends and I frequented pubs and clubs in London and other cities, where the revelry was often interrupted with public announcements that another pub had just been blown up somewhere by the Irish Republican Army. We were so wasted by the greatest blotter, barrel and other acids sent from Germany that these announcements did nothing to dampen our spirits. "Blow the world up! We're staying right here and partying! Far out!"

We would go into churches in small towns and grab the ropes of the church bells, swinging wildly up and down and making a thunderous racket until a friar or minister chased us off. Once, in a famous London graveyard, I stood atop the long gravestone of a sailor/mutineer-type scary dude and called his spirit out. Either I was tripping or I actually made contact; either way, I was transfixed for a long time, hypnotized by the incredible essence of this spirit. Tripping or not, I treated graves and spirits with great respect after this.

My brother Mark came to visit us, and I took him to see the sights in London. This, of course, had to be accompanied with a hit of LSD. We went on a great, two-day adventure to all of the popular tourist spots, where we generally acted disrespectful and boorish. We passed some bobbies, or English policemen, and Mark said loudly, "Are those the pigs?" Embarrassed, I hurriedly explained that Brits had a different relationship with their police than we did. We then took in the play, "Hair," which was a hilarious production. We were new to the theater routine, so when ushers cleared the theater at intermission, we thought the play was over.

We also visited the Tower of London, famed historically for many things, but best-known for its use as a prison and the execution site of two of Henry VIII's queens. We mistakenly thought the queens were beheaded in the chapel itself, so we giggled loudly about it. "They actually had the balls to chop her head off in a church!" one of us said. The other visitors shushed us and reacted as if we were the ones disrespecting the chapel, much to our misinformed amusement. Later, I learned the beheadings actually occurred outside the Chapel. Wish we'd known that then.

Despite my intoxicated disregard for the facts, I actually loved that England was steeped in ancient history. Mark and I visited the gates of the castle on the River Thames where condemned men were chained and drowned. We crossed the Tower Bridge and saw Big Ben. The biggest thrill of our visit to the Tower of London was seeing the Crown Jewels. These objects are incredibly beautiful by any standard, but to a couple of teen-age boys on acid, the visual spectacle was almost unbearable. We were so tripped out, we made people nervous with our ooh-ing, aah-ing and drooling at every display case. Looking back on this visit, it was one of the most pleasant, peaceful times my brother and I ever spent together.

I was proficient at talking up blokes in pubs to get my drug needs met. One night, I met some guys at a pub who were making fun of Americans and talking about our beers as if they were cat piss. I had to agree that a Budweiser was no match for Guinness Stout. We got real drunk, and I found out that the reason three of them had casts on their arms was because they were members of a famous soccer team. We had a good time bonding, but a couple of them were mean-mugging me all night, muttering things under their breath like, "Piss off, matey," "Fuck off and die, you bloody wanker," and "Fuckin' bloody Yanks." Their brogue was so thick and I was so drunk, I couldn't be sure of these insults, so I just let it ride. Then I went to take a piss, and in the bathroom I noticed four big soccer guys standing around me.

"Don't bother flushin' the loo," one of them said, smiling.

I smiled back and tried to walk past them when they each grabbed one of my limbs, flipped me upside-down over the toilet, and gave my head one warning bang on the porcelain. One of them yelled, "If you don't move, you won't get any teeth busted, matey!" In a Zen moment of clarity, I took heed of this warning and held still as they slowly lowered my head into my own piss. The drinking establishment was raucous; the toilet amenities, atrocious. I held my breath as long as I could and began struggling wildly, just about to run out of air, when someone flushed. Next thing I knew, I was standing upright with urine running from my head down onto my clothes, and all my new friends were laughing wildly. I was told that I had just been welcomed with the time-honored rite of passage known as a swirly. Drunk and bewildered by the broken trust, I left and spent most of the night freezing outside, waiting for the bus service to start. When a bus finally arrived, I was greeted with looks of disgust by the driver and the morning commuters as I made my way home.

More and more, my memorable events in England revolved around being completely drugged out and miraculously not getting busted. I once bought a big bag of mandrix, also known as Rohrer 714s. We thought they were just like Quaaludes. We were told they originally were meant to be used as horse tranquilizers. We took too many, got drunk, and went to a bowling alley, where the manager ejected us after we made a ruckus and rolled nothing but gutterballs. We hitched back to the base in the back of an open truck, laughing wildly and howling at the moon like mad dogs. When we arrived at the base, we noisily climbed over the fence near the Officer's Quarters. Such a low-key entrance got us surrounded by military police, which made us sweat over the hash and drugs we were carrying. While the police questioned us, the guy who was carrying dropped the drugs out the bathroom window. We were off the hook.

I got more and more careless with my drug abuse. I thought it was OK to use and smoke whenever and wherever I wanted. I would drop acid and drive on the right side of the road. I have hazy memories of many near-misses on the roadways on these crazy acid trips, when I nearly killed myself and many other innocent people. I was the poster child for the evolution of drug abuse: It starts out as fun, fun, fun. Then it's fun, fun, fun, with consequences. Then it devolves into a little fun and a lot of consequences, until finally, it leaves you in a crumpled heap of incomprehensible demoralization and a heap of trouble with the law.

Case in point: our class trip – and I do mean trip. We pulled together a motley assortment of eight unlikely companions and planned a journey on the Norfolk Broads, a scenic waterway that meandered through the English countryside, ending at the oceanside town of Lowestoft. We rented a boat and pulled together sailing fortifications for a six-day trip: six cases of beer, some hard liquor, speed, hash and LSD. Oh yeah, did anybody bring any food?

We arrived at the dock to get on our boat, which we expected would be a high-falutin' speed demon. Instead, we discovered that we'd rented a barge-like vessel with the controls and kitchen above deck and some beds below. We quickly learned that this large, slow-moving boat was hell to steer, and we endangered many sailors with our inexperience and impatience. Only a few of us had any water experience, but all of us drove that barge as fast as it could go in our drunken, drugged-out revelry.

The trip started out with easy-going, relaxing sails, interspersed with stops by the windmills along the twisting waterway. We would visit local gardens to pick our vegetables right out of the ground and pay for them. This was quite a challenge for young men who knew little about cooking. We'd clean and cut up the vegetables, throw them in a pot and cook them, along with leeks and chronically undercooked beans. You know what happened after that – we tooted along the Norfolk Broads with a real gas problem. In our haze of drugs and undigested fart blossoms, the passing windmills, big blue sky and giant, puffy clouds still gave us quite a beautiful experience.

About four days in, we started taking LSD en masse. Some of the new guys had no experience with this powerful drug, and things quickly got out of control. They would try to drive the boat up onto dry land, and we would collide with the shore because of their enthusiasm to mix physics and peripheral distortions. At times, we would have to take over the helm with stern warnings such as, "No, we cannot take off and fly!" Beer, vegetable soup, LSD, speed and hash were not good sailing partners. In no time, the inexperienced "travelers" among us were no longer available to this planet. Tired of baby-sitting the greenhorns, my friend Steve and I couldn't wait to arrive in Lowestoft and get away from the madness of our cloistered environment. We took a hit of LSD, did a line of coke and went off to sight-see.

We visited pubs and markets and picked up bags of all kinds of things while we tripped our asses off. Bobbies kept whizzing by in wailing squad cars. We paid them no mind until we seemed to be surrounded by bobbies on foot. We overheard someone say the police were searching for some young American men in the area. Alarmed, we ducked out and headed back to the marina, running down

alleys and trying to keep out of sight. We paused on a
hilltop that looked down onto the marina where our boat
was docked and saw four constable vehicles parked nearby.
We were tripping, with everything we looked at leaving
trails and every sound leaving a spiraling echo of "ch-ch-
ch-ch-ch-ch." In our altered states, we wondered if one
of our party had drowned. Finally, we walked nervously
downhill to find a bobby and ask what the commotion was
about. The next thing we knew, we were driven with most
of our traveling companions to the police station, where
we were seated around a table in an interrogation room.
I finally realized who was missing: Derek*, the officer's
kid. We were extremely nervous, which – considering our
leek-soup and undercooked-vegetable diet – soon filled the
interrogation room with deadly methane gas. The police
would ask questions and we would fart in response and
laugh uncontrollably. Some of us made light of this deadly
serious situation by trying on the bobbies' hats. We acted
like the terrified children we were.

Finally, the police laid out what they knew. Derek had
been found sitting naked at the end of a city pier. He was
talking to Jesus and aliens when they found him, and now
he was in the infirmary, recovering from exposure to water
and cold weather. Goddamn it – the officer's kid, I thought.
We never should have brought him on board. Leave it up
to officers to raise their kids to get enlisted people's kids in
real trouble.

In their search of our boat, they had found a pile of
drugs and a piece of paper on which someone had written,
"17 lbs of hash." They asked us whose handwriting it was.
No one said a word as the paper was passed around the
table. Finally, the paper came to me, and I was astounded to
see it was my own handwriting. Astonished, I babbled that
I meant "17 quid of hash," meaning I had bought about 40
American dollars worth. This misunderstanding explained
the three police divers we saw looking under our boat for

massive quantities of dope.

After hours of questioning, the police released us but intended to file some type of charges related to the speed and LSD they found. Most of the guys were picked up by their parents, and the rest of us soberly took the boat back to its home port. Not long after, all of us except Derek – who'd been excused as the innocent victim of our malevolent natures – gathered in court to hear a judge review charges of possession of controlled substances and malicious intent to harm. The judge said the police had found three hits of LSD saturated with a large amount of speed. The drugs must have melted into each other; that meant only one of us could get hung with a possession charge. The judge asked each of us what our plans were, and we all replied that we planned to return to the States immediately and attend college. Apparently relieved that we were getting out of his country, he dropped the charges and let us go. Derek, the officer's kid, was sent back to the U.S. immediately, and the rest of us finished the term. During the last months of school, we were the brunt of many jokes and felt guilt and shame for dishonoring our school and our parents.

Music provided most of my positive experiences at school. I was invited to play a drum solo during Lakenheath's commencement ceremonies. I decided to do it with some Kowalski flair. Streaking was at the height of its British popularity that year, and I greatly enjoyed watching these prim and proper people, from the football team to my dorm counselors, experience the great outdoors in the buff. So I dressed in farmer's overalls for my drum solo and, when I was done, I stood up in front of the entire student body and said, "I hear there's a lot of talk about streaking and naked people." I unclipped my overalls as students gasped, bracing themselves to see me strip at such an important event. As my overalls hit the ground, there was dead silence, and then a collective, "Eeeeeeeeewwwwww!" I was wearing flesh-colored nylons. Just something for them to remember me by!

My favorite thing about England was the tradition of ringing church bells three times a day. No matter where you were, you could count on hearing the soothing sounds of those bells. For a lifelong wanderer, I really appreciated the feeling of connectedness the bells gave me. It was one thing I could share with all the unknown people around me.

– 16 –

Draft Number: 114

At the Philadelphia airport, I stepped off the plane from England wearing my Harris Tweed suit, looking like Sherlock Holmes. It was a 90-degree summer day. I got the opportunity to cool off immediately when I was strip-searched by the inspectors. They pulled my luggage completely apart, scattering my belongings everywhere. At first, I thought I was finally getting busted for the music-store heist. But then I remembered the English marijuana seeds I had hidden in the aluminum frame of my pack. Pot was so rare in England that I decided to bring home some of these exotic seeds and grow a little crop on American soil.

While I was being searched, I could hear my father yelling at the officers outside the door. "I was an American serviceman who served for 20 years protecting this country, and this is how you treat my son?!" he bellowed. Meanwhile, I realized the precious marijuana seeds were also packed in my socks. I re-dressed and re-packed my bags. Welcome back to America!

My brother Mark and his friends handled the rest of my homecoming. We snuck back into the camper on Dad's property for some real catch-up partying. They were huffing Pam cooking spray in sandwich bags, a quick and cheap high that can be extremely damaging to your health. I finally took a drag and my mind went "ring-ring-ring-ring-ring" faster and faster. It was a dark, ugly high that got uglier when Mark told me to lie down on the floor and try it. I did, and he and his friends yelled that I was at a race track and horses were running over me. They proceeded to stomp on and around me as I lay helpless on the floor. I went to bed greatly disturbed, praying to God that I hadn't done permanent damage to my brain.

The Vietnam War draft was still going on, and I was prime, 19-year-old soldier material with a draft number – 114. Told that I was next in line for the draft, I started applying to colleges to avoid the war. I'd heard more than enough about Vietnam from my dad, who'd flown home so many thousands of our finest and youngest in aluminum coffins. I wasn't sure if any college would take me with my sporadic high-school attendance and grades to match. But just as I was about to give up, I was accepted by Delaware State College, an all-black school in Dover. Considering my bond and history with black people, there certainly couldn't have been any school that would have commanded more of my respect than one founded as the State College for Colored Students in 1890.

I signed up for a double major of music and therapy. I decided that I wanted to introduce the transformative power of music to persons with disabilities.

I began each school day with a beer or some weed before class. On one typical day, I cleaned the resin from my pipe before my piano lesson. My teacher took one look at my black fingernails and unkempt hair and asked, "What's that terrible smell?" She told me to go scrub the black residue off my fingers before continuing with the lesson. I once again started a fresh, new opportunity with destructive self-sabotage, which always got in the way of any excitement or hope I had for myself in new ventures. I didn't seem able to accept that anything good or lasting could happen for me, and my drug and alcohol addictions made sure I always fulfilled that prophecy. Of course, I wasn't hip to all that yet – I thought I was just having the "good time" I so richly deserved.

Even while my self-destructive practices went into full swing, there was so much I loved about Delaware State College. This was higher education from an African-American perspective. I was taught about a black God who existed for thousands of years before religions were organized. The Black History classes were incredible, loaded with amazing contributors such as Frederick Douglass, Sojourner Truth, Booker T. Washington, Rosa Parks, George Washington Carver, and so many others whose names were rarely mentioned in the white schools I'd attended. The school's music program added jazz, African rhythms and a fantastic high-stepping marching band to its classical training. I felt I was part of something special. I also took a particular interest in my geology class, fascinated by plate tectonics and the way the Earth was formed and stays in constant motion.

Music composition was one area where my rebellion was inspired by pure creativity. I strove to break all the rules, incorporating everything the teacher said not to use. I wrote using those sounds on purpose to create my original sound. I would never make it to the top of the classical-composing food chain with this attitude, but at least this sound was mine.

For about a year and a half, I carried 18 credits per semester, drove affordable cars and worked side jobs. Soon enough, wanderlust and lack of faith in my own ability to set and reach goals undermined my industriousness. I packed up my tiny Opal Cadet for the drive south to my old familiar vacation destination, Pensacola, Fla. I'd gone there before to visit my three Seventh-Day Adventist sister friends, but now Pensacola had some added attractions. First, I had reunited with my England friend, Steve. He was joining me on this adventure, much as he had accompanied me on the ill-fated class boating trip on the Norfolk Broads. Second, the sisters were still there. Somehow, I thought they had put their lives on hold, and I could just show up and get a relationship going with magical thinking and fantasy.

And third, my mother and her husband Ron had moved from England and bought a house in Pensacola. Steve and I loaded up the Cadet and a U-Haul trailer with my large drum set, PA, guitars, and clothes – and speed, and weed, and LSD, and beer – and hit the road. We stopped at a bluegrass festival on our way out of town, and then we went over the 20-mile Chesapeake Bay Bridge-Tunnel. We tripped along the countryside uneventfully for several hours, looking at the houses with their honeyed hams hanging outside for sale. Late at night we cruised down a small highway with a grass meridian between the lanes. The quiet was shattered when a Cadillac squealed onto the freeway traveling in the wrong direction, constantly forcing other drivers to skid out of its way. Finally, we heard through the open window the sound of cars and metal crunching, as the Cadillac hit the back of another car and spun it into the grass. Then the Caddy veered off the road into the woods and hit a tree. We were still tripping our asses off and seeing trails and colors, and our senses were heightened. I pulled over onto the meridian, and we ran to check the people in the first car. Except for being frightened, their seat belts had saved them from major injuries. We ran to the Cadillac, its horn blaring and its headlights wrapped around the tree and aiming eerily into the woods. We got the back doors opened, and the stunned passengers spilled out like agitated ants. The smell of perfume, alcohol and cigarettes was pervasive to my senses. Steve had a scared look on his face as I beckoned him to help me with the driver, who gasped quietly through the blood and gurgled, "Help me," over and over. His torso was pinned to the seat by the steering wheel, his arms dangling, his face contorted. I tried to move the seat back, but he was a large man, and I could not reach around him. Steve extinguished a lit cigarette he found on the back seat, in case any gasoline was leaking from the car. As I kept struggling to move the front seat back, the driver began screaming in agony. Now all I could see in the darkness were the white teeth and white eyes of the family of African-American passengers who were finally coming around. They were angry, drunk and concerned that I was trying to cause harm to their uncle. Suddenly, I heard sirens. Way too high to talk to officers for a police report, Steve and I slipped into the darkness, got in our car, and reviewed the incredible feelings we were having.

After pulling over to calm down from this drama and sleep for a few hours, we soldiered on until we hit Benson, S.C., where I left the highway to get gas. The exit ramp led to a T intersection, and I didn't slow down my car and trailer quickly enough. We barreled into a corn field beyond the roadway, and the corn slowed us down enough that I could plow through the field and get back on the road. After stopping at a nearby service station for gas and beer, I turned the key in the ignition, and the car was dead. We looked for people to ask for help, but the mechanic had just gone home. That just left a bunch of rednecks standing around looking at the two of us – Steve, a person of color, and me, a white guy who picked a person of color as a friend – like we were pond scum. I could hear people muttering things like "half-breed" and "white nigger" under their breath.

It was late, dark, and steamy-humid, and the only offer

of help we got was from the driver of a giant, 16-wheeler tow-truck who tried to jump-start the car. When that didn't work, he offered to push the car down the road so I could try to crank up the engine that way. We detached the U-Haul, and Steve stayed to watch it while I got in the car. The tow-truck driver pulled up behind me with his lights off and rammed the back of my tiny car with such force, I thought he might crush it. He pushed it along and then rammed it again. Finally, I pulled off to the side and he continued down the road with his lights off, yelling expletives like a madman. I was scared and shaking. Looking back down the road at the service station's lights in the distance, I had a bad feeling. I didn't want to leave my car, but I had to go back and get Steve. Back at the station, one other guy invited us to pile into his Mustang while he looked for someone to assist us. He drove us all over the area at speeds exceeding 100 mph until finally he dropped us back at the station. Worn out from this series of near-death experiences, we rolled into the woods and collapsed.

The next morning, we flagged down a black man with two kids in his truck cab and a flatbed full of chickens in crates. He listened silently as we told our tale, and then he took a look under the hood. He pulled out a pack of hand-rolled cigarettes of homegrown weed. We took this as a sign from God that we were safe. As we exuberantly thanked him for caring enough to stop, he slowly drawled that black people didn't really talk to whites too much in those parts. Then, he hit the starter and rewired a few things, and voila, the Cadet started up. He warned us that we should lose the U-Haul, because the tiny car couldn't handle that much weight. He didn't ask for anything in return for his aid, so I gave him a guitar and some canned food, and he gave us a little weed. Off we went, slow and easy.

We pulled over in Georgia that night in an area full of

creepy-looking trees with Spanish moss. We drank beers and smoked our bong until the weed ran out. Then I threw the bong, cans and bottles as far as I could into the field, so we would look like regular travelers who were camping by the side of the road. In the morning, I awoke from my paranoid stupor to see a patrol car with its lights on and no one near the vehicle. Several hundred yards away, I saw an officer looking for something out in the field. I started looking nervously in another direction, hoping he would walk away from where I had thrown the bong. He finally came up to us, satisfied with himself, and asked what we were doing on the side of the road. Steve and I blurted different stories at the same time, and then we both fell silent. I explained that we were on our way to Florida, and that we would be out of his state within an hour, and if that was all right with him, we would be on our way. So ended the journey to Florida.

Upon arrival, I headed over to the high-class Gulf Breeze neighborhood where Mom and Ron had bought a swanky house upon their return from England. They both were working two jobs, and I made myself scarce when they were around. I was the invisible man; the only evidence of my presence was a lot of missing food and beer and the mess I left behind. I felt out of place in this chic area, and I realized what a bum and a burden I was. I had easy access to my "angry young man" attitude and took full advantage of everything offered, as if it was owed to me. When Mom invited me to join them for Thanksgiving, I arrived drunk, threw up and disappeared, ruining the holiday for her.

The Vietnam draft was still on, so I registered for classes at Pensacola Junior College to avoid the call. Inexplicably, I chose business as my major. One of the first facts I learned was that most businesses fail in the first year. No longer needing much proof that I was doomed to fail no matter what I tried, I took this as my cue to start flunking my business classes right away and avoid the middleman. I found personal lessons in some of my other classes, though, such as the phrase, "Ontogeny recapitulates phylogeny." This simply means the birth of something new creates the need for it. This theory was the basis of the evolution of the species. I personalized this scientific concept as, "Evolution of the feces – I shit; therefore, I am! I must be flushed!" This sort of self-degradation masked as comedy contributed to years of failure and mental poverty. It's the worst conditioned reflex available on the planet, leading to my decades-long diatribe, "Why bother? Who gives a shit? Give up! Fuck it! Miss me with that! I'm not the one!" In other words, I told myself, don't dare to dream or aspire, because you can't take the pain of your inevitable failure. Tragically, I bought this line of shit for many years.

As usual, I required funds to cover my substance needs, so I got a job at the Pizza Wagon. This was the beginning of a longtime "pizza-based economy" for me. Not only did I earn cash, I also built a nutrition pyramid made entirely of pizza. One of the side effects of this was acne in a 20-year-old, hormone-laden man like me, but it was a price I was willing to pay. Our delivery area covered a 50-mile radius along the beach road almost to Panama City. The beach and dunes at night were a white and clear quartz crystal, illuminating the area as if it were a snowy winter scene. It was beautiful day or night.

I made some new friends who were my kind of party people. They led what I considered to be charmed lives and were still available for serious substance abuse. One new friend was Conrad*, a sweet guy who'd lost a chunk of his calf while playing chicken with a slow-moving train. No one seemed to notice his mutilation, though, and he was popular among the beachfront party set. Conrad and I played guitar together, and we started playing music at beach parties and private houses along the waterfront. This was another opportunity to try to fit in and be part of an attractive crowd. When someone gave me $200 and told me to go buy the liquor for a big party one night, I thought it might be a good chance to prove my worth. I loaded cases and kegs of beer and about 10 different kinds of hard liquor into my new/used Ford Maverick and headed back toward the party in a torrential Florida downpour. A one-lane bridge stood between me and the beach house, and in the rain, the traffic ground to a standstill. Cars behind me began honking, and I got so frustrated and agitated, I tried to make an opportunity where there was none and gunned my engine. A Cadillac nailed me and spun me into a Lincoln and a few other big cars until my Maverick came to a stop. The smell of alcohol from the broken bottles was overpowering. Back at the party, the rich kids improvised and had a great time. My shot at a foothold in that crowd was over, and I felt ostracized. I wound up in court, where the judge kindly excused the charges against me on account of the weather. But my car was gone, and I had canceled my car insurance the minute after I registered the vehicle, as was my cost-cutting custom.

My next job was waiting tables at a top restaurant called Rosie O'Grady's. This was a fast-moving place, and here I developed my skill set as a five-star waiter serving a high-end crowd. I spent every spare moment at the beach and met the regulars, one of whom took me to several places out in the country where psilocybin mushrooms grew. We would fill 55-gallon trash bags with mushrooms, then make mushroom Kool-Aid and party for days on end. Once, we shared a giant mushroom out in the field, and some nearby cows mooed at us as if to say, "We know what you're doing, and that shit will fuck you up." We had trans-species conversations with the cows that day. Suddenly it was all so clear!

I invited my mother to dinner at a friend's house, and we made spaghetti with mushrooms – guess what kind. We all laughed and smiled until Mom finally asked what was up. I told her she was tripping on a hallucinogen and finally drove her home. She never brought this up afterward. It was yet another result of my low-impulse inability to engage in a normal social situation without using thrill-seeking as a default.

I spent more and more time in the water. I would bring a gallon of psilocybin Kool-Aid to the beach, get in the water and snorkel for hours, sometimes diving to 40 or 50 feet. I would lower my pulse rate and avoid struggling with the fear of drowning until I could stay underwater for unusually long periods of time. At such depths, the water was clear and I sometimes could see for hundreds of feet with the reflection of the sunlight off the crystal-white sand. Schools of fish would hang around me with curiosity. It was one of the rare activities that gave me peace with my own existence.

Once, I snorkeled near the pier with my "Singapore Sling" spear gun, and I noticed a high number of schools of barracudas in the area. These fish like shiny objects, are easily attracted and attack at 35 miles per hour, so I moved cautiously. Suddenly, I noticed splashes near my head. I looked up and saw big-looking, long-haired, drunken rednecks throwing beer bottles in the water at me and the barracudas. They yelled at me to get the barracudas with my spear gun. I got the hell out of the water. Later that day, I heard that members of Lynyrd Skynyrd had been arrested for being drunk and disorderly on the pier and resisting arrest. They missed that night's gig in Mobile, Ala.

Around this time, the movie "Jaws" was released, and everyone started freaking out about a species that actually kills only a small number of people each year. In return, we kill about a zillion sharks annually. One day I was swimming near the 600-foot pier and saw something that looked like a shark. I high-tailed it back to shore and told people I'd seen a shark, but no one paid any mind. I swam back to the spot, and there, motionless in the water, was a magnificent, 12-foot, hammerhead shark. I knew sharks had to move to breathe, but even if this shark was sick or dying, it could still expend its last bit of life force to chase me and chew my leg off! However, no matter what, I decided I wanted the jaws of this massive creature as my prize.

I got my military bayonet from my car and dove about 20 feet near the shark. Then I thought the better of that plan. I found some macho-looking guys on the beach and convinced them to bring the 50 feet of rope they had in their pickup and come into the water to help me haul the shark to shore. They maintained every bit of that 50-foot distance while I dove and tied the rope around the shark's tail. By then, it was obvious the shark was dead. Dragging the enormous carcass to the beach was a serious undertaking, and after about two hours, we used our last shred of strength to pull the animal onto land. Word spread on the beach like wildfire, and people came from the concession stands, the parking lots and water to see for themselves. We strained to turn the creature over so I could finally claim my hard-won prize – those beautiful teeth. But once the shark was rolled over, it was obvious that someone had already hacked out its jaws and then discarded its body back in the water.

I did have one consolation for all of my efforts: The epic struggle to bring the shark to shore had attracted the attention of a young woman I had seen many times but was afraid to approach. We struck up a conversation and hit it off. Her name was Lisa, and her older sister drove an MG Midget that provided a place where we could get it on. A few weeks after we met, a hurricane approached Gulf Breeze, and vehicles equipped with loud speakers drove around town urging residents to evacuate immediately. Lisa's sister was dating a crazy guy who ran a gas station, and the four of us decided to have a "hurricane party" instead of evacuating. The booze and weed flowed as the storm approached, only 30 miles off-shore. We got into the crazy guy's van, paired off and had sex right next to each other while wild winds buffeted the vehicle from all sides. Then we changed partners. I could smell the sex of another man on Lisa while her sister, now getting it hard from the gas station attendant, gave me a forlorn look. Obviously she was not enjoying her circumstances any longer. The wind changed direction, and the storm made land 50 miles down the coast. Stone-cold sober once our near-death experience was over, we were extremely uneasy with each other and what we had just done. After that, I didn't see Lisa anymore beyond a quick hello.

By now, my guitar-playing had parlayed into the formation of a little band of musical misfits. We got a gig at a Holiday Inn about 50 miles away at Panama Beach. Just as we started playing our first set, I noticed a friend of ours playing the harmonica in the audience. The bartender emerged from behind the bar carrying a short bat, which he used to beat the back of our friend's legs until he fell over. The bartender noticed our stunned faces and motioned for us to continue to play. Who could refuse an offer like that! We played for quite a while, and then Johnny Cash's "Folsom Prison Blues" came up in our set list. The rowdy, drunken rednecks liked it so much, they insisted that we play it four times in a row.

When the rednecks turned abusive, the bartender came out with his bat again, and we decided it was a good time to pack up and run for it. As our beach crowd loaded up our cars and hit the road, the rednecks were right behind us, climbing into their pickups with loaded gun racks and CB radios. Our rich friends drove expensive, high-octane cars, and they were gone in a flash. My friend and I were left behind in a jeep, and the pickups were closing in on us fast. We pulled off the road onto a beach, killed the jeep's lights, grabbed the rest of the Mogen David ("Mad Dog 20/20," we called it) and our guitars, and belly-crawled along the beach to wait out the manhunt. Once the rednecks gave up the chase, we got back into the jeep. Not that this was any safer – my friend was plastered and weaving around on the beach without headlights, but his big belly kept him wedged in behind the steering wheel so he couldn't be ejected. I, on the other hand, got thrown from the vehicle every time he hit a big dune, which was cheap entertainment until I kneed myself in the face and badly split my lip. The rednecks couldn't have beaten me up worse than we did ourselves.

Around this time, I was looking for work again and applied for a waiter job at a high-class joint on the beach called the Galatea. When the manager rejected my application, I looked around and noticed that every single employee I could see was African-American. So I pointed out that he may want to reconsider his decision, since it looked like he might need a little ethnic diversity on the staff. Feeling pressured, he hired me, and the other waiters made it part of their job to try to harass me into quitting. That only egged me on, though, and I soon added even more finesse to my five-star skill set. I learned to serve dishes like chateaubriand, flaming red snapper, and elaborate flaming desserts with real flair. When preparing doggy bags, I made masterpiece versions of swans and other animals out of aluminum foil. Going the extra mile like that, I'd earn $125 for four or five hours of work. In 1976, this was bank.

Most of the clientele were "new money" oil guys. They were the richest men in town, with a lot of new prosperity but the same old simple tastes in entertainment. A few of us waiters were invited one night to join some of the customers at a strip club. I got drunk and felt awkward staring at women in front of a bunch of other men. Just then, a beautiful woman dressed in jeans and a flannel shirt walked up to me and took my face in her hands. She gently stroked my cheek and gazed into my eyes, then walked away. I couldn't believe my luck. A while later, much to my surprise, my wholesome farm girl took the stage and did a wild routine. On one hand, I was disappointed to see her modesty shattered, but of course, she was very entertaining. I went home alone, drunk and frustrated, and forgot all about her.

Not long after, I was working at the Galatea when a buzz went around the room. One of the country's first black three-star generals had just walked in. People strained to get a good look at him, but I was looking at his gorgeous companion, who was wearing a racy dress. My jaw dropped – it was the farm-girl stripper! The general looked around the room to choose a table, noticed that I was the lone white waiter, and said, "I'll take the white boy." I couldn't help but blurt out the general's secret to the older woman who worked there as hostess. She scolded me for disrespecting a member of our nation's military. I was still way too excited and had too much of my low-impulse behavior to access, so I waited until the general went to the restroom and then made up some reason to visit the table.

"My, my, my," I said. "You are a very busy woman!"

"You have no idea," she replied, without missing a beat.

As always, I was plenty busy myself. More than once, I woke up reeling from a hangover in the hotel room of someone I'd served at the Galatea the night before. During the year and a half I spent in Florida, I had the usual chaotic jumble of jobs. As a break from food service, I took a job as a longshoreman. It took some getting used to. Just walking to work, I would pass men on the docks playing cards, sneaking drinks and roughing each other up to collect debts. Once, I saw one guy hold another guy by his ankles and shake him upside down to claim whatever fell out of his pockets. The perfume of the docks was potent, between the hot contents of the ships' holds, the diesel fuel of ship exhaust, and the smell of men working in 100-degree weather. I was one of the youngest workers and by far the smallest. Every three minutes, I had to carry my own body weight of 150 pounds as the unending pallets moved in and out of the ships' holds. We filled ships from the bottom to the top, walking on the cargo as we laid it down.

For weeks on end, I would work like that, then go home, eat, wash and fall asleep. The pace was crushing. Sometimes, I couldn't help but wish that a pallet would break and dump 24 sacks of something heavy on an unsuspecting worker, because then we got a 15-minute break to honor the lost brother. The other guys were short-tempered when I couldn't keep up, swearing at me and calling me names. My only ally was an African-American man called Night Train. He liked that I was the odd man out, fighting against all odds to keep my job. Now and then, Night Train would carry a sack for me and save my ass. When I found out that Night Train was nicknamed in honor of a certain type of cheap wine that really packed a punch, I sometimes would give him a bottle at lunchtime. It was a way to thank him while reassuring myself that at least one person cared about me. I slowly became aware of all the infirmities that afflicted the longshoremen around me – back problems, hernias, bad knees, wrist splints. The money was good, but after four months, I chose my health and quit.

Unemployed again, I returned to playing and singing at beach parties for booze money. I'd become pretty good on the guitar by now and was acting as lead singer. I started hanging out with some Vietnam vets who'd served as Airborne Rangers. These guys raised thrill-seeking behavior to a downright psychotic level, and I kept up with them every step of the way. We would do insane things like dive off of bridges. My favorite version of this game was played on a wooden train trestle that was 60 feet above the water. The idea was to be the last guy to jump, just before the train hit you. The rickety old trestle would shimmy and shake like an old roller coaster as the train approached, and as the deafening whistle screamed, we would look each other in the eye to see who would jump and who would wait. It got real close to stupid and even closer to death, as we jumped and tried to avoid hitting the people who were taunting us from below. For added flair, you could try to land inside truck-tire inner tubes that we'd strewn on the water.

I was now a long-time, full-blown alcoholic, drinking morning, noon and night. I got a new job as a "litter gitter" with one of my veteran buddies. We joined a bunch of college kids in picking up litter along a popular, five-mile stretch of beach. Anytime of day or night, there would be 20 or 30 parties jumping on the beach. Using a jeep and a truck, we drove down the beach periodically to pick up whatever was left behind. This job had two impressive perks. First, there often were nude sunbathers on the beach, which afforded us an enjoyable view. Second, wasted partiers often left behind full or partial bottles of hard liquor. We did our best to take advantage of both of these opportunities. We would approach the nude sunbathers and cordially ask whether they had anything we might throw away for them. This was not merely a cheap thrill – it was absolutely free. Then, we all chipped in to buy a blender, drink mixes and ice, and someone on the crew would act as bartender, mixing up our found liquor and bringing pitchers of mixed drinks to us. What the heck, we'd take swimming breaks, too. It was hot, hard work but with gratifying benefits.

The Vietnam vet and I would sometimes go thrill-seeking during breaks, and the bridge across the bay was a great place for this. Partial remains of the old bridge stood about 60 feet above the water, and towering above that was the modern, 250-foot-high bridge. We jumped off the old bridge structure for the first few weeks. Then we got bolder and started jumping and diving from the lower part of the new bridge. One day, the vet and I were drunk and doing 60- to 80-foot crowd-pleaser dives to entertain a crowd of onlookers. People standing below us on the older bridge structure called out, "Higher! Higher!" The vet was used to jumping out of planes, so he was fearless. He jumped with his shoes on to break the fall, while I dove head-first. Higher and higher we went, gauging our ascent by the platforms that appeared every 20 feet on the megastructure.

Suddenly, the weather changed from dead calm to windy. The swell of the waves was harder to read, the higher we went. If you hit a wave wrong, it was game-over. At about 120 feet, the old bridge structure and the people on it looked tiny. Without batting an eye, the vet jumped. I counted the seconds as he fell – one-thousand, two-thousand, three-thousand … I lost count, mesmerized by his long drop. He hit the water and disappeared under the surface for a long time. Just as I feared the worst, he surfaced, and the crowd cheered as he swam toward the bridge ladder.

Now it was my turn. I felt like I was in a wind tunnel under the bridge. My mind kept pleading, "No! No! No! This is much too dangerous!" That was diametrically opposed to the messages the alcohol was sending: "Go ahead! You can do it!" I stood and shivered in the chilly wind, trying in vain to see the waves. Finally, frustrated and with no control over my low-impulse, thrill-seeking behavior, I dove headfirst. The wind buffeted me this way and that, and I couldn't control the way my body would hit the water. I hit the surface of the water with the force of a peach hitting a windshield. I blacked out for a few seconds and opened my eyes to see my turquoise necklace slowly floating down, down, down, down … until it disappeared into the darkness below. I was terrified to discover that I could move nothing except my left hand. Paralyzed, I drifted from face-down into an upright position and saw that I was about 25 feet below the surface. Using my left hand as a paddle, I desperately tried to maneuver upward to save myself. In my slow ascent, I exhaled as little as possible, but I was suffocating. My trunks, torn off of me in the fall, floated past me. Time stopped, until I finally managed to rise to the surface with one side of my face. Various parts of my stunned body were slowly recovering from the shock of impact, but I was barely treading water, looking up sideways through one eye and whispering, "Help me, please help me," to the onlookers who cheered from the bridge. Realizing that no one was coming to my aid, I made it to the ladder somehow and clung to it until I regained enough mobility to climb out of the water. Most of the spectators had left. I realized how close I had come to death with a large audience of witnesses who would not have saved me. The experience forced me to take a hard look at how I lived. But it wasn't harrowing enough to force me to change.

– 17 –

Cross-Country
to San Francisco

I had a red 1969 3-speed Firebird with racing tires. I got it cheap from my neighbors, who had to sell it to send their son to college. It was such a cheap deal, in fact, that I didn't care that everyone would drive it and burn rubber in all three gears while they were high and drunk.

My Pensacola friends discovered MDA, a horse tranquilizer also known as Angel Dust. This spelled the beginning of the end of our relatively carefree days having beach parties, lying in the sun, working, playing music and swimming. They were ending up in car wrecks and emergency rooms. I had to revive two people by sticking them in cold showers for 30 minutes, holding them down and slapping them around. A funny thing happens when you're on MDA: You can access your adrenaline and attain super powers. One guy of slim proportions had six cops struggling to restrain him. We got him to the emergency room and he broke his restraints, stood up on the gurney and fell backwards. You could hear his head hit the linoleum floor like a melon. Amazingly, like a drunk in a car wreck, all he had was a headache after that encounter.

Right about then, I met a gorgeous model at the beach. We had many strange sexual encounters like I had read about in magazines. We did it in the water, in restrooms, on the beach at night, at parties. When she moved to San Francisco, I decided to follow her. I'd had enough of the MDA carnage anyway, and I needed what Alcoholics Anonymous calls a "geographic." In other words, I would try to run away from myself, only to run into myself wherever I landed in that river of denial, where my misery would be cheerfully refunded. And wherever I ended up, there I was again with the same incomprehensible demoralization.

I seriously considered driving the Firebird to California, but I couldn't afford the gas. Besides, I didn't enjoy the empty prestige of driving a car that made people look at you with bedroom eyes. I never really got any more action with the car than I did without it. I found a small Kawasaki KZ400 twin-cylinder street motorcycle. I had only a small amount of experience on motorcycles, and the guy who sold it to me gave me a hit of amyl nitrite as I was riding off. Stoned and flipping from the huffer, I let go of the accelerator, went 20 feet and crashed ever so gently into a car.

Before the motorcycle, I'd owned and driven seven heavily armored crash-dummy-mobiles that were waiting to blossom into the wrecks they were meant to be. They all had magnetic bumpers that liked to seek expensive cars and hit them. It was tough to make the transition to driving drunk on a motorcycle. When I stopped at a stop sign and didn't put my foot down, the bike would fall on my leg. The muffler would burn my flesh as if it were a piece of barbecued chicken. In the rain, I would often skid around, trying to slide safely away from big objects as I crouched on the side of the engine, with the wheels spinning wildly close to my hands and legs. Sparks were skidding off the pavement from the crash bars. This thing even had a windshield. The good part about it was the bike barely went over 100 miles an hour.

After a few months learning to ride, I packed my guitar and my backpack on my sissy bar, said goodbye and set off on my wondrous journey with $120 in my pocket. It must have been around September or October 1976. In the South, these were still good months for sporadic warm weather. Heading out of Florida, the bugs were relentless, splattering my face, stinging my eyes and coating my windshield. At night, they lit up the sky with a luminous glow that stung at 60 miles an hour.

I looked like Easy Rider with my guitar sitting on the sissy bar on the back of my seat. I rested on my pack. I had a sticky accelerator from crashing the handlebars, and I could set the speed by jiggling it just right. I would ride with no hands, looking deceptively like I knew what I was doing. I stopped at a few places and mostly slept outside, but my $120 for the journey quickly petered out. Out of money for gas and food, it wasn't long before my excursion came to a halt. I learned about Manpower, a temporary employment agency prevalent throughout the South. I began to make my way from place to place by taking a string of jobs for Manpower – packing frozen meat in meat factories, working in refrigerated cheese warehouses, moving and stacking 400-pound mag wheels for 18-wheelers, landscaping. The work was back-breaking, and sometimes I would come to work with my clothes still soaked from whatever weather I slept in (or not) the night before. Often I would work with little or no sleep.

Texas seemed to take forever to get through. During a thunderstorm, I got stuck behind a gasoline tanker. I watched as the lightning filled the sky for 50 miles and

started coming toward us. It would rain, then dry off
in minutes, then rain again. The traffic was thick and
unmovable. I hoped we wouldn't be struck by lightning and
that the tanker would not explode.

Often on my journey, I would have a 40-ouncer of
Budweiser or Coors tucked under my T-shirt, between
my legs, and use a super-long twist straw. That way I
could drink and drive with no hands in the long, hot days
of Indian summer without stirring the attention of police
officers along the way. That night, somewhere outside
of Lubbock, Texas, I decided to pull over to sleep. There
was this roadside place with about eight rest areas where
you could picnic off the freeway. The small structures in
the rest areas had the Mexican adobe, reddish, half-round,
tiled roofs. I wanted to be safe, so I decided to sleep on this
dangerous perch. I was exhausted. I settled into the very
uncomfortable, roughshod bed of tiles in the air, on the side
of the roof that was not visible from the road, and went to
sleep with my guitar beside me.

I woke up startled by the sound of multiple gunshots. I
realized I was up in the air and hung over from drinking.
My life crystallized before me, and I broke out in a sweat.
I looked over the top of the little roof to see two cars full
of crazy-looking men shooting toward me. It looked like
shotguns and rifles – lots of muzzle flash lighting the sky.
They sounded drunk, yelling obscenities and firing at will
as they drove past and turned around. Frantically watching
my life drain before me, shaking in shock, I jumped down
with my sleeping bag and guitar. I put on two bungee cords
to hold my pack and guitar, with my sleeping bag hanging
out between them like a giant scarf. I fumbled for the keys
and tried starting the bike. It was then that I noticed they
were coming back toward me on their second assault.

The bike wouldn't kick over. I started running alongside
the bike, then jumped on and kicked the clutch. It caught,
and slowly the tired little motorcycle gained momentum.

Then the lonesome sound of a train whistle and the roar of rushing engine mixed with the sounds of gunshots as the cars got closer and closer. With my heart beating so fast it felt like it could explode, I was in a three-way race with the train and the cars moving alongside the road. The train was deafening. As the cars edged closer, I could see red muzzle flashes in my vibrating mirror. Up ahead, I could see in the night sky that the road and the train track intersected at a crossing. With my sleeping bag flopping wildly in the wind, whipping back and forth, I knew if I stopped, I was dead. I raced the train for what seemed like an eternity. The train engineer and I were abreast, and he could tell I wasn't stopping. He screeched his air horn to try to blast some sense into me.

We got closer and closer to the crossing. I tried to gain more speed. In a race for my life, I made the decision to try to outrun the train and cross the tracks. These split-second decisions were made in terrorized agony. The train grew even louder; the whistle shrieked. The crossing where the track and the road intersected edged closer, and so did the cars behind me. In a second, my life flashed before me. In shock, I beat the train across the tracks, and the cars had to stop. I floored the bike to its limit. The long train seemed to take forever and gave me the precious time I needed, all the way to Lubbock.

I arrived in an unforgiving town and went to the store for some much-needed beer. To my surprise, it was a dry county. You could not get liquor. Imagine the look on my face when I had to deal with this dilemma stone-cold sober. Pissed off, I rode for another eternity and passed out from delirium along the roadside the next morning. I woke up dehydrated with my face burned in the noonday sun.

On my travels, I usually would find kindred drug spirits. For years, I had been a drug chameleon: Whatever drugs were flowing in whatever crowd I happened to be with, I would flow with the drugs. Speed had always been a favorite, whenever it was available. Now, on the road, I was alone and had to make friends quickly wherever I wound up. I met a henchman who made his living in the "Collection Agency" part of drug use. I decided to work for him and try my hand at it. This income opportunity didn't last long as, before I knew it, guns were being drawn. I was outclassed, outbullied and outgunned by several members of the opposing team. After a couple of episodes involving loaded weapons being pointed at me, I gave it up.

During my brief tenure as Henchman in Training, I joined my friend in shooting speed daily. The thin line between what I would and wouldn't do grew thinner, and I started doing anything that was available. I didn't have anything holding me back – I had no job, no roots, no hope, and no beer money. The next thing I knew, I had become a very cheap speed addict. I could shoot up an amount of speed the size of a match head and get a real good rush. I shared eyedropper needles, shot up with no sanitation, participated in unintentional blood-to-blood contamination – ahhh, don't you just miss the good ole days of drug addiction?

With my collection job finished, I hit the road again. A couple of days later, I was sitting back and no-hands-driving along when a car full of girls drove by. They sounded like they were making fun of me as they passed. I forgot about them. Then up ahead, there they were again. This time, they chatted back and forth with me and smiled, and I smiled back, acting like I was someone who could pull off this deal. They motioned me to pull over, and we talked. They quickly asked if I would like to come over to where they lived in some small town and go skinny-dipping at a quarry. What luck!

I was terrified and in over my head. These girls were in charge and I was faking my bravado, but I couldn't resist the temptation of getting some action. We went to their place in a nearby college town, where we ate, drank beer, smoked some weed, and headed to the quarry.

We got naked and jumped in fast. Then, as we were more comfortable and felt safe with each other, we just relaxed, jumping off ropes and small cliffs around the quarry. They were nice, and in that moment, I got a fleeting glimpse of living a peaceful, beautiful, hopeful life. I was intoxicated by the young women spending time with me. I liked one of them, but she wasn't interested. The one who picked me assured me of happiness and comfort. We went back to their house as the night sky filled with colors that only the desert can bring, and night blurred into day.

In the morning, the girls seemed like different animals. I rode away after quietly thanking them for a wonderful time.

My head spinning in wonder and serendipity, I started singing a song I hated but couldn't get out of my head: "Everything is beautiful in its own way." After I started my bike, I forgot to click my kickstand up. I headed around a curve and noticed 12 warning reflectors. My bike rode right into them. My crash bars knocked a few down, and then I crashed. Stunned, I looked around in shock. I was right next to an old folks' home. They started hobbling out to see if I was OK. One of them asked me if I had insurance and said they would call the police for me. The police? Insurance? Who did they think I was?

Through the torn, bloodied right knee of my blue jeans, I could see that a piece of my kneecap was missing. I limped around, trying to get my things back on my motorcycle before the cops showed up. My gloveless hands were bloody and shook uncontrollably. Glass and gravel came out of my hands for 20 years after this, slowly surfacing, painfully reminding me of this crash. I checked out my bike and realized it took an even harder hit than I did. It had only one spark plug; the other was broken, cracked and misfiring, irregular and sputtering. Still in shock, I started the bike on one-quarter of its regular power and rolled slowly out of town on two cylinders. I headed toward the mountains at 35 miles an hour. Driving up and up to the high desert of New Mexico, I slowly limped along on the damaged bike while cars whipped past me.

The cold was unbearable. I put on every piece of clothing I owned. I inched my way through the mountainous terrain forever that night and finally reached the top. With the last money I had, I filled up at a gas station. Penniless and freezing, I climbed into my cheap, thin sleeping bag and slept out in the high desert plateau, damning myself for being so unprepared. Hell, I didn't know I was going to get stuck in the mountains. I didn't even know there were mountains in the Southwest! My body in agony, my stomach wanting nourishment, I pulled the bag over my head and began breathing on myself to warm up. Delirious from the cold, I noticed frost on the ground as my body stiffened. I kept my core warm by staying in a fetal position.

Finally, light broke the dark, foreboding silence, and cars started passing by the gas station with more frequency. It was too cold to stay outside. The gas station's store clerk let me hang out for a few hours. Then, after I wore out my welcome, I headed onward toward my destiny.

As you get higher in altitude, a funny thing happens to an engine. The high desert air has less oxygen, and unless you adjust the carburetor, your engine can't burn with the rich combustion available at lower altitudes. I hobbled on at 15 to 20 miles an hour till I almost gave up. The bike went slower and slower – was I going to be stranded? Finally, the mountains started heading downward, and I coasted downhill as fast as I could without crashing. The front fork of my bike had been bent in the accident. I prayed the brakes would hold out. Numb from the cold, I took more chances as I grew more delirious and tired. Then at last – warm, flatter ground.

After what seemed like forever, I got to a truck stop, where I met a compassionate Christian man named Paul.

He noticed my broken, disheveled condition and offered to buy me breakfast. I scarfed the food down so fast, he looked at me with surprise and asked what happened. We drank coffee, and he listened to my story. Paul offered to let me stay in his hotel room but, fearing an unwanted sexual liaison, I was wary. He explained that a similar thing happened to him when he was young, and someone had shown him compassion. Now it was his calling to extend such kindness when he met people who were struggling as he once had.

Paul took a look at my bike and said it wasn't going anywhere in that condition. After we took it to a mechanic, he invited me to share a day of his vacation with him. He planned to ride a tram up to a peak of the Sandia Mountains and eat lunch in a mountaintop restaurant. Unaccustomed to unconditional generosity, I didn't even know how to respond. When I explained that my injuries were causing me real pain and I was concerned about my bike, he said he wouldn't take no for an answer. I would be missing a great time and a wonderful view of God's country, he said. I gratefully accepted his kindness. In that moment, I felt a higher power was looking out for me.

The gondola afforded me a majestic view of the mountains where I'd almost frozen to death. The glory of the terrain, the wildlife and the wind at the top were exhilarating. We ate in the blissfully warm restaurant and looked around, trying to time our return to coincide with the closing of the motorcycle shop. The next day, with my motorcycle fixed, Paul and I parted company. He gave me $50 to pay for enough gas to get to California. I'm sure he knew the odds were slim that I would use the money for gas instead of alcohol or drugs. The fact that he gave it to me anyway somehow kept alive the tiny flicker of faith I still carried inside – faith that people could be kind, trustworthy and compassionate to others just because it was right.

Back on the road, I traveled through the sun-blistered country until I arrived in Los Angeles. After visiting people I knew, I turned north toward San Francisco. Along the way, I stopped to visit my old girlfriend from England, Raven. My habit of popping in without warning to surprise past sexual or romantic partners usually had dubious results, and this time was no different. Things had changed, and after some awkward moments, I rolled on toward my supermodel flame and my San Francisco destiny. The fog was on the horizon as I crossed the San Francisco-Oakland Bay Bridge. Most people stop to pay tolls, but I was able to take advantage of the toll-dodging technique I developed in Florida. I would floor it and blast right through the toll booth, cross and then disappear into any side road I could find.

It didn't matter which side road I took – the city was like a wonderland to me. The smell of saltwater was refreshing, and the skyline and cool fog, hanging motionless like clouds of cotton candy, were invigorating. I saw the Golden Gate Bridge, the trolleys on Market Street, Chinatown and the ocean. I did note one hazard on the city's streets: the trolley tracks. In the fog, you could easily get a wheel caught in the track groove, slide around and lose your bike and/or your life. This would become a constant worry, since I usually drove drunk or drugged, and I did dump my motorcycle on several occasions.

I was excited to finally reach my destination. Now what? I knew where the model from Florida lived, and I drove around for hours until I found her neighborhood. I parked at Lone Mountain College and spent the night in view of her house. I now had misgivings about appearing on the model's doorstep, dirty, tired, hungry and broke. Those few weeks of wild and crazy sex on the beach seemed like the distant past. I realized that we really didn't know anything about each other. I drove around for two days before I built up the courage to knock on her door. Then I had to return and knock again and again every few hours until finally, the next morning, she opened it. Wearing a towel, she said, "What are you doing here? You interrupted my bath." Long stare. "You weren't really supposed to show up here." The blistering heat of our summer fling was ice-cold.

She casually got back in the tub as I sat, hot and horny, on the ceramic throne and tried to get her to share my magical thinking and give me shelter and sex. I wanted to jump on her and remind her of all the good times she had coming. Not a chance. She was working as a call girl now and had to get ready for her next client. She said I could stay for a week or two, but then I had to go.

During my brief stay, I stood in the window and timidly watched her get into a parade of luxury cars – Cadillacs, BMWs, Jaguars, you name it. I felt outclassed, helpless and rejected. She did take me along to several Halloween parties, and there, among those people, I felt at home. I thought, "I've finally arrived. These are my people. I belong here." Finally, though, my time at her place was up. She showed me a Jimi Hendrix album cover with the "Haight/Ashbury" street sign on it and said, "I don't care where you go, as long as it's not here." Suddenly, the scene changed from escort-funded luxury to the unwashed homeless on Haight Street.

Before long, I found a cult of people led by a big Filipino man named Peter. They lived in a strange commune where every single square foot of attic, closet and basement was occupied by squatters. Every day, people would panhandle to raise money. Communal meals were served, and everyone was required to pay up one way or another, whether through sex, drugs or construction talent. I chose to work a few hours each day doing carpentry, and then I could enjoy the rest of the day with a few bucks in my pocket and my "rent" covered. I met a young woman there and, while we were having sex, she introduced me to her older sister. Her sister really knew all the nooks and crannies of San Francisco, so she would choose adventure destinations for us to have casual sex in strange places. Once, we were getting busy on Mount Tamalpais when we heard giggles. We couldn't find the giggler until he sailed over our heads on a hang-glider. I had never seen or heard of anything like it.

I couldn't live off of panhandling forever, so when it was time for me to go job-hunting in earnest, I went to the street I knew best – the Haight. In the midst of the thousands of unemployed, I visited every little shop from one end of the street to the other, seeking my fortune. I ended up at the last of the businesses on the edge of Golden Gate Park. It was a hole in the wall called Hurley's Pizza*. The owner, Sean*, led me to a table with a job application. My gaze moved from Sean's face, which was covered with fresh burn scars, down to the tabletop, which had pot, stems, seeds and rolling papers casually strewn across it. I gulped and hurriedly explained that the pot was not mine. He laughed and said, "Don't worry. Just fill out the paper." I later found out he burned his face trying to light his pizza oven while high on cocaine. Sean told me to come back every few days and check for job openings. Soon enough, a slot opened, and I returned to my old familiar "pizza for life" program.

Sean was the author of two cookbooks and had celebrity status with San Francisco's In Crowd. I was a nobody and worked hard to fit in with the hip, slick and cool freaksters who frequented Hurley's. The party was on 24/7 at this place, and I practically lived there. I took over all the prep for the pizza and learned to make four 55-gallon drums of pizza sauce every couple of weeks. He used massive amounts of about 10 ingredients to make his sauce, and the pizza was the best I've ever tasted. We made our own dough and tossed the pies high in the air. It was a real circus show for those who could afford to pay. The workers' pay was low, but pizza could be traded for heroin, speed, weed, LSD, opium, and every imaginable type of pharmaceutical.

Our hard-working crew started the morning with mixed drinks to get us going. Sean would cook us a great meal, and then the drugs began in earnest, with music blasting from the speakers. Once a week, the Brownie Lady would come through and sell incredible brownies that lasted for a few days of total, wasted, lethargic marijuana magic.

Sean eventually trusted me enough to watch his two children. Sometimes I would sleep on his floor and watch the kids for days between work. They would steal my cocaine, and I would beg them to please give me my "headache powders." I was sick and I needed my "medicine." Truer words were never spoken. They also would do things like take the parking brakes off of cars and let them roll down the hill near their house. Sean's kids were a dynamic duo of troublemaking.

Sean knew all kinds of movers and shakers, such as an outlandish insurance salesman who called himself Auto Graph. A smallish, older man, he would get drunk and grope women outrageously, often until he got slapped. He exemplified all the beliefs I learned to advocate: misogyny, chauvinistic womanizing (or manizing, for that matter), the eternal quest to conquer the elusive and unreachable 1 percent of physical perfection. Sean and Auto would take me to clubs on Union Street where the cool, older crowd hung out. I would try to pick up rich older women, but I got far too drunk to have any real gigolo value. These were smoky, fragranced, alcohol dens where the restrooms became cocaine nasal depositories and quick pit stops.

On one memorable night, I was passed out under Sean's dining room table on Quaaludes and marijuana brownies when a boot nudged my ass. "Get up! Get up!" Sean yelled. "Get up, the sheriff's here!"

I sat up with glazed eyes and hit my head on the table, then raised my hands and said, "OK, OK, take me! I'm ready, let's go!" They played along and laughed for a minute and then let me in on the joke. It was the sheriff of

San Francisco, all right, but it wasn't a bust – he was Sean's guest for dinner.

The sheriff turned out to be a real nice guy. Sean was a great cook, so everyone wanted to eat his culinary creations, no matter who they were. We ate and drank; some of us smoked weed, and then Sean and I slipped away to another room to snort "Scarface"-style long lines of coke with Sean's friends. Then we drank some more. We had what seemed at the time like a series of fascinating conversations in which we resolved many hard-hitting issues of the day. In truth, I'm sure we blathered like idiots. When the long evening was over, talk turned to Sean's latest questionable acquisition from some of his equally questionable friends. He had access to a whole tractor-trailer full of stolen vintage wines. They could be had for $1 a bottle or $12 a case. Even I, on my meager salary, bought a few cases. The sheriff wanted a few cases, too, so I loaded them into his trunk.

When it was time for the lawman to leave, someone said, "We can't let you drive in this condition! You can't even walk straight! You might get in real trouble!"

He retorted with a laugh, "What are they gonna do, arrest me? I'm the goddamn sheriff of San Francisco!"

– 18 –

Unraveling

I spent my off hours on Hippy Hill in Golden Gate Park. I played my guitar and joined drum circles, smoking and drinking until I was wasted late at night. I would stumble back to wherever I was flopping at the time, or sleep in the park, or go to strangers' houses for casual sex. When it was time for work, I would get loaded and report for duty. I would throw pizza crust high in the air while on LSD, watching the trailers and listening to the "ch-ch-ch-ch-ch." If a spinning disc of crust glanced off the greasy, filthy oven hood, no problem – a little sauce would cover the skid mark, and into the oven it would go, none the worse for wear.

At one point, Hurley's staff included four people from New York City, and one of them was a fast-talking Golden Glove boxer named Johnnie. This guy had fighting in his DNA. He was talented and driven, but he didn't know where to drive himself. Johnnie was a nice person, but the burdens of life had destroyed his ability to set or reach goals of any kind. He had the kind of abusive, dysfunctional personality I could relate to, and we started hanging out. Our friendship deteriorated rapidly into shooting Ritalin, which was so harsh it pushed you to the edge of cardiac arrest. Johnnie got fired and became volatile and threatening. He would drive stolen vehicles onto sidewalks to menace anyone who messed with him. Sometimes I would ride with him. I had a buck knife, and I was still clever with a blade since my days at Shorgood Poultry. I also was loaded out of my mind. What little judgment I had was terrible.

I sat in Hurley's one night, drinking Velvet Hammers with Kahlua and cream and playing with my buck knife, flicking the blade opened and closed – in and out, opened and closed -- like a real street thug. I really thought I was something. I was trying to impress a new hire, an innocent and friendly 17-year-old girl, and show her what a hotshot I was with a blade. I dropped the knife and as I reached down to pick it up, I noticed the horrified look on her face. She pointed to my leg, and I saw a tear in the fabric of my pants. Then, I looked more closely and spotted a 1½-inch stab wound in my leg.

Off I went for my first visit to San Francisco General Hospital. Accustomed to treating gunshot and stab wounds all day long, they casually packed my excruciating injury with gauze but withheld all pain medication because I was so drunk. That's how they sent me home. I had just moved into the front room of a Victorian on Delmar Street in the Haight, and that's where I woke up in blinding pain. Now how was I going to pay the rent?

My dad came out to visit and make sure I was all right. I took him on my usual routes, which were all in the most crime-ridden, impoverished parts of the city. He was amazed that we would emerge alive from these neighborhoods, especially when we were the only white people and I would be staggeringly drunk and yelling things at the top of my lungs like, "Niggerrrrr! See? No one will fuck with me!" All during his visit, I drank nonstop and destroyed this opportunity to bond or communicate. He would sit and watch as I would chug down anything I could get my hands on and babble into oblivion.

On one day of his visit, someone got the dubious idea to ride motorcycles up Mount Tamalpais. I was still healing my leg wound and had no business riding a motorcycle. And of course, I was drunk. Beyond that, I decided it was a good time to ride like a daredevil without the benefit of any experience to qualify as one. We borrowed a motorcycle for Dad and raced up the mountain road, dodging oncoming traffic. I almost wiped out several times, and Dad kept trying to offer life-saving tips that I would ignore until the next time I almost wiped out and killed myself.

Once we reached the top, we decided to kill the engines and coast back down the mountain. We rode with only the sounds of the bikes' chains and the wind blowing through our hair. After 70 or 80 hairpin turns at high speeds, I was getting sloppy and just barely maintaining control of my motorcycle. When I ended up on the wrong side of the road for the last time, facing oncoming traffic and endangering innocent people, we agreed to take it slow and easy the rest of the way down. I appreciated that we collectively agreed that life was more precious than ego or thrills. He gave me $200 and went back home. I still owe him that money.

Delmar Street was a Wild West drug atmosphere, and it was always High Noon at my house. It was plenty crazy all by itself, but the insanity was helped along by three of my housemates, Billy*, Hank* and John*. Billy and Hank were wild and crazy nurses and made sure I had all the heroin, opium, weed and prescription drugs I could handle, and then some. John worked at Hurley's and grew pot up north. He introduced me to sinsemilla, a type of marijuana I called "heroweed" because just one toke could blow you away for hours. This was long before this type of high-octane weed was readily available. Meanwhile, Hank introduced me to opium – the hard way. He told me to drop my pants if I wanted to take opium as it was meant to be taken. After much negotiation, I dropped my pants and bent over, and he thrust his opium-coated thumb into my rectum. I screamed and cried from the pain. It took me a while to recover. If there was any benefit to being drunk and high all the time, at least I was partially numb during episodes like this. Problem is, this kind of numbness wears off sooner or later.

A new age of punk music was dawning in San Francisco and around the world, and it was my kind of music. I'd been writing songs and playing with as many people as I could. The scene was just getting started, and I was in it for once. No more same-old rock and roll; this music was fresh and raw, and I started writing in earnest. One of my frequent partners was an older man named Peter, who made antique lampshades up the street. This small man was a master of slide guitar and had played with many famous blues musicians at the Fillmore through the years. Peter took me under his wing. On many nights, we would shoot speed, share a bottle of Old Crow, and play blues all night long until my fingers were blistered. I got good at the blues. I would sit for hours on LSD, and we would play and sing like Ol' Yeller howling at the moon.

Around this time, a woman named Tara* moved into the Delmar house. I immediately became obsessed with her. Although (or maybe because) I was unstable, violent, jealous, desperate, needy, and always looking for the next victim to love, she took me on, and we began a relationship. She didn't do drugs, and she was smart. She wanted to be a physical therapist, so she enrolled at John Adams Community College. I followed her there and enrolled in classes to become a nurse's aide. At this point, I realized the importance of health and nutrition. I wasn't about to stop drinking and doing drugs, so I made it a point to start taking better nutritional care of myself.

As part of my training, I began working at San Francisco

hospitals as a nurse's aide. On one of my first days on the job, I was assigned to care for a patient who needed to have Hydrocortisone cream applied to his whole body from a gallon jug. Due to some strange ailment, his body was covered with blistering sores. I was applying the cream to his skin with ungloved hands when the head nurse walked in and freaked out. She dragged me out of the room to disinfect my hands and taught me about the disease whose name I didn't recognize – herpes. There were many incidents like this. Looking back, I shiver to contemplate the various forms of pestilence to which I was exposed.

I continued my training at Veterans Hospital in San Francisco, and while caring for patients I would try to figure out why these people ended up with the diseases they had. One cancer patient told me that after World War II, he had steered an aircraft carrier into port at Hiroshima. Everyone else was drunk, and he knocked out about 600 feet of pier trying to slow down the carrier. We agreed that radiation exposure might have contributed to the deteriorating skin condition he developed later in life. To treat the pain of his terminal cancer, he took Brompton cocktails every four hours. These were a potent mix of morphine, cocaine, alcohol and sometimes Thorazine.

One day, sick of being debilitated by his disease and its treatment, he growled at me, "If you're gonna be a goddamn nurse, you should know what you're givin' people. You should try takin' this shit." I looked around and then downed his cup of woe like a shot of whiskey. The stuff was so powerful, I staggered half-awake through my activities for the rest of the day. His influence raised my compassion and empathy for all the patients I met in the future. My understanding was that doctors got three months of pharmaceutical training, and then they would commence to prescribing drugs that had an average of seven to 10 side effects each. They'd prescribe five drugs to a trusting patient and seem oblivious to the 35 potential side effects the patient was left with. Meanwhile, the pharmaceutical industry was raking in the profits.

My medical experience, along with my rage at the manipulative and greedy pharmaceutical industry, inspired me to start a New Wave punk band called the DOKTORS. We would rally against the machine of the American Medical Association, I decided; we would change the world by imparting real information about the way the medical industry was really run. After all the street bands and house parties and jamming I'd done since arriving in San Francisco, the DOKTORS was the first of my bands that got attention on the music scene. We started getting gigs, and I often would go to shows late after work wearing my nursing uniform with white shoes. The punks in black leather jackets and spiked hairdos would look at me funny.

It was 1978 then. I was 22 years old. My life started to truly go insane and unravel at a faster rate. A friend of mine, Ezra*, worked in house painting and property management, and I started working for him on the side. Before long, he made me foreman of his property management jobs so he had more time to shoot heroin. When I completed my training as a nurse's aide, I also started working for a nursing temp agency. So when I wasn't working and playing music, I was partying, getting high and getting laid. I still lived on Delmar Street, but I usually was home only long enough to shoot speed, drink and set up multiple opportunities for sex.

On those rare occasions when I could have gone home, I was too high to hold still in an enclosed space. So I began to wander the streets all night, talking to myself, yelling, babbling incoherently. Thus began my curious double-shifts of working all day and speeding all night, working all day and speeding all night – and then finally, sleeping every few days. I slowly extended these periods until I was a full-fledged junkie, awake and tweaking for more and more days until the periods between sleeping lasted up to a few months. In San Francisco, people threw everything away in large debris boxes on the street, and these boxes became my nighttime home. I started needing a home less, and needing more the freedom to do my business in the night air until 5 or 6 in the morning. Then I would rest for a few hours before shooting up and doing my day job.

I cultivated marijuana plants in every place I lived or wherever I could access the back yard. Eventually, I had eight houses where I grew marijuana, and it became one of my favorite pastimes. I remember sending my mom and dad photos of myself posing naked with my pot plants, along with lyrics of the scores of songs I was writing during that time. I looked like a counter-revolutionary, hippy-punk bastard in my little jungles of weed.

I had a Quaalude connection for a while, but that drug was too dangerous even for me. I'd get loaded and then wander groggily into dangerous neighborhoods, only to snap out of my stupor and find myself in hazardous situations. Once I woke up next to someone who was having his head beaten to a pulp; other times, I'd come to with a gun pointing at my face. Then came the time I woke up to discover that a man was penetrating me anally from behind. I tried to keep my cool as I stammered, "Hey, hey, hey, what's – what – who are you? HEY, WHAT IN THE HELL ARE YOU DOING, ASSHOLE? AND – WHO ARE YOU??"

My most compelling – and final – experience involving Quaaludes happened the night I combined the 'Ludes with speed. In my altered state, I apparently was overcome by my great love for green and flowering plants. All night long, I gathered every plant in a 20-block radius and brought them all back to our house. As the sun rose, I realized with horror and shame what I had done. Our front stairs were full of plants in pots of all sizes, some of them cracked from being dragged. Dirt trails led from our front porch and down the street for blocks in all directions. In the weeks after that, I would walk in any direction and pass houses with dirt rings on their stairs where their potted plants used to be, and I knew what happened to them. I decided that I couldn't afford the risk of Quaaludes anymore. The price was too high for others, as well as myself.

I consoled myself with the pharmaceutical speed that my nursing friends brought home. We would break it down into spoons and get wasted with the government's best. Everyone was hooked on something. Me, I was a trashcan of immediate gratification and convenience. My nursing friends and I would drink and get stoned out of our minds and then go to see movies or get naked and sunbathe together. Once, we took the party to Angel Island, where my housemate, Hank, and I drank a whole bottle of Cuervo Gold on top of a rocky embankment. We passed out, and when we awoke hours later, Hank was gone. Just when we decided he'd left, someone noticed a stick-figure body with a red head at the bottom of the embankment. We headed down the embankment screaming his name. His eye socket was full of blood and he looked dead. Blood had partially dried on his face from lying outside so long. We were vastly relieved when our shaking and screaming roused him from his blood-covered stupor. He was alive but no picnic to be around, as the only thing he could say was, "Yer mother." Evening was coming, and the last ferry had already departed, so the Coast Guard had to rescue us and take us back to Fisherman's Wharf. Hank kept muttering, "Yer mother," to everyone we met, until he escalated to yelling, "Fuck you and yer mother!" on the Coast Guard ship. To their credit, the Coast Guard people kept trying to treat Hank's wounds despite his verbal assaults.

The last months of 1978 were tragic and tumultuous for all of San Francisco. The mass murder-suicide of more than 900 members of Jim Jones' Peoples Temple occurred on Nov. 18, 1978. Many of those who moved to Guyana with

Jones the year before were from the San Francisco Bay
Area, so hundreds of local families were thrust into shock
and grief by this event. The city was still reeling from the
Jonestown tragedy when, only nine days later, something
equally unthinkable occurred: Recently resigned City
Supervisor Dan White assassinated San Francisco Mayor
George Moscone and Supervisor Harvey Milk at City
Hall. The whole city seemed wounded and sensitive as the
holiday season approached.

Around that time, I was working a house-painting job at
Green and Leavenworth, the area that had the only working
fire hydrant during the Great Earthquake of 1906. This
historic Victorian house, which extended down the side
of a hill, was owned by a developer and architect named
Akihiro Adachi*. Adachi had three kids, ranging in age
from about 13 to 6. His 6-year-old son was notorious for
getting six work crews fired from this painting job before
I came onto the scene. He would say, "I'm telling my dad
you're not working, and you're gonna get fired!" This kid
and I became fast friends. Then I met the rest of his family
– all Americans from one of the Southern states. This was
quite a mix of Chinese culture and the Deep South. Adachi
and I made a bet that if I survived to the end of the painting
job, he would buy me a bottle of Chivas Regal. I'd seen the
commercials all over, and I wanted to enjoy the good life
that I could not afford.

I went at the painting job in my usual manner, drinking
heavily while five stories up. One time, my friend Jim and
I were standing on the same scaffold plank, painting in
the fog, when we each slipped. Somehow, we both caught
ourselves on the way down. The other notable thing about
this job was that I learned my first real trade. This house
had about 80 windows that needed new ropes, so an old
man taught me the Victorian window trade. I learned with
workaholic fervor.

Mr. Adachi's kids had never been to a real rock concert,

and I was voted most likely to succeed in taking them to one. I had been to a few, but they were boisterous, drugged-out, drunken affairs from which I had to struggle my way home. This time, I took the kids to see Earth Quake and Sammy Hagar. These young ruffian kids carried small bottles of airline liquor and somehow smuggled in pot, too. Despite their best efforts to get me lost and have a wild time, the concert was a success.

I was caught off-guard when the Adachis invited Tara and me to share their Christmas dinner and gift exchange. It was a powerful thing to be included in a personal family event of such significance and grandeur. When I was given a large gold chain as a gift, I felt I was being recognized as a person of worth. This Christmas experience lit a small flame somewhere inside my addict's soul that maybe, just maybe, it was possible for me to make lasting, positive progress for the first time in my life. After the new year began, things continued much the same as they had before. My alcoholism and drug abuse raged on unchecked, but that little flicker of hope remained.

Months later, I traveled to Detroit to visit my father and meet his new wife, Alice. The occasion was a family reunion, which for my volatile clan always carried an element of risk. Sitting and drinking in Dad's living room, I was jarred by news coverage of the White Night Riots that erupted in San Francisco after Dan White was convicted of manslaughter, not murder, in the deaths of Moscone and Milk, and sentenced to only seven years in prison. As we watched the news footage of protesters rioting and burning police cars, I got foul-mouthed and began drunkenly declaring that I should be back with "my people," taking part in these righteous riots. Dad would have none of it. He felt no pity for those "faggots" who were mourning the openly gay Harvey Milk, or for the crazy people who got themselves killed in Guyana because they bought into the rantings of a religious zealot. As an atheist, nothing made less sense to him.

This face-off in Dad's living room, in front of his new wife, erupted into the last severe beating my father would ever give me. It was the same old dynamic all over again: He hit me, and I yelled things like, "Fuck you, asshole!" until he hit me again, and on it went. The beating spilled into the street in front of their house until finally, I walked away and wandered, lost, through the streets of Dad's neighborhood. I grabbed my gold chain, which represented my fragile sense of being and self-worth, wrenched it from my neck and threw it into the freeway. The next day, every inch of my head was swollen, red and bruised, and my body was sore. I felt empathy with every vulnerable person who had ever been beaten like this. I felt so ashamed that I had let my guard down and my father had violated me again. My self-esteem shattered, I didn't care about anything anymore. I slipped into becoming a dedicated, hopeless, full-time, motherfucking junkie.

Before I left Detroit, I hooked up with my brother Mark, and we bought some cocaine. We took it back to Mark's house, where our mother was visiting. After hours of persuasion, including telling Mom that Sigmund Freud had done coke, we all snorted lines together and got high as a drug-induced family. I repressed this memory for years. It was the last shot our original nuclear family had for any kind of decent gathering, and it was not a pretty sight. But it was the best we could do. The only way our mother could spend time with us was by letting us hold her hostage with drugs. And I was the ringleader, disguised as a victim.

– 19 –

Suicide Club

Back in San Francisco, I moved into a new place at 607
Masonic St. with my construction partner, Ezra. He still
was smooth-talking his way into gig after gig, then buying
all new tools and turning the job over to me. His crews
were always rag-tag groups of guys who were fresh out of
prison and ready to do anything to make up for lost time.
The house on Masonic had a quirky history. First, it was
available to us because its owner, a man in his 60s, had
been busted for selling the largest amount of LSD on record
to a bunch of undercover cops. He left behind a young,
pregnant, Latina wife who went into labor just when I
was giving her a lower-back massage to relieve pressure.
I got dragged along to the hospital to be the guy she dug
her fingernails into every time she had a contraction. Just
another day in the life. A member of the Mafia died at 607
Masonic under mysterious circumstances and left behind
treasures galore. My friends wasted no time walking off
with art, guns, and anything else they could carry. My

selection was the 100-pound fossilized bone from the leg of a Triceratops, which I proudly displayed near my bed. All was well until the Mafiosi dispatched the dead man's brother and two unbelievably ugly armed men to gather up the belongings of their fallen comrade. They held everyone in the house hostage at gunpoint and released people a few at a time to go retrieve the objects they'd stolen. Drug dealers, junkies and hangers-on were summoned to bring back their bootie under the threat of death. Finally, enough stuff was returned, and the thugs let us all go. I had waited out the siege and hung onto my treasure, though – no way were those guys going to get their hands on my trophy. Much later, I traded my dinosaur bone for a second-century Roman short sword, but that's another story.

I met an ambitious man named Francisco who wanted to build an empire of music studios throughout San Francisco, and I decided to help him reach his goal. We started with the Venetian Bakery Studios in North Beach. The long-running musical revue, "Beach Blanket Babylon," played upstairs every night, and "Star Wars" was rolling at the North Point Theatre next door. It was a hopping neighborhood, with people always lined up around the block. I eventually helped to build about 100 studios all over the city. This, I thought, was my claim to fame. I knew all the bands in town, and I felt like I was hot shit. I auditioned for band after band and tried to get gigs at the biggest San Francisco venues for punk and New Wave, Mabuhay Gardens and On Broadway. The city's punk-music scene revolved around the man who operated both venues: Dirk Dirksen.

Dirk infuriated and alienated many people with the cynical/comical way he communicated and did business. I didn't care about that. I knocked myself out trying to get an audience with our powerful Godfather of Punk, but he was always surrounded by 20 bands and their entourages, all vying for his attention. Finally, tired of waiting, I strode into the packed room and said loudly, "If you want me to give you that blow job, you better get these faggots out of here!" Dirk looked up, surprised, then sized me up and said, "Everybody out!"

Just like that, it was Dirk and me in an empty room. Shaking, I stammered that I only wanted to get his attention so my band could play at Mabuhay Gardens. He laughed and commended me for my originality. This was the beginning of my friendship with a wonderful man who became a loving father figure to me. Dirk wanted to see me succeed, so he put me on stage with whatever band I was playing with at the moment – Lurid Tales, the Tongues, the Organ Grinders, Ruen, Nothing Sacred, the DOKTORS, the Tibetan Boy Scouts, and Greed Incorporated, to name a few. Dirk was a master promoter and sometimes managed to get air time on the local network stations. He used this opportunity twice to showcase the bands in which I played. I showed up late both times, and he kicked my ass all the way up to the stage. My pre-show regimen included drinking a six-pack and sometimes getting head before I took the stage, and Dirk knew it. He was one of many people over the years who saw my potential and tried in vain to keep me from self-destructing. More than once, Dirk would introduce me to some new rising star on the avant-garde scene, and instead of offering my hand to shake, I would expose myself.

To make up for these transgressions, I would do handyman work at Dirk's venues, like replacing the toilets that were shattered by customers almost every night. I felt I was supporting the arts in a real and valuable way.

My search for stardom and fame led me on an illusory trail of auditions for more than 30 bands in the Bay Area. Along the way, I fostered and enjoyed many incredible musical experiences, and I met family friends who would weather all of my lives and behaviors. In Ruen, I played with Greg on drums, Chuck on bass, Dwight on keyboards, and Ruen on guitar. Dwight and Ruen were brothers. These guys were really nice and supported themselves with legit day jobs. Dwight, Ruen and I wrote the songs, and I played some guitar and sang lead. With the multiple lives I was living, they got to see only the best I could manage to serve up. But this was still great rock and roll.

I was running around the punk scene with my fingers in as many musical pies as I could find. The lyrics I sang were autobiographical, such as one song I loved that was popular at the time: Split personality/Why won't you let me be? I was living marginally, sleeping with different people and shooting speed, snorting cocaine, and drinking till I passed out. After all, All my heroes up and died taking drugs and suicide/Left us here all alone, left us here to carry on.

One of the songs I wrote, "Suicide Club," was a sign-of-the-times kind of song.

Suicide Club
She was a black-haired loser
from Atlantic City, New Jersey,
Mom and Dad was New York City at night.
Manhattan was romantic till you got mugged in transit
42nd Street was better than dying.
Got the West Coast blues, off you flew,
Dyed your puberty and black roots blonde,
Snorting cocaine, shooting the shit with anything
On your knees and crying.
I just want to make you think
About what you're going to do
I just want to penetrate,
That's all I want to doo.
In the suicide club you jumped and got caught,
A net under the bridge.
They put you in leather jackets,
Thought they were so attractive,
Four times a day they gave you your pills.
Getting along in years, everyone looks younger,

Your last wish was hell bent,
And when you died, you had
A shit-eatin' grin on your face.
I just want to make you think
About what you're going to do
I just want to penetrate,
That's all I want to doo.

I met Dwight's girlfriend, Linda, around this time. She treated me like a normal person no matter what I did to act out. Dwight and Linda have been close friends of mine for the past 30 years. I was not able to access this friendship for more than half that time because I was way gone … I was touched a bit too much. Linda and I first really connected when we talked about spiritual matters, and she mentioned St. Germain. I suddenly remembered that while digging in a debris box, one of the hundred thousand stamps I'd collected was a handmade stamp of St. Germain. I went looking and somehow found it, out of boxes and boxes of crap. I brought it to her. We were both just amazed at how God's coincidences show that he is working in your life. It was a great bonding opportunity for both of us.

Then I experienced a rare, rare occurrence in my life: I met three people who wanted to play my music. I met Symon first. The first time I saw Symon, he was playing music across the street from 1019 Haight St., where I had a horrible room. I yelled up at the window like a crazy man, "Hey, you! Hey! Hey! You wanna play music?"

Symon looked out and probably was startled, because what weirdo would come yell up at your window on Haight Street? We didn't get together then, but about a month later, a mutual friend introduced us formally. It turned out Symon's girlfriend lived in a building I was managing. I was playing in a group called Nothing Sacred at the time (I called it Nothing Scarred Yet). This was a death-rock glam band, with eyeliner, mascara, and tight-fitting clothes. We played Bauhaus-type music.

Eventually, Symon and I started jamming at the studios, and we formed the Tibetan Boy Scouts soon after that. I was playing in a couple of other bands at the time – the Organ Grinders and the first incarnation of Greed Incorporated, a bike-messenger band. (All the other members were bike messengers except me.) The Tibetan Boy Scouts played cool, fun music. In that group, my music really started to become hearable and likeable. We called ourselves "pop music of the '80s," but it was really punk rock.

Sometimes I stayed in a back-porch room at Market and Dubose. It was actually an outdoor porch. It was freezing cold, but I never slept anyway. I was a drug dealer by this time. I was always at a dealer's house, on the streets, playing music, or fucking someone. A guy named Larry lived downstairs with a bunch of youngsters. I had heard that he played drums, and my idea was to train him to play my weird music. Larry was an innocent kid with good morals. We started playing music together, and I went through the painful learning curve of being patient while someone learns. He was patient and kind and willing to learn my crazy music.

Then, I met Kimba while I was running crews of men at construction jobs. I would teach men how to do plumbing, electrical, sheetrock, demolition, whatever was needed. Kimba wanted to work. Kimba was also a bass player and a real nice guy who introduced me to all of his nice friends. We started hanging out as best buds, although he was 10 or more years younger than me. He was kind, soft, trustworthy and gentle, and he really made me feel good about myself. About this time, the movie "Bad Boys" came out. People told me a lot that I looked like Sean Penn. Except I wasn't in the movies – I was for real. I thought I was a badass myself, but Kimba saw the soft side of me. I was very alone, high on drugs, and trusted no one. But I trusted him. And so our friendship began, and has lasted till now. Together, Symon, Larry, Kimba and I formed the longest-lasting, permanent lineup of Greed Incorporated.

Meanwhile, through my work with Ezra, I also was beginning to dabble in property management, which gave me the chance to support the refugees floating over from Vietnam en masse to escape the killing there. We moved about 25 complete families of refugees into apartments in downtown San Francisco, where they would sleep up to eight per room. During the day, their mattresses would be lined up against the wall. These were resourceful, educated, middle-class people who quickly acclimated to this new country of opportunity. They went crabbing and fishing to survive until they found paying jobs. For all the damage we did to their country, I felt proud to offer them this little bit of help upon their arrival. I also felt shame watching them use their perseverance, family unity and education to quickly pass me by on their way to the top of the economic food chain, after being here such a short time.

The rest of my personal experience of property management in San Francisco involved much less noble and enterprising situations. The buildings I managed were often crack houses being rehabbed for re-sale, so I would move in and squat with the squatters while I repaired the dilapidated structures. Then, I'd strong-arm all of us out the house and move on to the next seedy place. Even I had to leave. A typical experience happened in a multi-unit building one night, when I heard the man across the hall being choked to death by an assailant yelling expletives. I ran to find the gun I kept for property-management protection, but my friends had taken it from me to keep me from killing someone in a drunken rage. So I ran into the hallway, got into shooting position without the gun, and pounded on the door, screaming with all the badass I could muster, "I got a gun and I'm gonna shot your motherfucking ass, bitch! You better run!" I heard the window open and footsteps scrambling down the fire escape. I called an ambulance and used my master key to open the door, where I was greeted by a beaten and grateful man who was still breathing.

The .22-caliber Beretta I didn't have for protection that night was most often used for my drunken expressions of rage; thus, my friends' decision to take it from me, since I was a danger to myself and a menace to society. I would have them drive me on the freeway while I unloaded clip after clip into the giant Coca-Cola sign that had about 10,000 light bulbs on it. Sometimes, I climbed the fire escape to the studios I'd help build on Market Street, across from a huge auto dealership. Between songs, I would shoot out windows of nearby office buildings. Eventually, the dealership put up 20-foot-wide window covers around the whole block. Twenty years later, when I was sober, I went to the dealership to apologize and make amends for my dangerous and destructive madness. They looked at me like I was still crazy for even talking to them.

While I worked various construction jobs, I would always do death-wish demolition – tearing things apart and seeing the inner workings of buildings and machines. Through the act of destroying, I found strange objects that made everything work. Under stairways, in attics of buildings I worked on, in music studios I built, I always made or found storage areas. I would haphazardly store things all over San Francisco this way. I saved objects that caught my eye or that I thought were precious.

Around this time, fluorescent colors became popular and readily available in aerosol cans. I love the brilliance of fluorescents. I get the same kick out of fluorescent shades that others get out of normal colors. I need more color! I need more excitement! I got my hands on several spray cans of paint in these shades, and I felt compelled to use them. So I gathered some of my found objects and sprayed the colors onto the objects. Then, I needed a place to press the objects. I pressed them onto paper, T-shirts, bed sheets, car hoods, sides of buildings – anything I could reach became a handy canvas.

Suddenly, I started feeling mental relief from the repetitive quality of this art. I had found a way to release my inner anguish. It gave me a sense of freedom. I felt like I was doing something with my wasted life. I couldn't do much, but I could do this. I got into rhythms and almost attained a mantra state. It was like chanting with objects and colors. And it momentarily relieved my very serious and untreated mental-health problems. I named my art practice "Radical Relief."

The first times I remember making Radical Relief paintings were at Turk Street Studios in San Francisco. We had an old cash register from the turn of the century and tore it apart. I would get parking meters from outside and destroy them with sledgehammers to get the parts and the loose change. I would tear apart early-model computers, VCRs, televisions, any electrical equipment, irons, hot-tub filters – anything that had a unique shape. Turk Street Studios' long basement hallway seemed the perfect place to do my work. I would lay out my paper all the way down the hallway outside the studio doors. I threw the objects over the paper, and I'd spray them with one color. Then, I would throw the objects in different positions, and spray another color. If the object had too much paint on it, I would reverse it and print it onto the paper or a T-shirt so I didn't waste paint. There was no ventilation in the basement, but that didn't concern me at the time. All of the bands had to breathe my furious malaise.

I scavenged constantly for paper and objects to do my art. Kinko's and printing places discarded all kinds of paper I could use. The San Francisco Chronicle threw away huge sheets of paper. I scoured through debris boxes all over downtown. I never missed what San Francisco calls "Put Out Night": Throughout the year, different residential areas are invited to put large items on the curb to be picked up with their trash. I plundered through street after street of curbside discards. Soon, I was producing prolific piles of work.

The part I never figured out was what to do with finished pieces of art. Friends would sometimes take them home. I couldn't keep them, because I constantly moved, so they would get destroyed. I'd be kicked out of places where I was squatting or working, have to throw away all of my models and paper and paints, and then start all over again. Being homeless, that's the way it was. But that's also what made Radical Relief the perfect form of artistic expression for me. It was a portable activity I could do anywhere. Everywhere I went, there was always garbage.

I still was working as a nurse's aide for 15 major hospitals through a temp agency, which exposed me to a lot of sad and ugly situations and fueled my addictions. This kind of work had a high burnout rate, so if you showed any initiative at all, you were given responsibility. I was a real go-getter at this job; I wanted to know how to do it all, do drugs and live forever, and stay healthy and young. I also felt I was put on the Earth to heal the people who were seemingly discarded into these facilities like human trash and left to suffer.

I worked as an orthopedic technician at one hospital; in pediatrics at another, and in the psychiatric ward of a third. Sometimes I was assigned to a skilled nursing facility called Hillhaven, where I cared for a lot of wonderful older people who'd been forgotten by society. The most common issue I resolved for these patients was extreme constipation caused by dehydrating medications and water restriction. I devised a way to manually remove these intestinal blockages, to the great relief and gratitude of many an uncomfortable patient. I don't know how legal that was, and I'm sure it isn't lovely to read about, but it was a frequent occurrence and it was real. I was passionate about working with these older people, who shared a lot of their wisdom, knowledge and experience with me. I accepted as much of this positive energy as I could, overwhelmed with the daily traumas and infinite sadness of working in San Francisco's hospital wards.

In my early days as a nurse's aide, I had an experience at one hospital that shook me to the core. Another aide and I were taking a deceased man down to the morgue when I felt the man's ankle and detected a weak pedal pulse. We stopped the gurney at the nurse's station to report this, and one of the nurses said this patient had a history of seizures that put him into shock and mimicked death. Then, the head nurse said calmly that the man's medical insurance had run out. He was "expired," she said, and if I ever wanted to work in this town again, I better get busy taking this body down to the morgue, STAT. I was brand-new and nervous, so down we went to roll this man onto the stainless-steel morgue tray and slide him into the refrigerated compartment. Needless to say, I felt a lot of conflict about working as a nurse's aide for a long time after this, and I medicated myself heavily with drinking and drugs. I also wrote this song.

Boney Bones
I don't remember seeing your boney bones
I do not recall your boney bones
But everywhere I go
Your boney bones, ah!
Your boney bones, ah ah!
Your boney bones, ah!
Your boney bones, ah ah ah ah!
All the people know your boney bones
Everywhere I go, your boney bones
They're dancing in the street
Your boney bones, ah!
Your boney bones, ah ah!

Your boney bones, ah!
Your boney bones, ah ah ah ah!
Lucky stiffs! Jive cadavers! Cold cuts! Meat on a
platter!
All on a skeleton cruise
Your boney bones, ah!
Your boney bones, ah ah!
Your boney bones, ah!
Your boney bones, ah ah ah ah!

My youngest patient was a 6-year-old African-American boy who'd been passed around the foster-care system by people who accepted foster children just to get the state's payments. He had been locked in a closet where he started eating the lead paint chips off the walls; he now had the highest levels of lead in his body that had ever been recorded. He was a classic abused child, lashing out at the other kids on the ward, hurting them, pulling IVs out of children's heads and ankles, and threatening them. As an abuse survivor myself, I knew he would respond only to the kind of punishment he was used to, so I threatened him and acted like a badass until I gained his trust and respect. Then, during the five weeks I spent as his nurse, I gave him every opportunity to participate in a positive way. Sometimes I would dress him up in an isolation gown, gloves, mask and stethoscope and bring him on rounds with me to care for the other children. He would offer the children ice cream instead of threatening them or stealing their candy. By the time he left the hospital, he was the best-behaved darling of the ward. Upon release, he went back into the foster-care system. I tracked him down at his new address and saw that he was back to living in a trashed-out house in a drug-infested neighborhood that I knew well. I was despondent and wept that this was the best we could offer such a bright and intelligent young person who was caught in our diseased system.

I would leave the hospital after shifts like this and look for the quickest possible escapes from reality. Once, I went from work to a yacht party where I got so drunk, I was arrested on my way home and wound up in jail with my first DUI. Then, fresh from jail, I'd go back to another day of caring for Hell's Angels who'd wrecked their bikes and wound up in traction, getting my attention by yelling, "Hey, faggot," or "Hey, you fucking queer." I'd wait until their badass brothers left, and then I'd let them know who was a great candidate for them to treat with respect. I'd adjust the traction for their broken limbs with just a little added pressure, or I'd make sure I was extra late returning to their rooms to remove their stainless-steel bed pans. "Faggot that, motherfucker – talk to me now, big man."

That said, there were many opportunities for me to do nursing my own way. With the staff's blessing, I sometimes smoked medicinal marijuana with patients. That stuff was powerful. One New Year's Eve, at a dying patient's request, I put on a yellow isolation gown and mask and played the guitar all night along with the Grateful Dead, who were on TV. I once cared for a wealthy Japanese patient who did not like me to wear white, because it was a Japanese belief that the angels of death wore white. I wore casual clothes when caring for him. He would not sleep unless I slept with him at night, so I was paid to spend nights with him. We tied a string between my finger and his wrist, so he could tug it to wake me for bathroom breaks.

Occasionally, someone would die on my shift. Sometimes the family would gather and become overwhelmed with the emotion of the moment, unable to stay present with their dying loved one. Once, an elderly female patient asked me to send her bickering family out in the hall so she could die in peace. I stayed and took gentle breaths with her, holding her hand and maintaining eye contact until her eyes closed and her breaths grew shallower and farther apart. As the hand I held grew colder,

I could feel her soul leaving the flesh and dispersing into the universe. Finally, she took her last breath and her heart stopped beating. After sitting with her for one more quiet moment, I began prepping her body for the family to see before it was taken to the morgue. I removed the oxygen clip and the IV, but when it came time to gently tug the catheter from between her legs, the catheter was stuck fast. I braced one foot on the bed rail and gave a mighty tug, and the catheter came loose and smacked me in the cheek, spraying urine across my face. I could have sworn I heard quiet laughter in the room as I realized I was so overcome with emotion, I'd forgotten to release the bubble of air that holds the catheter in the bladder. Sharing the moment of this woman's death with her had been one of the most beautiful experiences of my life, and I was grateful for the little wakeup "slap" at the end.

Presbyterian Hospital was my favorite medical facility in San Francisco, being the most modern and well-run. My work in orthopedics gave me the unexpected opportunity to share my knowledge with the African-American patients who came through with broken bones. I saw so many African-American patients who never were given complete information about the possibilities of healing. They wound up limping and using canes for the rest of their lives, not knowing that they could take advantage of physical therapy to regain their full range of motion. Care for black patients was notoriously unfair, and I tried to be a freedom fighter for change in the way our system treated people of color. I personally made sure that all people of color I worked with knew not to believe the lie that they were doomed to walk with a cane for the rest of their lives.

Considering the way I lived my life, it seemed inevitable that I would wind up on the other side of the cast plaster one day. That day arrived when I was working with Ezra to install a sprinkler system in the Berkeley hills. As I drove across the Bay Bridge toward home, a truck swerved in

front of me. As the passenger side of my car glanced off
the side of the truck, Ezra – a Black Belt in martial arts
– instinctively jerked his body toward me. My right arm,
taut with my vice-like grip on the steering wheel, snapped
in five places as Ezra blasted through it like a cannonball.
I swerved to a stop in rush-hour traffic and tumbled out
of the car, holding the limp pieces of my splintered arm
and screaming in pain. Looking down from the bridge
to the white-capped waves of the water 250 feet below, I
considered jumping, then burst into crazed laughter and
decided the water was too cold.

I waited for six hours at Highland Hospital in Oakland
until finally a doctor examined me. He smelled like a
brewery, and the nurses said he'd just come from a party.
He put an inflatable doughnut on my arm to slow the
swelling and then disappeared for another hour; a helpful
nurse told me he'd passed out. By the time he returned,
I was in pure agony. He set the five breaks in my arm at
what seemed like unnatural angles, but by then I was worn
out from pain and screaming and just wanted to get out of
there. When I awoke the next morning, the pain in my arm
was unbearable. I went to San Francisco General, where
they weren't surprised to hear that a slobbering drunk was
responsible for this travesty of a job. They re-broke my
wrist in three places and re-set it properly. I was shaking
with rage. This was the arm I shot dope in! How was I
supposed to get high?? Back at home, I used my Sawzall
to cut the cast back far enough that I could inject myself
with speed. Not able to sit still with that much speed in
my system, I bought a whole garage worth of broken
furniture and started sanding it with my good arm, using
the cast on the broken arm to hold each piece steady. I was
drunk, drugged-out and crazed with pain – and I had no
misgivings about medicating myself as often as possible.

– 20 –

Punk Musician, Thug Enforcer

I continued playing music with my arm in a cast. One person I jammed with regularly was my friend Terry*. I met Terry at a mutual acquaintance's house on Haight Street. They were all playing Grateful Dead music, which I abhorred. I was an original music man. I didn't like things like the Grateful Dead or any of those old bands. Terry and I were smoking some joints and talking about women. We were both womanizers. We had a lot more talk in us than we had action, and Lord knows if we had connected with any women, they would be damaged for life. We started playing music and writing original songs, and eventually I played in three or four bands with Terry.

One day, after Terry and I jammed, we took a walk around the Mission. Terry saw his friend Cindy* at a garage sale at Dolores and 17th and pointed her out. On a dare, I went over to meet her and bought some stuff. We started talking, and I liked her a lot. We decided to meet again. She was breaking up with somebody. She had moved to San Francisco from Virginia, and she wasn't like the crowd I hung around with. She didn't know about drugs or drinking. We started seeing each other, and I introduced her to my crazy lifestyle. We kept it at a casual, social, fun level.

As the 1980s commenced, part of my responsibility as a Viking Ostrich, full-metal-jacket junkie was to make sure I had relationships with several dealers, and to always pursue connections with new ones. I discovered that frequenting the bars and bath houses on Castro Street satisfied several needs at once – I could drink, have all the casual sex I could handle, and meet new speed dealers, all at the same time. I began noticing unusual purplish splotches on the legs of some of the gay men, and as a nurse's aide, I wondered what caused these splotches and whether it was contagious.

Working for a temp agency, I usually would be assigned the most hostile or unpleasant duties at each hospital, and in those days, I found myself in room after room of emaciated young men dying from rare infections and pneumonias. At shift change, the nurses would say these men were gay and/or drug users, and no one knew if their disease was airborne, bloodborne or transmitted some other way. Most nurses wanted no part of these patients and took a hands-off approach to their care. I would walk in to find these patients spitting up blood all over their bedsheets or covered with pale-colored, bloody stool because they had hepatitis C in addition to this mysterious illness. I would clean up these weakened patients by myself and tell them everything would be all right – even while I was stunned and bewildered at the knowledge that I was doing every risky behavior they were doing. Hell, I was high right there on the shift. What was this new pestilence? Why was it killing the young and adventurous? Why gay men? Why not me?

I tried to emulate Mother Teresa and just care for these patients without fear, but I was emotionally and mentally bankrupt, without the skills to deal with the scope of this plague. The dead were quietly removed and replaced with scores more until the wards were overburdened. Finally, the disease was given a name, and facts about AIDS and HIV began to replace fear, thank God.

All through my nursing career, I was a favorite of the psych patients, because they liked my style. The nurses usually liked that I could deal with the "unreachable" crazy patients, and that I wasn't afraid to do something like lie down with them to get them to sleep. If there was one thing I could always do well, it was relate to unstable, disenfranchised people. I was crazier than a loon and more like our mentally unstable patients than anyone knew.

My property management career took a dramatic and all-consuming turn when I started working for a man named Charles*, a well-connected owner of numerous properties in San Francisco. This silver-haired fox seemed to know every loophole and tax break in existence to maximize his income opportunities. He lived on a prestigious estate in Spain and hired me as a property manager/fix-it man. By now, I had christened myself "the Nigger Nose" to honor my affinity with people of color, as well as my hard-earned knowledge of survival on the mean streets. It simply meant, "Don't fuck with the Nigger, 'cause the Nigger Nose." It also meant "black man's knowledge," as the word "gnosis" means "knowledge."

I had honed my skills as a thug-enforcer property manager who hired all those considered the throwaway dregs of society to form my rag-tag construction and demolition crews. For potential employers, I described my preferred crew members as "niggers, spics, punks and hicks/ robbers, rapists, muggers and thieves/ whackers, crackers and thugs." I also hired as many starving musicians as I could, as well as women who were willing to work hard for good pay and were sick of being shut out of these good-ol'-boy job networks. I taught all of my workers every construction skill they could handle, and they were allowed to drink and use drugs all they wanted, as long as they could produce quality results (and I didn't see them do it). I could outbid any competing contractor by doing jobs for one-tenth the market price, and I paid my workers under the table.

One advantage of property management was the ability to move drug dealers into pivotal locations all over town, so in the course of a normal day of checking properties, I could get high – real high – as high as one could get. Staying this loaded kept my crazed eyes on the prize 24 hours a day. I would check properties and supervise crews all day, then take advantage of the night shift to use the element of surprise on squatters I needed to evict. Once, I climbed through a window at 5 in the morning and began kicking bed frames and bellowing, "Get up and get the fuck out of here now!" I walked each person out the door in whatever clothes they could grab on the move. "What about my money? What about my dope?" they'd ask groggily.

"Get your money! Leave the dope!" I'd bark. "Get out now!"

In sleepy, drug-induced wonder, some would ask who I was and what right I had to kick them out in the middle of the night. "I'm God, and it's time to get the fuck out!" My status as a crazed, needle-fueled nemesis was obvious, and my methods met with little resistance.

Once I'd emptied a flat this way, I would summon a crew of rogue workers who would respond immediately, no matter what the job was, always ready to earn money to get high or pay rent. We'd clean out apartments and prepare them for paying tenants. On one occasion, when a dealer was among those I'd evicted, a worker came upon a half-ounce of cocaine, so we took a break and got out some soup

spoons to shoot up the bounty. We got some needles from
a responsible, rent-paying dealer I'd moved in upstairs;
pulled the drug up into the needles, and had a needlefest.
We almost lost our minds on cocaine, with bells ringing in
our ears and the sounds of the city magnified 1,000 percent
in our ears. Our eyes clouded from the high concentration
of the drug in our bloodstreams. I got more fucked up than
I'd ever been and was nearly unable to move, while the
workers stumbled around like stunned bees who'd just been
subdued by a smoker. Just then, someone pounded on the
door, the sound of which magnified to the level of a train
wreck in my ears. "This is the police! Open up!"

I struggled to my feet, swearing. "You guys get in the
back room and look busy! Get rid of the needles and the
dope now! Dump them in the trash in the back of the
building!" I wobbled toward the blurry door and opened it
to find four angry, frustrated undercover officers, most of
whom I recognized from the hundreds of nighttime hours
I spent on the streets. "Hey, what's up?" I said, striving to
sound casual.

"Why'd you kick them out?" the lead cop demanded.
I explained the former tenants were about three months
behind in their rent. "You can't just break in and kick
them out – it's against the law!" he said. It turned out the
police had the place under surveillance for months, and my
housecleaning ruined their case. But there wasn't much
they could do, especially since much of the evidence was
now floating through my retinal blood vessels.

As I handled the property management duties in
Charles' office, it quickly became apparent that he did not
restrict his business dealings to real estate. Charles owned
sole distribution rights for the three main gun companies
that supplied Indonesia. His Telex machine rattled off
order after order from untraceable black ops governed by
agencies like the CIA, which were selling shipments of
firearms to militant groups that supported U.S. interests. I

watched our office distribute death and destruction to the Sandinistas, Afghans, Filipinos, and groups all over Africa. My rampant, obsessive, speed-fueled paranoia reached new heights in this environment. I already suspected I was being personally surveilled by undercover cops and ultra-ultra-conservatives. I could only guess at the government agencies that would be interested in these gun-running activities.

Living in this constant state of compulsive suspicion and fear strained my tenuous grasp on reality. It also strained my on-again, off-again relationship with Cindy. Of all the people I'd done hit-and-run, short-term engagements and one-night stands with, Cindy was one of the few constant relationships I managed to maintain. I still adhered to my philosophy of pursuing two or three relationships at a time and avoiding commitment, so I would live with her for a while, then go on a speed bender and disappear into my cycle of working, drinking and using all day; shooting speed and walking the streets all night, and staying awake for six or seven weeks at a time. When I was near collapse, I would return to Cindy, who would take me in and give me food, comfort, and a safe place to sleep until I was ready to start the cycle of dangerous street life again.

There was a lot of unconditional love and tenderness between us, but at this point, we both were drinking and I was using drugs, which sometimes escalated our conflicts into violence. As an alcoholic junkie with multiple untreated mental illnesses, I often reacted to conflict with anger, threats, controlling demands, and violence toward Cindy. One such episode ignited when we attend a friend's beach wedding, where we both got drunk. Emulating a frequent control maneuver used by my dad during my childhood, I dragged Cindy into the ocean. She got so angry, she insisted that we leave the reception. We got into the red VW Karmann Ghia we'd bought together, and we began physically brawling as she drove us through the park.

She pulled the car over as I tore at her clothes, trying to rip off her blouse. Two men approached to see if Cindy needed help. As I tore off the rest of her blouse and left her topless, I threatened to kick their asses next. We got back in the car, and she tried to scare me by driving too fast. She drove over a curb, launching the car 20 feet through the air over marshes and cattails, and landed in a pond.

The violence continued at home, where I destroyed the apartment in a rage. When our fighting spilled out onto the street, a neighbor called the police. One of the officers who arrived to break up our fight started to arrest me and then stopped short when he heard my name. "Are you Captain Kowalski's son?" he asked. I lied by omission, and he let me go with a warning. We cooled off, but we didn't find our car for two days, since it was in a spot obscured by reeds. I had thrown the keys into the pond anyway.

Around the time I worked for Charles, I returned to Cindy's place after one of my typical weeks-long disappearances, and she told me she'd had an abortion in my absence. I was devastated that she'd done it without telling me and felt that my child had been killed without my knowledge. The logistics of notifying me of anything when I was impossible to find for weeks at a time meant nothing to me then. News of the abortion put me over the edge. I disappeared again, throwing myself headlong into the abyss of hardcore drug and alcohol abuse, sex and overwork.

One morning, the San Francisco Chronicle hit the front porch of Charles' office with a scathing expose by columnist Herb Caen. He blasted the owner of a bombed-out eyesore at Market and Sutter, asking how anyone could let such a monstrosity mar the landscape of our beautiful city. As the owner of the monstrosity in question, Charles was up in arms over Caen's column. But the building was tied up in litigation between several family members, and no one wanted to bankroll the expensive repairs. When I offered to get a crew together and rehab the place,

Charles accepted and lined up architects, contractors and subcontractors. In no time, word got out, and I had every hulking, drugged-out felon in the Bay Area on my crew. We filled 80 debris boxes as we gutted the building. I paid daily or weekly, and I always had to have that cash on hand, which put a slightly built guy like me in a precarious position. But I knew if something happened to me – the guy who paid good money to musicians, minorities, women, felons, and other needy people – the culprit would be hunted down and punished.

We cut corners and broke so many rules that we earned 14 pages of violations from the OSHA inspector. But the mayor wanted this three-story wreck rehabbed, and Charles knew how to dance us in and out of the system and around all the red tape. A revolving door of inspectors visited constantly and tried to train us in safety procedures, such as the proper removal of the asbestos that lined the heating system of the building. While the inspector demonstrated the safe handling of hazardous materials, I would be whooshing asbestos into the air like snowflakes and catching them on my tongue. My crew lived a wild life, and any of us easily could have died at any time from any number of our professional and leisure choices. Our motto was, "Whaddya want – to live forever? Get to work!"

An OSHA inspector was assigned to visit the worksite each Tuesday. He would hang out for a few hours and point out what I was doing that absolutely crazy, then digress into endless war stories about people who had been maimed, electrocuted, crushed or dropped to grisly deaths. Then we'd have lunch. The work chugged forward relentlessly, and the workers who couldn't keep up were weeded out, no matter how big they were or how much dope they had. My discipline and guidance of the crew consisted of yelling, "Bang – you're fired! Now get back to work!" or "You hired yourself, and now you done fired yourself!"

The biggest threat to the project came when 50 or 60

union guys picketed the worksite. They threatened and intimidated the "scab" crew so much that some workers got scared and stopped showing up. I couldn't let that stand, so I walked out front to talk to the union leader in front of all the angry, yelling protesters on the street who wanted to kick my ass. I was scared, but I knew my crew was watching from windows above. When I knew most of the crowd was paying attention, I did the only thing I could think of to express my feelings on this matter: I dropped my pants, swung my penis in their direction and yelled, "I got your scabs hangin' – scab this, you mothers!" Seeing that dialogue was not an option, the union crowd dispersed but promised to return and keep fighting us. It was just an old rock 'n' roll move, but at least my crew felt vindicated. Later that night, the protesters returned and tried to set the building on fire with our welding and cutting tanks, but it didn't catch. It just scared the hell out of us.

I remember two other incidents that occurred during the project that I regret now. In one, an elderly woman fell and broke her hip on the sidewalk in front of the building because a small water-cover plate had been removed, leaving a hole in the pavement. Before the insurance company came to inspect the area, I grabbed a water-cover plate from another area, rusty screw and all, and filled the hole. I now regret that my misplaced loyalty prevented this deserving woman from suing the hell out of us. In the second incident, a Latina woman fell in 6 inches of water in the alley near the building and cut her arm on some glass. The cut extended from her wrist to her elbow. Wanting to make the matter go away, I acted like a dick and asked, "Do you have your green card?" I pray for forgiveness for those two misdeeds.

My substance abuse, personal relationships and job performance rolled along this way for the next few years. As the end of the decade approached, I primarily played with three bands, most notably Greed Incorporated, the

XyPhoids and the Tibetan Boy Scouts. I usually put the people in my bands on my construction crew, too, so we all made $12 to $15 an hour. For a bunch of punks and slam dancers, making this much money was a great thing. For me, this influx of cash went straight into my veins.

– 21 –

Homelessexual

By 1985, I knew thousands of people whose lives revolved around drugs, alcohol and sex. Adoring followers would swarm around certain dealers, such as one delicious young thing known as "Sean* the Androgynous." Although I was 37 – an old man in junkie years – I began to keep company with Sean and one of his followers, a teen-age boy called "Robin Homes." Robin would take anything from anyone, sometimes pausing in the homes he was burglarizing long enough to enjoy a leisurely meal and a nap until the residents came home and called the police. One night after shooting two quarters of speed, I walked down the street with Robin at about 2 a.m. when he decided to gain entry into a car owned by a death-rocker chick who was always trying to commit suicide.

"Robin," I said, "I'm an old man. I can't be around you when you're committing dangerous acts that could be construed as crimes." He laughed with the invincibility of youth. "If you're going to do this, please put the big bag of dope in your pocket under the car. Then at least we won't get arrested for the drugs." Reluctantly, he agreed.

Just then, an elderly man called from a nearby window, "What are you boys doing out there?"

"Nothing," we replied. The cops were on us in about 12 seconds. Since I considered myself somewhat arrest-proof after a lifetime of many near-misses, I was shocked to find myself being dragged down to the Haight-Ashbury station with Robin the Cop Magnet. I stood in the station and saw all the officers who passed me day and night, year after year. One officer walked by with a bindle of dope on his tongue and stuck it out so only I could see it. "Mmm, good," he said. Another walked by with two fistfuls of bindles, flashing them at me. I was flying way higher than normal, and they were trying to get a reaction out of me. No doubt, I was transfixed. They transferred me to a holding cell that was a filthy disgrace. I began loudly imploring them to give me a mop and bucket and then a can of paint so I could try to make this cell respectable. They laughed at my bravado and let me go a few hours later. Robin was arrested and went downtown for a week.

The next morning, I went back to the car to get the dope, and I met the elderly man who called the police. His name was Carl, and he became a treasured friend. Carl taught me that integrity was important even in a dysfunctional life of addiction. "The way you leave one place is the way you'll go into the next," he would say, "and the way you end one relationship is the way you'll begin the next." Unbeknownst to me (and his wife), Carl was a regular with the prostitutes down on 16th Street. But his lessons of integrity stuck with me anyway. Carl was a country man who knew the dangerous street life I was living. When he made sausage and jerky from deer meat, he would give me some, and I would carry it with me to nourish myself on my long journeys through the city. The greatest experience I shared with Carl was emptying out a huge warehouse full of items stockpiled by families during the tumultuous decades following the 1906 San Francisco Earthquake and Fire. Being an amateur anthropologist, it was heaven for me to help Carl sift through the clothing, household effects, papers and other items. Unfortunately, we threw most of it away, but I was still collecting stamps, so I grabbed all the envelopes I found and stashed them all over town in every hiding place I had, like a squirrel storing nuts for winter. I also took moccasins and medical equipment purported to belong to an Indian healer who treated the dying wife of a San Francisco mayor around the turn of the century. From her collection, I took about 100 bottles still filled with circa-1900 medicines such as laudanum and morphine. I stashed these as well.

My infatuation with Sean the Androgynous indirectly led to my nurturing friendship with Carl, but soon after that, it led to a violent incident that dropped me a few more rungs down the ladder of utter, self-destructive insanity. One night, several dealers were rounded up by a gang of thugs called the "Slay Team" and brutally victimized in the apartment directly below Sean's. The dealers were forced to perform lascivious and demeaning acts on each other for their assailants' entertainment. The police came and arrested the dealers and a few of the perpetrators. Everyone fled the building, but I chose to stay and guard Sean's place until the trouble passed. One of the worst perpetrators kept calling Sean's apartment from jail, threatening to bring his "Slay Team" of thugs to clear out the building and grind up anyone they found there, especially me. Wasted and worn out, I took his calls and responded to his violent imagery by saying things like, "Jesus will be here, my son," in the most beatific voice I could muster. Because I considered it a good investment to take care of my dealers' belongings, I decided to stay at Sean's apartment until he returned, even after the "Slay Team" guy was released from jail. He wasted no time calling me to let me know he and his partners were on their way to finish me off.

I was scared and out of dope. In my commitment to stay with Sean's valuables, I had shot up every bit of speed I had and was reduced to scavenging the contaminated, bloody residue from about 15 baggies strewn on the floor. While I did this, I gathered every instrument of death I could find – several pieces of iron and six big knives. The irony of gathering weapons for self-defense while endangering my own life with contaminated dope was lost on me at the time. I also took advantage of a common feature of dope dens – 12 large, full bags of garbage that hadn't been taken out. I barricaded the doors with the trash bags and any furniture I could budge.

When the time drew near for their late-night assault, I prepared to greet them in the method I had perfected over the years: I got naked and turned off all the lights. I often passed long nights "on guard" in unsafe areas by sitting with knives in the dark, ready to hit any suspected target by sound and feel. Sitting in front of a reflective chrome ball that enabled me to see above and behind me, I went into a trance-like state, all my senses focused on the movement, sounds or vibrations the gang would make as they entered the building. I wished I could have accessed my favorite monitoring method: lying in a tub of warm water and using the plumbing as a vibration amplifier of the whole house. When I had a hearing aid handy, I used it at times like this. I was fastidious in my mania and hysterical paranoia. I am alive today because of it.

At last, I heard noises on the front stairs and in the back alley. I rushed to the back door and saw six shadowy figures climbing the back steps. Madman that I was, I grabbed two large kitchen knives and rubbed them together repeatedly, quietly saying, "Ninja … Ninja … Ninja …," out the kitchen window. Rather than deterring them, that made them take the back steps two at a time, so I moved to Plan B and deployed my impressive arsenal of smelly trash. At the top of the stairs, I kicked over five or six of my 33-gallon-size trash bags, raining down rotted food and many pounds of used cat litter onto my aspiring assailants. When I heard them shriek on the steps, swearing about the coating of cat feces and urine they were wearing, I responded by throwing every object I could reach down on them. They scrambled back down the stairs, and I heard the alley door to the street slam shut behind them.

My adrenaline was pumping. Still terrified, I wondered if they were backing down only to re-emerge through the front door. I crept to the front of the house and listened. Nothing. I felt trapped, and I figured my chances of survival were slim. But they didn't come back. I laughed that my flimsy litter-box scheme had deterred them. Eventually, I found out I knew some of these guys from around town, and they weren't bad guys. The ring leader was later found murdered and eviscerated near 16th and Shotwell.

I was becoming more of a danger to myself and others, losing my grip on any reality that was not based on anger, attachment, victimhood, perpetration, or sick ideas about love. I talked mostly in metaphors, parables, double non sequiturs and secret codes, and no one could understand what I was babbling about. I believed I could read people's minds and thoughts; I thought they communicated with me in code using gestures and eye movements. I tried to use my bipolar depression as armor to protect myself, but really it just kept me separated from reality.

One cold night, tweaking my brains out, I wandered the streets for hours playing my flute. My playing was muted by the fog as I started out in the Tenderloin downtown and headed toward the Sunset area and Golden Gate Park. The gracious thing about San Francisco is that its residents regularly put clean clothes and shoes out on the curb, so I could always find something clean and keep layering to avoid catching my death of cold. Around 5:30 in the morning, I ended up near Kezar Stadium in the Haight, where abandoned school buildings took up a whole block. I got inside an empty auditorium that had been a squat for homeless people for some time. Somehow, I never thought of myself as one, even when I wandered aimlessly night after night with no reason for living and found myself in places like this. I enjoyed the perfect acoustics for my flute's sweet timbre for a while, marveling that I had this whole place to myself. I got onto the stage to play, and my music echoed throughout the auditorium. There were giant, 4-foot holes in the stage that you had to walk carefully around to avoid getting seriously hurt.

I was playing like Jethro Tull, twirling the flute and having a one-man show, and trying to keep warm in the morning chill when I noticed a few punks with mohawks and Army/Navy Surplus jackets standing near the pitch-black entrances. Then, I saw a few more, wearing black leather jackets and green military jackets made for cold weather. I kept playing like the Pied Piper of the Living Dead, as more people streamed out of the darkness and walked slowly toward me in a drunken death march. These were not happy, smiling faces; they were unhappy people I had accidentally roused from the safety of their respective stupors. I had violated the peace, safety and silence of this stolid crypt.

Likes bats in a belfry, there were now about several people shuffling toward me who had reached the stage. I kept playing and moved around the holes in the stage like an actor, dancing and weaving in the darkness and desperately seeking a place to "exit stage left" and lose them. But they picked up their pace to match mine. Finally, I had to stop playing the flute, switch into survival mode, and run for my life. It was fortunate for me that I was on speed and moving at 1,000 miles per hour. I bolted toward a pair of chained but unlocked doors, and they followed in hot pursuit. The chain had just enough slack to let one person at a time squeeze through. I burst through, and once outside in the dim light, I picked up a large boulder lying nearby and hurled it with all my might at the door, aiming at the three people who were struggling to get out. The metallic clank of the rock against the doors stunned us all. I grabbed my flute and ran for my life, while they made only a feeble attempt to follow and just stood and watched me get away.

My eyes blurry with drugs, I resumed playing my flute, giggling like a madman at my brush with death. This was not just depression; I got a real rush from thrill-seeking behavior, and I got my fix.

A few days later, I told my friend and music promoter, Dirk Dirksen, about my latest adventures. He knew my mental state was getting worse and that I was surviving by eating food out of cans and drinking cheap beers. In a desperate attempt to slow my downward spiral, Dirk helped me pack a bag of survival gear and took me to Crockett, a small, unincorporated community north of San Francisco. His plan was that I would dry out and rehabilitate myself while I repaired an auditorium that had been donated to the community.

In autumn of 1985, Crockett was a favorite hangout of the Hell's Angels, one reason being it took the Contra Costa County Sheriff's Department about an hour to respond to calls there. I had also heard that it got its start as an unprincipled community in the late 1800s, when someone shot the sheriff and a deputy. Now, Crockett was home to a C&H Sugar factory, which employed most of the area's residents. I moved into a small room in a dilapidated hotel across the street from C&H and the auditorium and got to work familiarizing myself with the important landmarks in town – namely, the two bars. I walked in, approached the biggest bad-ass biker I could see, and said, "You probably don't believe me, but soon I'll be buying speed from you guys. I was wondering if we could cut the shit and skip the formalities of me having to prove myself and get to know you guys personally." I was dismissed as a crazy person at first, but soon enough, my prophecy came true, and the speed was flowing again. Meanwhile, ever on the prowl for tasks to maintain my workaholic pace, I volunteered to rehab a storefront on the main drag for the Sheriff's Department to use as a substation. It was harder to score dope from the locals while fixing up a place for the cops, but I managed. I was still a junkie, but once again I was walking both sides of the gossamer thread that holds us all together, stretching and stretching but never breaking.

Like-minded people find each other in any given community, and before long, I found my usual netherworld companions with whom to drink, shoot up, and have sex. The same behavior inevitably led to the same results, and before long, I was in enough confrontational situations with violent people that I again lived in fear for my life. I was able to maintain my dysfunctional routine until the night a friend of mine, an African-American musician in a band called the Black Athletes, came to visit from Vallejo. As we walked down the main drag in Crockett, some Hell's Angels came out of a bar and stopped us. "Why don't you get your motherfuckin' faggot ass back to San Francisco?" one of them said. "And don't bring no niggers around this town again – you got a free pass this time."

Embarrassed, shaken and, of course, drunk, I escorted my friend safely out of town. Then I drank real heavily, real fast, and went back to the bar to call them out, pitchfork in hand. When they emerged, I rushed them and pinned one against the wall, pressing the sharp prongs of the pitchfork into his neck.

"If you ever call me a faggot again, I'm gonna stick this pitchfork through your friend's neck," I said calmly to the big, beefy Angel next to him. Then, without flinching, I stuck the pitchfork into the neck of the observing biker and screamed, "Now, look at me real good! If your friend ever calls my friend a nigger again, I'm gonna kill both of your asses, you hear, you fucking assholes??" The bar's patrons had poured out onto the street, and someone called the police. I took off into the night, a light rain falling. I hid my pitchfork in a 4-foot hedge and then took my flute and sat near the rear of the building where I rented a room. When the cops pulled up an hour later, I was playing my flute, waiting for them. Guns drawn and flashlights scanning the area, the police searched for me. One cop tried to step down a retaining wall near me, and I popped out at him and trilled the highest, fastest, staccato notes I could, trying to play like a madman. He jumped and lost his footing, landing face down in the mud, right next to his fallen gun and flashlight. A younger, more agile cop right behind him saw me and said, "Don't move!" I obliged. He grabbed me and called, "I got him! I got him! I got my first one!" The older, muddied-up cop wanted to bash my head in, but the younger one, delighted with his prize, wouldn't let him near me. They called an ambulance to 51-50 me to the crazy house.

After about 25 years on the streets, I was finally caught in the act of being crazy. I took the hour-long ride to Contra Costa County's mental observation lockdown unit, where they usually observe patients for 30 to 60 days to determine how nuts we are and whether we are dangers to ourselves or others. They tucked me in that night with restraints and an injection of Thorazine that knocked me out cold until the next morning. When I woke up, I was choking on a huge object stuffed in my mouth; it took me a minute to realize it was my own tongue, swollen to elephantine size because of the Thorazine.

I was used to working and playing while I was high and out of my mind, so I struggled to function through the heavy Thorazine haze. I read every piece of reading material I could find, and when I ran out, I slurred around my swollen tongue to tell the nurse I needed more National Geographics, which she kindly brought. As I slowly came to my senses, I knew something obviously was wrong with my meds. The lead nurse came to interview me and read my police report, which stated I had been running around Crockett with a pitchfork saying I wanted to kill somebody, anybody! After calmly saying that never happened, I went on to slur my entire anti-American-Medical-Association diatribe at her and question the meds I was being given.

Then it was time for music therapy hour. I called on my experience as a musician to engage everyone in a jamming, smiling good time. Afterward, everyone shared what they would do when they were released from this facility. I listened intently to their goals, and then I announced that I was going to pursue SSI for being crazy. Once I had that income, I would work under the table for a regular paycheck and make lots of money. Everyone's eyes lit up, even some of the nurses'. The next day, I got a free ride back to Crockett. The staff told me they'd concluded I was a danger to myself and others in the mental-health system, so I had to go.

Back in Crockett, a small architectural firm was rehabbing the downtown area, and the staff was headquartered right next to the auditorium where I worked and played music. I started making small talk with Meredith*, one of the architects, and the chit-chat turned into lunches and then dating. I put on my best "look-good" and wined and dined her with all the smooth talk I could muster. Meanwhile, I became convinced that the Hell's Angels were manufacturing speed in the basement of my auditorium. I could never prove it, but when the auditorium burst into flames one day and was destroyed, I wondered if the infamously volatile chemicals used to make speed might have been a factor.

I had enough of Crockett and decided to return to San Francisco. I began a strange relationship with Meredith and my old friend, Cindy: I would spend a few nights at one woman's house; then, with both of their knowledge,

I would go to the other woman's house. This plan worked out great until I messed around with some younger women and got scabies. Both Cindy and Meredith had to spend hundreds of dollars to fumigate their entire wardrobes and homes. I was so ashamed, I broke it off with Meredith. She couldn't understand why I wouldn't just straighten myself out and go on with our relationship. I could see that she didn't realize what a sick person I was, so one night, in her car in the rain, I ended the discussion by striking myself in the head over and over and verbally abusing myself. She got the message. And I was alone once again.

Oct. 17, 1989, began like any other day. I woke up at Cindy's house, where she let me rent a room, and I did a shot of speed and drank some beers on the way to a job site at Sixth and Howard streets. It was the Defenestration building, famous for the furniture attached to its exterior walls. I knew a dealer who lived right upstairs, so it was convenient for me to work the morning and then go upstairs and get high during lunch. My crew of about eight dedicated misfits and I worked all morning, then headed to the roof to eat lunch. It was such a beautiful day, the crew decided we all should go to Baker Beach and do some nude sunbathing. We piled into my white Toyota truck with some beers, weed and speed and headed to the ocean, where we got loaded all afternoon, taking occasional breaks to jump in the surf. As 5 o'clock approached, we headed to the Jack in the Box at Lombard and Divisadero for some burgers.

We were just stumbling out of the truck at the burger joint, all tired, sunburned and drunk, when the Loma Prieta earthquake hit. Confused at first, I yelled at passing drivers to straighten themselves out and stop driving so crazy! Then we walked into the Jack in the Box and ordered our food, failing to notice that the power had gone out and all the workers were staring at us in shock. The cashier apologized and said she couldn't serve us at the moment, since (for starters) the cash register wouldn't work. Before

I could escalate from irate to abusive, my crew loaded me into the back of my truck and drove off. We rolled through the shaken city, with people crowding the streets and fires erupting here and there, and I yelled like a lunatic as we passed people.

After stopping to buy more beer, we arrived at the house I shared with Cindy. On the ground floor, nothing was out of place except one blue vase that was knocked to the floor but didn't break. Upstairs in my room, however, everything of value was splattered all over the floor. I took it as a personal affront from God. So what else could I do? I found the expensive bottle of champagne Cindy was saving for a special occasion and popped it open. I realized I was out of speed, and all the dealers I called were out except one, who lived in North Beach. We headed downstairs to the truck, and on the way, I greeted Burt, our downstairs neighbor. A San Francisco police officer, he sat on the front steps putting on his riot gear to go out and face this crazy evening. Then we drove down Divisadero Street toward the Marina, where the biggest damage and fires were. We zigged and zagged through the surrounding neighborhoods until we finally made the dealer's house, where he reluctantly gave me his last eight ball on credit, since the ATMs were out of service.

Back at my house, we sat in my room getting high and listened to the news. When I heard about the collapse of a segment of the freeway in Oakland, I realized it was only a few blocks from a major job I was doing for another employer at a printing factory. I worried about a three-wall architectural design I had created without permits and hoped no one had been hurt in the rooms where I installed a colonnade of 6-by-10-foot windows to create a natural-light effect popular at the time. I was distracted from my professional concerns when we dropped acid and started really partying like it was the end of the world. The next few hours passed happily as we played music, did art projects and saw trails. At some point, Cindy got home and discovered that her champagne was gone and wisely demanded $60 in cash on the spot.

At one point, we all went to the roof to survey the city. I was looking around with binoculars when I noticed a man waving flares on a distant street. Suddenly, I heard a gunshot and saw the flares roll down the street in the dark. I later learned that I had witnessed the fatal shooting of someone I knew – a young African-American man named DeSoto Barker. I wondered why God seemed to train my lens on death like finding a needle in a haystack.

The earthquake led to a more personal milestone when my phone rang at about 3:30 a.m. It was my mother, calling to make sure I was all right. Apparently she'd called many numbers before she finally tracked me down, which was nothing new. I'd talked to her only three times in the past 15 years and sadly, whenever we spoke, I was wasted. This time, she had no hope of getting coherent answers to any of her heartfelt questions. The party was still rollicking on, and we were playing Scrabble, a game we'd played a lot when I was a child. I screamed into the phone, "I need a seven-letter word, and here are the letters!" With a rare opportunity to talk to my mother, that was best I had to offer.

– 22 –

After the Quake

After the earthquake, I began doing one repair job after another in the East Bay cities of Oakland and Emeryville. In crime-ridden West Oakland, I fit right in and began hiring anyone who wanted to work, including a man we believed was an ax murderer. I met a lot of African-American parents with young adult sons who were unemployed, and they welcomed me to their neighborhoods when they saw that I offered many of their kids the chance to earn decent pay while restoring damaged buildings in their communities. I often was the only white person I saw in these areas, which were notoriously dangerous. Firearms were everywhere; the sound of Uzi spray was not uncommon during an average workday. All of this work was done quickly without the proper permits, and when inspectors visited my work sites in the months after the earthquake, I was proud that all of the projects passed inspection.

At this time, I added something new to my regular diet

of alcohol and speed – crack, which was cheap and easy to find. Before long, I had developed a $500-a-week crack habit, along with drinking one or two cases of beer per day and shooting speed. Ingesting this amount of drugs and alcohol was life-threatening in itself, but I also had frequent close calls while buying crack from dangerous brothers with guns. Needless to say, I was a real mess. Finally, after smoking crack for weeks, my body couldn't take the strain anymore. I knew something was seriously wrong and wound up at San Francisco General's Emergency Room with EKG wires all over me. They told me I had suffered a small heart attack and damaged some heart muscle. I recognized some of the nurses from the days when I worked as a nurse's aide. They laughed at how pitiful I looked. When I asked if I was going to be there all right, one nurse assumed the half-paralyzed pose of a stroke patient and retorted, "Sure, you'll be OK, if you don't mind the consequences." This wakeup call was dramatic enough to get through even to me, at least somewhat: I decided my crack days were over. Yup, it was back to the relative safety of alcohol and shooting speed.

Around that time, I was supervising a motley collection of musicians and locals in re-roofing about a quarter of a square block in Oakland. One day, these amateurs started to get careless and a little crazy with buckets of hot tar. I knew they had no idea of the agonizing damage hot tar could cause if it landed on their skin, where it would melt, sink in and harden. I didn't want anyone to be hurt, so with my usual patience and self-control, I snatched a full, steaming bucket out of someone's hands. Screaming and cursing about how dangerous tar was, I splashed the hot tar across the roof and yelled, "See? That's how it's done! Gimme another bucket!" I demonstrated again and then motioned for a third bucket, impatiently yelling at them to back away and observe the proper handling of roofing tar. Unfortunately, I was standing too close to a wall this time, and some of the hot tar splashed back onto my skin. My safety lessons didn't include the fact that one should never splash buckets of hot tar while shirtless, so about 20 bits of blistering hot tar spattered across my bare chest and stuck there.

I screamed in burning agony and then sputtered in a blind rage, "Goddamn it! Gimme another bucket! Son of a bitch!" Sploosh – more bits of tar rained onto my face, hands, nose, hair, and near my eyes. Now it was time for Kowalski First Aid. I shouted at my workers to bring me a case of beer, which I gulped down as fast as I could. Then I put another case under my arm and headed home to rest. A woman named Lara*, whose boyfriend was a bandmate of mine, offered to come along and take care of me. I soon learned that all she was interested in was taking advantage of the sado-masochistic opportunity to have sex with someone who was in agonizing pain. With both of us drugged and drunk, we went at it. Why not, I figured – if beer was good first aid for third-degree burns, then beer AND sex was even better. As soon as her skin rubbed against my burned stomach, my brain exploded from the pain and I passed out.

When I woke up, I gingerly peeled away the bedsheet that was adhered to my skin, and the tar left an imprint of my burned body on the sheet. This "shroud of Kowalski" was evidence of my total disregard for any level of self-care. I "medicated" my worsening pain with alcohol for about a week until I noticed that several of the burns were getting red and infected from lack of treatment. When I finally went to the hospital, the only option left was to cut the tar out of my skin, bit by bit. I was temporarily sober for that moment and went through it cursing and screaming, much the same as I had when I'd injured myself in the first place.

After years of junkie life, I was mentally challenged beyond belief, and I had no skills to cope with anything. I was perhaps most dangerous behind the wheel, being drunk and high most of the time. On my way to buy dope one night, I rear-ended a vehicle with no tail lights. I waited around for about 10 minutes, but I had a dealer with dope waiting for me, and that was my priority. I took off.

Not long after that came the next time my rampant addictions and carelessness almost killed innocent people. I did a job applying a thick coat of acrylic to the top of a bar at a San Francisco nightclub called Lips Underground. There were two big problems with this job opportunity: I applied a highly toxic substance in an enclosed area with no respirator, and I had full access to the alcohol behind the bar. I drove home down Divisadero at 4 in the morning and plowed into the back of a car, pushing it into an intersection. Dazed, I found myself staring at the totaled front of my truck and shredded back of their car. I staggered to the car and did a quick drunken welfare check: Can you move your arms and legs? What day is it? Everybody OK? Good! Then I got the hell out of there, parking my truck in a bank parking lot about a block away. It took me about three days of aimless wandering to find my truck again, which I was surprised to discover hadn't been towed from the lot where I parked it.

I didn't need a car to endanger myself. I also frequently placed myself at risk in hand-to-hand combat situations on the street. When my truck was stolen, my friends called me repeatedly to tell me they'd seen it around town. Finally, I got a call that the truck was close by, and I found it and staked it out, waiting for its driver. When he walked up, I jumped him and wound up holding him over the tailgate of my truck with his windpipe exposed.

"Do you have any weapons?" I demanded. He nodded, and I yelled, "Well, use 'em!" He slowly and cautiously offered his knife, which I grabbed and tossed away. Then I waited for the police … and waited … and waited. After about 15 minutes, a nearby store owner who'd been watching us came out and said he'd called the police. As my adrenaline slowly faded, I started to notice my suspect's hugely muscled arms, which were covered with Nazi tattoos, and his scarred hands, which wore several skull rings. I kept a firm hold on his ponytail and kept barking at him to hold still or I'd crush his larynx. But I could feel the strength draining from my body, and I realized what an opponent this guy was. I normally never would have screwed with a person like this.

Finally, just as I was desperately trying to decide how to severely injure him before he overpowered and killed me, the police arrived. Of course, they had a hard time figuring out whom to arrest. I'd been awake and high for weeks, and I wasn't exactly the poster child for law and order. In the end, it had been more than 24 hours since the truck was stolen, and there was no way to prove whether he was the thief or just a guy who bought it from the thief. So after booking him, the police let him go. I was outraged.

Soon after that, I got my second DUI when a disgruntled employee broke out the windshield of my truck, and I insisted on driving it across the San Francisco-Oakland Bay Bridge that way. At that point, my workers started to drive me around, and I began to lose it for real.

The next near-death event occurred when I began hanging out with wanna-be bikers in a thin-walled warehouse in the city and doing drugs there. During one of these visits, everyone could hear that a biker was beating his screaming girlfriend in the next room. Unable to take it anymore, I bellowed, "Hey, why don't you come out here with the men, if you can't be nice to your woman!" I repeated it until the raging bull emerged and asked who said it. From my reclining position on the ground, I identified myself. He walked over, bent down and punched me in the side of the face. But beating my ass wasn't enough of a distraction from his displeasure with his girlfriend, so he returned to the other room and resumed beating her.

The second time I baited him enough to come after me, he did it with a 5-pound barbell in his hand. He threw it from across the room, a distance of about 25 feet. I had just stood up, and I saw it approaching in the din light just in time to dodge it, narrowly avoiding a broken leg. But it did clip my calf, which left me deeply bruised and limping for weeks. He ran at me like a charging bull and jumped me. I got him into a scissor-lock between my legs; this was the one wrestling move I knew that enabled me to squeeze the air out of anybody. I grabbed handfuls of his hair and beat on his head, but he kept freeing himself by wrenching away and leaving his hair in my fists. I called desperately to the other bikers for help while he thrashed us all over the room. I begged the bikers to help me, but they had witnessed his temper before, and they just looked at me liked scared deer and apologized for not being able to intervene in the fatal beating I was about to receive.

By now, his girlfriend emerged and watched me pull handfuls of hair out of the raging biker's head. When he called to her for help, she looked at him with disdain. Then she walked over to us and, with all the power she had, smashed her fists into his face over and over again and connected real good. This disgrace made the biker crumble in my grip. I maintained my hold on him until I somehow managed to persuade him that I truly was psychotic and I needed to leave now before I ended him. He agreed to let me go. I ran down the stairs of the warehouse, and the door was double-locked. Now I felt real fear.

I screamed, "Open the fucking door! Open the fucking door!" And someone finally came with keys and opened it. I stood on a nearby bridge and watched the cops show up and haul him off. The wanna-be bikers kept asking, "Why don't you press charges??" I replied that I wasn't going to press charges because it was their fight, not mine – they let it happen in their domain.

Unable to drive because of my latest DUI and without car keys, it was harder to keep track of my house keys. I lost them repeatedly and would get inside the Victorian where I lived by climbing, drunk and angry, up the gingerbread trim on the side. After doing this several times and alienating all of my roommates with my drunken, public tirades, I grabbed a loose piece of gingerbread one night and fell backwards 20 feet onto the concrete below. My left foot took most of the impact, and my heel felt like it exploded. Still locked out, I crawled up the front steps and knocked on the door until one of my pissed-off roommates finally opened it.

In shock, I crawled up three flights of stairs to the bathroom, where I filled the tub and took a bath as my leg swelled to twice its normal size. I knew I had to go to the hospital, but I was filthy and drunk, and when you went to the ER looking like a homeless bum, you got treated like shit. Now clean and wearing the least-dirty clothes I could dig out of my dirty laundry, I went to the hospital. In the X-ray, my foot looked like a grenade exploded and left a thousand fragments where my heel used to be.

At this time of my life, I no longer had any friends I could trust to help me while I was injured. I couldn't be sure they wouldn't steal from me or burglarize my roommates' rooms. So I tied a bucket to a rope, and I called acquaintances to bring me food, booze and drugs. I would lower the bucket from my window, and they would put the stuff in the bucket. That way, I could stay fed and high without having to go up and down three flights of stairs. To avoid trips to the bathroom, I urinated into bottles. Sometimes I was so high, I drank my own urine by accident. I had been a nurse's aide, but now that I was unable to take care of myself, I had no one in my life I could trust to help me.

Cindy, who also lived in the house, went on vacation. While she was gone, one of my supposed friends stole a diamond ring that her grandmother had given her, along with other valuables. After several years of love and friendship marred by dysfunction and addiction, this ruined me yet again in Cindy's eyes. For all of our damaged history, she had seen the worst of me and loved me through it all, and I owed my life to her for taking me in so many times after I'd been awake and tweaking for weeks on end. She told me I had ruined the best years of her life. I realized later that she always had the choice to stay or go in our relationship, but her heart was big. My heart broke at the renewed loss of her friendship, and I hit an even lower low.

To heal my shattered leg, I permitted a doctor to put on a cast, but I refused the pins he recommended. I sawed the cast off three times to make sure my ankle and foot were healing properly. I handled the injury in my own way, swimming in the ocean and the Russian River to regain the range of motion in my leg and taking way too many drugs to obscure the pain before I returned to the doctor and had another cast put on. Finally, the injury healed and the cast came off for good.

In the same way I maintained two or three relationships at a time with women, I took that approach with my speed dealers. I rotated among three major dealers, so my high-volume needs were always met, whether I had cash or not, without burning out my supply. I was the worst violator of boundaries, especially if I was low on funds. I would demand to be served or threaten to return drunk and abusive. I was a well-known nasty drunk, so this threat almost always worked. I also had racked up a lot of fully paid "Frequent Flier Miles" with these dealers, so I figured I earned a free trip once in a while. Sometimes, with no money and no "goodwill" service, I would shoot up blood-laden speedballs that some dealers kept in their freezers. The freezer dope was left over when dealers failed to hit a vein, but couldn't bear to throw away the $100 worth of cocaine, speed and heroin. Warmed up, these syringes full of hazardous waste provided quick fixes for me. This method was horribly dangerous, and for reasons known only to God, I do not have HIV as I tell this story today.

Around this time, I began to keep company with a dealer named Eve* who lived on Divisadero. I met Eve's teen-age daughter first, but after some awkward close encounters, the girl "gave" me to her mother. Eve was surrounded by an entourage of the seemingly cool, quirky speed freaks – art students and other greenhorns who were experimenting with drugs. They were devoted to Eve, of course – she had all the drugs. This was a sweet fix for me: Every day I would shoot four quarters of speed for free, work a full-time job, play music in one of my bands, then have sex for hours with Eve and/or her young, adoring ladies in waiting. Then I'd sleep for a couple of hours and start the routine again.

This ideal situation started to grow dull when Eve confronted the dilemma of most female junkies. Women usually blow out all of their veins in a short amount of time because of the extra layer of fat in their skin. Eve would sit for hours, night after night, trying to hit the tiny veins in her fingers and wrists. Hour after hour, she would be hypnotized by the delusion that she could find the lucky vein, only to blow another vein out of commission with a massive hit of speed. This obsession started to cut into our quality time for late-night sex. Finally, I decided to take my "star fucker" status somewhere else.

Looking for Diamonds

I was deep into drugs, living out of a bus parked in a lot outside some music studios in an industrial part of town at Third and Hudson. People died daily there from drive-by shootings and drug deals. Once, I was painting a warehouse wall at about 3 in the morning when a car full of armed men drove by. Someone fired an automatic weapon in my direction, spraying bullets into the wall where I'd been painting only moments earlier. I took my life into my hands every time I went down the street to buy beer. I always wore my tool belt in case I needed to defend myself in hand-to-hand combat. If I didn't have the tool belt handy, I picked up bottles from the gutter and was ready to use them.

These music studios were right next to a sewage treatment facility, so mosquitoes were a constant pain in the ass. I would drink a six-pack of Budweiser 16-ouncers and go to sleep. When I woke up, I had bruises on my face from beating myself up trying to hit the mosquitoes on my face and ears. One night, as I slept in my bus, a black man came around, looking for something to steal. I had no way of locking the door, which had been broken into so many times. I woke up and looked out the window just as he looked in, and we screamed in each other's faces. He ran off as if he'd seen a ghost, and I jumped up and hit my head. I ran outside half-naked, wanting to tell him to come back and not be afraid, but he was long gone. I also wanted to thank him for this chance meeting that turned out to be so funny, and how I appreciated the wakeup call on so many levels of life.

I did a construction job at a children's entertainment center in the area called Play and Leave. I was putting up a 4-foot-high barrier to keep the 16-and-older crowd from giving crack to the little kids. I was the only white man for miles. On a typical day, the police would show up with their guns drawn for a domestic call, like some guy holding his wife hostage with a shotgun. The cops would cordon off the area and look awkward, leaving us, the audience, with nothing better to do than watch to make sure there was no police brutality. I would always be the one screaming from an otherwise all-black crowd, "Kill Whitey!" The blacks would laugh, but I was for real.

Drive-by shootings and holdups were commonplace in our neighborhood. My favorite store was Kennedy's Liquors. I happened to be there when someone came in to hold it up and sprayed the room with bullets. We all huddled in the back of the store, doing our best to be invisible. We were skin-tight, packed in like sardines, waiting for the danger to pass. I welcomed the human smells of the other people in the pack; our bodies' needs for communal safety were being met. The bullets kept spraying to keep everyone scared, flinching and in a heightened state of Post-Traumatic Stress Disorder. The sound of gunfire was a repetitive-stress injury in this neighborhood.

By now, I was a drunk who would walk from one liquor

store to the next. I could find my way to any point in the city by charting how many liquor stores I would pass on the way. This mapping system meant I often would pass out during the day and sleep in parks where it seemed safe. My paranoia and status as an eternal outsider turned into full-fledged "institution-phobia." I was no longer willing to use public transportation or enter any public buildings. I had a hard time even entering a grocery store. This paralysis lifted only when alcohol was involved; if I was buying beer, I could walk into any structure without hesitation.

My speed-fueled nights were still spent digging through debris boxes, following the route of "Put Out Night." A network of dedicated junkies followed the "Put Out Night" route as it moved around the city. We would find cameras, computers, dishes, you name it. The junkies would descend on the trash and make an awful mess. I came along later than most and would clean up the night's disarray, usually finishing just as the garbage truck pulled up. The drivers were always grateful to see that at least one of these bottom-feeders was responsible. During this time of my addiction, it was the one accomplishment I could be proud of. As I dug through debris boxes in the dark, my hands and arms cut and bleeding from broken glass, I sometimes would notice shotgun shells left on top of the trash as a warning to people like me. I didn't care. Even when people yelled from windows that they were going to kill me if I didn't get out of their trash, I would dig onward. Delirious, deranged, I thought, "What are you gonna do, kill a dead man?"

Some days, I would go on job interviews. I'd start the day at the Goodwill to buy a suit, then have a beer and head for the interview. These interviews were for any kind of job that I'd heard of and thought I could do. Afterward, I'd stop at a dealer's house, and I'd look so nice in my suit, I'd usually get an especially good deal. I would do a hit of speed, and then it was off to the races. Three days and three nights later, I usually would still be in the same suit, now filthy and ragged, digging through the trash. Occasionally, a guy cruising for men would stop by a dumpster and inquire about my availability. My offer was always the same: If you want to be with a stinking mess, you're on, but only if you want to give me head and, of course, if you have drugs. Then it was back to a stranger's place for all-night sex that usually left me worn to the bone. But gays always had the best speed, so I would override my Catholic guilt and confusion for a good high.

My honesty and integrity became blurred, as my needs for drugs and sex became more desperate and the surroundings grew ever more violent and dangerous. One after another, I crossed line after line of "the things I would never do." I deteriorated into a babbling crazy man with no grip on reality. I could be found on my knees day and night, "looking for diamonds" among the endless shards of broken glass in the ghettos. To protect myself from the gang and drug violence around me, I would arm myself with a rolled-up Playboy to beat people with, or a stick that was 4 or 5 feet long that I would twirl like a baton at anyone who looked menacing. I looked like a ninja nut in the middle of the street, twirling my magic wand of protection. If I happened to be carrying a musical instrument, that would become my weapon. I might be found walking the streets in the dark of night, playing a sax with a bayonet stuck in its bell. My defense methods worked to repel people who preferred their victims to whimper with fear and beg for mercy.

I was the crazy guy who stared at the sidewalk, babbling incoherently to myself, shooting the occasional question at a passing stranger who would quicken his pace and look the other way. All I wanted was some help, some truth. I was tired. I would get on my knees and blow at the cracks in the sidewalk until the dirt covered my face and left raccoon circles around my eyes. I sometimes would see gang members committing crimes or violence, and if I failed to remain invisible, they would walk over to ask what I was doing. "Looking for diamonds," I would reply. They would usually laugh, or one would stir the dirt with his shoe and say, "Here's some diamonds, man!"

Once I was told they were going to kick my fucking ass. I looked up calmly and said, "I don't think so." I was crouched beneath a stop sign with a rolled-up magazine in my hand. Without warning, I jumped straight up and slammed the stop sign with the magazine with one forceful punch. The impact made a loud "bang" in the middle of the night. "OK, OK, crazy man," they said, backing away. "OK, bato. He's fuckin' loquito, man."

Usually the trauma of street life kept me from falling asleep on the pavement, but once, I did drop in my tracks from sheer exhaustion between two parked cars on Mission Street. I was awakened by the disjointed ramblings of a street wino known as Bear. He kicked me to get me up out of the street. If you value your life, one thing you never do is kick a sleeping street person. I jolted awake and yelled, "If you don't get the fuck away from me, I will kill you, motherfucker!"

He laughed and said in his gravelly voice, "Come on – you get up now, I got a great joke to tell you." I wearily stumbled to my feet and felt my body sweat out the last bit of water in my soul. The smell of the street, strewn with poppers, cigarette butts, and used rubbers, was on me and in me. My ears acclimated to the bus horns and car brakes, and I blinked in the bright sun of the Mission.

"Get the fuck away from me," I said feebly. But he just laughed again and launched into his joke. I didn't have the strength to resist, and nowhere to go except to dig through the trash of the nearby fruit stands to look for rotted fruit for breakfast. So I stood, blinking in the hot sun, and listened.

"A guy goes into a tattoo parlor and asks the artist to

tattoo a hundred-dollar bill on the end of his cock. The
artist goes, 'Hey, wait a minute, buddy, why do you want
a hundred-dollar bill tattooed on the end of your cock?'
'Well,' the guy says proudly, 'I like to pull my money out. I
like to play with my money and watch it grow. And I want
to see if my old lady can blow a hundred dollars without
leaving the house!'"

I looked at him with all the forlorn, infinite sadness
in my bones, and all of a sudden, laughter erupted from
me. We laughed until I cried. I swear that man saved my
life and gave me hope with his ridiculous, inappropriate,
gender-insensitive joke. I was saved, for another moment.

By now, I knew I was severely mentally challenged.
I knew a lot about the words used for people in my
condition. I lived in constant multi-personality, alcohol- and
speed-induced psychosis. I could create ways to be both
a hypochondriac and a healer, fooling myself into and out
of every form of pestilence known to man. I called myself
"double-psychotic paranoid schizophrenic." This pretty
much covered all the crazy feelings I had from one minute
to the next. I had panic attacks, rage disorders, institution-
phobia, authoritarian combative syndrome, bipolar
visions of hypergrandiosity and hypersexuality. At times
it was all I could do to aimlessly walk the streets, crying
uncontrollably, wanting people to understand, to know my
true worth, to venerate my real spirit. In my mind, I was
meant to protect and set to kill. Street poems would run
through my head. This is a street poem I turned into a song.

I Was a Spy for the UFO
I was a spy for the UFO, my mind was willing,
But my body wasn't into killing.
Time and time I had to figure you out.
I was a spy.
I spent my time living on the edge,
my mind clear as a bell,

But when I talked I sounded like a mental vegetarian.
Time and time I had to figure you out.
I was a spy for the UFO.
Time to kill, you know the drill
Where I've been, no one can follow
Can't lie, cheat, beg, steal or borrow
From what I've seen, you all got a long way to go.
I was a spy for the UFO.

Squats were still a prominent part of my life. At any given time, I would have three or four squats going throughout the city. I started a typical squat, known as "the Lord's House," with "Lord Spencer," an African-American man in his early 50s. Spencer was a Black Panther in the '60s, but he'd mellowed out. Now he had access to some of the worst biker bathtub speed on the planet. It seemed to be made of battery acid, Drano and lighter fluid. When cops saw this stuff, they wouldn't even arrest us. We chose this house because while Spencer and I were searching its basement, stuffed with 10 years worth of garbage about 7 feet high, we found a boot. It was brand-new, and the thought of finding its mate drove me to obsessively remove every bit of garbage from that cellar. In the end, we didn't find the other boot, but we had ourselves a house. So I fixed it up.

The next thing we knew, 50 people – pimps, dealers, runaways, criminals on the lam – were coming over to get a shower, do drugs, or just waste time. To claim a house as a squat, all I had to do was find an abandoned place, mail a letter to myself at that address, and voila, I had proof of residence. Eventually, the police, unhappy neighbors or a disgruntled squatter would burn or force us out, and we would move on to the next unoccupied house ripe for the picking.

Every now and then, my small-time junkie path would cross with that of a big-time dealer, catapulting me into a different netherworld where the stakes were higher. In the early '90s, I met a highly successful businessman with a massive speed operation. I'll call him John*. I was willing to do just about anything in exchange for speed, and thanks to my excellent reputation among many dealers as a trustworthy and multi-talented bum, John used me to do quasi-security jobs. He maintained several spots throughout the city to keep his drugs and other booty and moved it around to keep the police confused. Sometimes, he would post me at spots where he wanted to know who was coming and going and when.

Other times, he would give me painting, plumbing or electrical tasks at his businesses – a used furniture store, a record company, and a frame shop, to name a few – and I would greet all manner of people at the door and either admit or deflect. I could find myself at 4:30 in the morning telling police officers that I couldn't let them in because I was "just the maintenance man"; a few minutes later, I might be talking to liars, thieves, and other strange people who came looking for speed. John bought more of his inventory from the Hell's Angels, so I made sideline connections that grew increasingly more dangerous. Whenever the Angels were the cooks, you knew people would be dying and disappearing all around you.

I had been up for weeks when a friend of mine named Winthrop* invited me to join him on a weekend trip to Reno. Winthrop liked to go jogging in Marin County and steal credit cards from mailboxes, so I knew how he was going to pay for our little getaway. He was a nefarious thief, bully and braggart. Whenever we were together, I considered us the modern-day equivalent of Barrabas and Jesus. (That made me "the little Jesus" – uh-huh, that's right.) Winthrop was always involved in activities in which people wound up getting ripped off or killed. When I heard that he pushed a friend of mine off of a roof in the Tenderloin, I made it my personal crusade to get to know him. I always took it upon myself to watch over these types of people – to make sure I didn't just look and wonder, but played an active role in their lives by caring enough to give a damn.

The trip to Reno turned out to be a typical Winthrop vacation: We enjoyed our penthouse suite just long enough for me to take a bath before the phone rang, announcing that the hotel already knew Winthrop was there on a stolen credit card. Still dripping from the bath, I ran out the door on Winthrop's heels into the cold night air. He went gambling, used our 18 bucks to win $2,400, and then proceeded to lose every cent while I begged him to stop. Winthrop wanted to stay and keep gambling and getting hotel rooms on credit, but I'd had enough. Stranded with no money, I called Cindy, who bought me a Greyhound bus ticket, and I rode home with my tail between my legs.

When I got back, I learned that John had been found murdered at one of his stores. His neck and knees had been broken, and he'd been rolled up in one of his own rugs. This meant all the cops, dopers and Hell's Angels were in disarray, trying to reposition themselves around this pusher's void, and some questioned why I had chosen that particular time to go out of town. Even without the paranoia and madness brought on by being constantly high and drunk, I knew it was a dangerous time. But on any given day, I was in contact with three or four different underground worlds of drugs, sex and danger, always drinking hard along the way. I lived in a dark, shady world where boundaries blurred and young people got compromised. It was a world of dealers and music and sex and violence and crime and homelessness and overwhelming danger from day to day. The most overwhelming force of all was the internalized oppression that goes with this lifestyle, wearing you down until you feel like a nobody. The reasons for living become fewer and farther between. But I was about to get a whole new reason to go on living, when I least expected it.

– 24 –

A Family of My Own

In early 1994, my old friend and property developer, Francisco Gamez, contacted me with an attractive offer: Help him clean out the squatter-infested Turk Street Studios in exchange for a room. Homeless and grateful for a place to live, I got down to the business of clearing the 20 or so young junkies out of the building's dozens of nooks and crannies. This turned out to be an absurdly difficult undertaking. These heroin-addicted homeless kids and runaways had decided the studio's hallways were their Neverland escape pod from the streets of the Tenderloin. Led by a young, crazy and stubborn junkie known as Pirate, these squatters were tenacious. First, I tried to drive them out of the basement hallway, but as soon as I got some out, others would let them back in. Then, I tried putting bleach on the basement floor where they slept and shot up, but the kids were oblivious; they just went and laid right on the bleach. Even when the bleach dissolved the fabric and their clothes fell right off their bodies, they didn't seem to notice. I graduated to using fake pipe bombs, making them all run for their lives by lighting them and yelling, "See you later! We're all gonna die!!" But when the bombs didn't go off, they'd run right back in. I screamed at them with a bullhorn; I changed the locks. Finally, they got smart and started crashing with dealers who had rooms, and the turf war ended.

Among these young people were two who stood out from the rank and file. Jane* and David* were educated people in their early 20s who seemed to come from nice, solid backgrounds and had been seduced by drugs. Their faces were on "Missing" posters throughout the Tenderloin, as their parents desperately searched for them. Jane had been a speed freak for a few years, and David was hooked on heroin. They had just come from Texas, where Jane became physically sick and then had a mental breakdown, lost and delirious from the devastating effects of the drug lifestyle. They lived out of cars and hotel rooms, and Jane had a storage unit at a seedy place in the Tenderloin. Jane said she was a lesbian, and David said he was gay, but they had formed an obvious partnership. They did what they had to do to feed their respective habits, while meeting several times each day to eat together and check in.

I rarely developed anything more than a casual relationship with young people on the street, but I was drawn to Jane and David. I appointed myself as Jane's "nurse" and tried to help heal all of her maladies, which were common among speed freaks. Emotional enmeshment was one of the few ways I knew to relate, and I entangled myself completely with Jane. We got high together, and slowly, Jane grew to trust me. I tried to get to know David better, but he was focused on the care and feeding of his heroin habit. I repeatedly attempted to get them to go back home to their parents, as I always did with young people who were not full-time, dedicated Spartan Junkies. We took David back to his parents in Sacramento twice, but he returned to the city both times to resume his lifestyle of choice. He would hang out in a room down the hall where about 15 heroin junkies would sit around in this eerily silent shooting gallery. It was like a cross between an opium den and a belfry full of sleeping bats. When you entered the room, all you could see in the dim light were people in trance-like states; all you could hear was their breathing. Gradually, the studio was emptying out, one room at a time, but it was a real Wild West show. Anyone who was anyone in the junkie world was trying to stay there and maintain this lifestyle. Guns were pulled and knives were thrown, and thugs sent to fuck me up would realize I was not the enemy and get me high instead.

In all my years on the street, I had never taken advantage of the young people I met there. I always tried to help them and encouraged them to go home and quit the junkie life. But the more time I spent with Jane, the more I found myself falling for her – her innocence, her education, her naiveté, her fall so far from her middle-class, educated background. It was another chance for me to find my own identity through helping another person instead of myself. And then, I became enamored.

Jane and I moved from one place to another from day to day, following the drug and work opportunities. We spent one night in a squat in the Haight, baby-sitting a dealer's small children. The apartment was full of garbage and broken dishes, and used dope baggies littered the floor. I gathered about 15 of the bags, combined the dregs and shot up. This was how low I'd fallen. The babies were still happily oblivious to the horrible atrocities surrounding them.

Jane told me she wanted to have a baby, but David could not give that to her at the time because of his sexual orientation to men. I was 38 and had no children; I had never been stable enough to build a family of my own and had no reason to believe I ever would be. Now, a young, intelligent, educated woman wanted me to make her pregnant. Sure, she was a speed freak, but with her stable upbringing and supportive parents, I believed she had a good chance of getting clean. It was clear in my mind that this might be my only chance to father a child. I agreed to try to get her pregnant and then let her and David raise the child. Jane wanted a child so much that she stopped using speed and improved her diet. Without drugs, she became depressed and unstable. But then, it happened – she was pregnant.

With a real baby on the way, I became more connected to wanting a child than ever before. Jane and David were getting excited about the idea of moving to Finland, where David's status as a Finnish citizen would provide valuable perks such as subsidized housing and education. We agreed that Jane, David and I would all move to Helsinki once the baby was born. We would get sober and start our lives over as an unconventional family. It's easy to look back now and see what an impossible long shot this shaky plan was, but at the time, it was the closest I had ever gotten to being part of a family of my own. After two and a half decades of being an invisible, homeless outsider, it seemed like the dream was within reach. Jane moved back to her parents' home in Vallejo, a much healthier environment than the squats we lived in. But then, she had a miscarriage. She returned to San Francisco, devastated.

Back in the city, we both struggled between the dream of a healthy pregnancy and a new beginning, and the pull of the old life of drugs and "free love." She quickly got pregnant a second time, and when she went back to her parents' home in Vallejo, I moved with her. Sweet and loving people, Frank* and Mary* were relieved beyond words to have their daughter home again and striving toward sobriety. We laughed at the irony of our situation: Jane and I were going almost cold turkey, while her father worked as a pharmacist and her mother kept a medicine cabinet loaded with prescription drugs for chronic back pain.

They took me in without batting an eye, even though I was in such pathetic condition that I was embarrassed to meet them. I was skinny, sucked up and dehydrated, with ragged teeth and bad breath, and I knew it. The day we met, I had a piece of metal in my eye after working with a grinder. They rushed me to the emergency room, and then an eye patch topped off my junkie ensemble. I had to stay sober in their house, but I had no way to fathom living without my morning ritual of alcohol, let alone my decades-old habit of quelling my racing mind and emotional discomfort with all the drugs I could find.

Hoping for the best, Frank and Mary began taking me along to their church services each Saturday. One Friday night, Jane waited for her mother to get out of the shower so she could paint Mary's nails. As a joke, Jane painted my toenails while she waited. The next day I was invited to join the men of the congregation in a back room for the ritual washing of feet. I thought nothing of it until I was paired with an elderly man who pulled off my socks and discovered my hot pink toenails. He pretended not to notice and calmly proceeded to wash my feet. I hope I gave him a good laugh once the service was over.

I didn't last long in Vallejo, going cold turkey with no recovery or support. I bolted and went back to the numbness of the drug and alcohol buffet available to me in the city. But when Jane, unable to cope with her parents, came back to the city, I wouldn't have it. I would hunt her down all over town until I found out where she was getting high with "my" baby. The cycle began of me capturing her like a cornered animal, then locking her in rooms of squats to keep her sober and under my complete control. She would try to escape any way she could, and I would become frustrated and violent, hitting and threatening her in a fruitless attempt to control her actions. I made it all about the baby, but in truth, I was a control freak who was terrified of being abandoned and losing this shot at having a family. I just wanted everything to "be OK," but the only ways I knew to interact poured kerosene on the situation and made the chaos expand exponentially. I even called her parents one night to meet me at a major dealer's drug warehouse, where I knew Jane was staying. We cornered her inside, and I warned everyone there that if they gave Jane any more drugs, I would personally kill them. She rebelled completely and ran away again. She got a place of her own in the city with a dealer. I went out of my mind with rage, jealousy and loss of control over her. I would stay up for days, wandering aimlessly and always winding up near her place, trying to manipulate my way back into her life without really giving anyone a choice in the matter.

Somehow after all this mayhem, Jane and I made a commitment to live together in Vallejo. Now I promised to find a place for us to live and to find a job to support us while staying clean and sober – none of which I had any idea how to do. Thanks to the welfare benefits to which Jane was entitled as a pregnant woman, we moved into a small apartment along the wetlands in Vallejo and were able to get food as well. Jane used every bit of credit she had to help pay our way. I had no idea what credit was or how it worked, since I'd never had it. I thought it was free money. Meanwhile, I felt overwhelmed by anxiety and panic attacks caused by my institution phobias, and I had no idea how to get help in any area. I tried to act like I had it all together when I applied for welfare. The welfare worker suggested I get some kind of help for my obvious mental distress. I already knew that I undoubtedly was a sick motherfucker, but now I was struggling to see over walls of paralyzing vulnerability as I tried to be a breadwinner. Anger, victimhood, confusion, inadequacy and resentment washed over me in smothering waves, and I couldn't numb out of any of it. I lashed out at the person closest to me – Jane, who had an unborn child and her own fragile sobriety to protect.

If all that wasn't enough to grapple with, all I had to do was take a step outside our apartment door for more self-destructive opportunities. Our particular neighborhood had already been featured in an episode of "Cops" for its rampant crime and drug trafficking. This neighborhood was pay dirt if I wanted to score drugs, but I was trying my best to be different. I would go to the nearby discount liquor store and sneak as much alcohol as 3 or 4 bucks could buy. I tried to quiet my mind enough to take the driver's license exam, as I couldn't apply for any decent jobs without a photo ID. I had been driving since I was a kid, but I couldn't get through the DMV test without getting lost in the metaphors and parables. Finally, on the third try, I passed by the skin of my teeth.

Jane kept improving and regaining the use of her considerable intellectual skills. She took the California teacher's test and scored in the top 10 percent. I got myself on the C List for the Hod Carriers Union and began dutifully showing up each day to gut through what threatened to be a six-month-long waiting period for work. Then one day, a guy on a motorcycle drove up to look at the red flags that were placed in advance of some type of utility work in our back yard. His name was Cassidy*. He had two wives and a bunch of kids, and he was on probation for trying to assault several police officers some months earlier. He set off all the wrong alarms in my head, and instead of running in the opposite direction like I should have, I became fast friends with him.

Cassidy got me a job as a cement laborer on a six-building school construction project in Santa Rosa. I made the hour-long drive each day in a Maverick with no windshield wipers. In the middle of winter, I would drive in the rain with the windows open so I could see outside and avoid driving into the roadside ditch. The work was tough and exhausting. For the first few months, all I could do was work, eat, have coerced sex and sleep. My whole life, I had lived on the reward system of working hard and rewarding myself. Now, earning more money than ever before, my alcoholism reared its ugly head and demanded to be paid. While I worked hard and clung desperately to my last shreds of self-control, I learned that David had finally made his way to Finland, where he was putting things in place so that Jane could join him there. With my fear of abandonment building, I channeled my discomfort into workaholism. I began making a huge bottle of Mah Huang tea every morning to drink on the way to work. Mah Huang, or ephedra in its herbal form, was an exotic, Chinese way to sneak my speed fix. Then, after a grueling day of work, I would drink beer all the way home, ensuring that I would be a violent drunk by the time I arrived. Around that time, I bought a Mustang 4.0, a car that was far too fast for me, even if I'd been driving sober.

When Christmas Eve arrived, Jane and I got together with Cassidy and one of his wives. Cassidy and I went out for "a drink" and got hammered for hours. Late at night, somehow Cassidy wound up behind the wheel of my Mustang when it was time to drive home. He detoured into a muddy field, where he thought it would be fun to do doughnuts, but in the process, he ran over a fire hydrant. Water shot 25 feet into the air as we struggled to push the car out of the mud. After we gave up and started the long walk home, Cassidy confided that if cops got involved, we had to say someone else was driving, because if he were arrested while on probation, he'd go to prison. We agreed to say an imaginary friend of ours named "Lenny" was driving the Mustang that night, if anyone asked. I threw my keys into the marshland just before some cops picked us up on the roadside and took us to a station in Fairfield.

When the time came to explain what happened with my Mustang, I told the police that "Lenny" was driving – and

Cassidy told them that I was driving. The police didn't like my version, so they sought a confession by giving me the worst beating of my life. They were professionals who knew how to use their night sticks in places that mostly wouldn't show – my kidneys, liver, bladder, a few cracked ribs, the back of my legs, and all of the painful pressure points. They finished with a crushing blow to my forehead. I had lost control of my bladder and bowels during the beating, and my clothes were covered with feces and urine. They took me to the emergency room for a few stitches, then returned me to the observation tank for the night. On the morning of Christmas Day, they released me on my own recognizance, and Jane's parents picked me up. They must have been aghast. I limped, shoeless, in unspeakably filthy clothes, to their SUV and climbed in, breathing shallowly because of my broken ribs. "Merry Christmas," they said feebly. I lived with chronic pain for months afterward.

Life went on like this through the next several months of Jane's pregnancy. I drank and worked full-time, in that order. Despite my desperate wish to be a father and have a partner, I was incapable of achieving either of those goals as long as I kept drinking. I was physically and verbally abusive to her constantly – hitting her in the head, screaming at her, threatening her. When Jane's water broke in the middle of a warm July night, she repeatedly tried to wake me up, but I was too drunk to rouse. We had no phone, so she got dressed and walked to a phone booth to call her parents, who drove her to the hospital. I stayed with her during her 16-hour labor, and it's only now that I can acknowledge the pride and happiness I felt as I watched Jane give birth to our healthy, strong, beautiful son.

The three of us lived together for a very short time, but my drinking and abuse gave Jane no choice. I was a danger to her and to the baby. One night I came home to find them gone. She had taken our son and moved back home with her parents. I was shattered. Alone in a town where I knew no one, I had made my fear of abandonment into a self-fulfilling prophecy. I had been convicted of driving under the influence after the Christmas Eve incident, so I had no license and couldn't drive for a year. I was desperate to speak to Jane or her parents, but they told me they would call the police if I didn't stay away. All I could do was cry. For the first three weeks, I cried myself to sleep and would wake up with blood-covered sheets, because crying made my coke-damaged nose bleed. For months, I cried at the drop of a pin, at the sight of a couple with their child, at the beauty of a sunset. I played out the next few months, trying unsuccessfully to see my child, but that didn't happen. Finally, I returned to shooting speed. Once again, I was medicated and distracted enough to not need alcohol 24/7. I went back to San Francisco alone.

– 25 –

You Are the Disease

As an adult, I have always believed I was a fairy who took people across the Lake of Death to the netherworld. There, with me by their sides, people had to decide whether they wanted to live or die. My personal philosophy at the time went like this: "The least amount of resistance from A to B is Nirvana. There is no mystery, magic or illusion that separates us. Begin now!"

Once people had been so informed, I believed they could not deny their own enlightenment. When they said "I'm sorry" or "I love you," I felt those were empty words they repeated over and over to avoid taking responsibility for changing their behaviors and to dodge their consequences. But those mindless repetitions just hoist them by their own petards. "Petard" is the French word for a cannon used to blow down doors. But in fact, when "I love you" or "I'm sorry" were deployed, the door stayed firm and the blast blew you up instead.

With a belief system like this, I was drawn to people

like my old friend Winthrop, renowned liar and thief. One day, not long after I returned to San Francisco, Winthrop noticed that I was so debilitated by depression that I couldn't function or think clearly. I had been up for weeks and was delirious from sleep deprivation and a serious case of pneumonia. To cheer me up, Winthrop invited me to join him on a trip to New Orleans. I was looking for any distraction from my own dismal failures at that point, so I packed my essentials – a needle and dope – in a paper sack, and loaded my bicycle into the back of his van. Off we went. I hadn't thought to ask him to reveal his revenue streams for this trip beforehand, but that became clear the first time he filled his gas tank and then drove away at a high rate of speed without paying. Same old Winthrop. Full of guilt and remorse, I realized what I was in for: stealing and running like madmen, all the way to Louisiana. The die was cast. We were in motion, headed toward Lake Tahoe.

We stopped at a restaurant to eat, and he got up to use the restroom, then took off. Unable to think straight, I sat there and tried to look cool. I knew if I got arrested, Winthrop would leave me there to rot. I created a diversion in the restroom, then ran for it when the staff was distracted. This trip wasted no time getting crazy. Meanwhile, I was feeling worse and worse, getting sicker and coming down from the drugs and alcohol. Sick as I was, with lungs full of mucus and green snot running freely down my face, I grabbed any chance I could to sleep.

We rolled into Reno. Feeling delirious, I went right to sleep while Winthrop broke into cars and trucks and grabbed whatever he could. He stole sleeping bags, sacks of personal belongings, cameras and other small electronics, all of which he pawned for quick cash so he could go gambling. He moved at a dizzying pace. When I could rouse myself from my near-death slumber, I would watch the master at his trade. At a bar, Winthrop created a distraction by spilling someone's drink at one end of the bar. While everyone was looking in that direction, he took tips off tables and grabbed people's money right out from under their noses.

In the restroom, I saw myself in the mirror – a skinny, sucked-up, dehydrated mess with a disgusting, punk-spiked haircut. Desperately, I tried to clean up my act so I could maintain some invisibility while I was with this crazy man. Really, all I wanted was for Winthrop to strand me in the snow so I could freeze to death and get this awful life over. I knew he was capable of great harm to me, and yet he needed my company. We made quite a strange team.

When we went to get dinner, I ate my steak and eggs right at the counter, looking like a mobile disaster unit. Winthrop ate and, as usual, took off. Before I knew it, the staff had my number and called a state cop. I told them my friend had all the money and had just gone gambling – he would be right back. Since we were in the vicinity of three gambling establishments, I asked them to use the intercom to page Winthrop. An hour later, they put me in handcuffs and prepared to carry me to jail for vagrancy. Right then, Winthrop showed up in a nice-looking jacket, full of apologies. By then, he had stolen enough money to pay for our food, so the cop let me go.

We went straight back to the tables with the windfall Winthrop had acquired by stealing the purses of two distracted gamblers. He would bet on blackjack tables and go on uncanny winning streaks – always immediately followed by agonizing losing streaks during which he couldn't stop playing. Whenever I could, I would grab his chips and go cash them in, and he would turn right around and cash them back into chips. He was totally out of control. But since he knew how to get us free meals and a room on credit, we lived a life of temporary luxury for one night. I drank all the little bottles of liquor and happily watched porn while Winthrop went out to fulfill his nightly destiny of stealing, gambling, and coming back penniless.

We went from town to town through the State of Nevada, and I discovered to my dismay that each city had its own gambling opportunities. I had to get creative to stop Winthrop from gambling. While he pilfered from cars outside of the next casino, I would walk in ahead of him and say loudly, "My husband is coming in here, and he has a real bad gambling problem. Please don't let him spend all his money, or we'll be stuck here in your town!" The people of this Podunk cow town were quite disconcerted to see a stark-raving mad gay man cross the threshold. Winthrop would walk in with fresh money, and they would take one look at his ethnic ass and refuse to open a blackjack table for him. Winthrop was bewildered, having no idea what precipitated this welcome.

By the time we got to Utah, we were desperate for cash. Winthrop walked into a store with a can of Mace and a survival knife and asked them to please buy these items, so we could get on down the road. They saw the red flag standing before them and told him to just take a few items and please leave the store. After getting two cups of coffee using this method, a state policeman pulled us over. He really didn't like Winthrop's lying and stealing demeanor.

"You won't believe this," I told the officer, "but I'm watching this maniac. I promise we will not be heard of again in this fine state of Utah if you let us go."

"You must be the silver-tongued devil boy," the officer replied. "I don't know why in Heaven's name I should let you go."

But he did. Winthrop, who was driving a van he'd stolen from his own sister, had an uncle with a high-profile job with the city. Winthrop's relatives habitually covered up the misdeeds of their black-sheep son. We played that card to qualify the registration and insurance of our vehicle. As for me, I was carrying no ID, but since I was raised in the military, I knew how to put on a good show, reassuring the inquiring party as to whom I was and how they could confirm I wasn't wanted by the law. So off we drove, wide-awake from the adrenaline rush of this encounter.

It was a crisp winter morning, and the snow-capped mountains were beautiful as we headed toward Salt Lake City. On the way, Winthrop pulled over to pick up some kids carrying skateboards. Runaways from Olympia, Wash., they were obviously under-age, maybe 14 to 16 years old. I really didn't want to get tangled up with laws about transporting minors across state lines. I didn't want to dump them out in the cold, but I didn't want to get arrested with them, either. We drove on with the five of them smoking cigarettes in a closed vehicle. I still had pneumonia and struggled to breathe with smoke permeating the air like a disease. I hate smoke and felt so disgusted, I wanted to die. Winthrop scraped together some money, and the kids kicked in their panhandling income, so we could get a hotel room to stay out of the cold. There, still tormented by smoke, I finally passed out.

When morning came, I woke up from a death-like slumber for the second time in months without a shot of speed waiting for me. We hit the road and got to Salt Lake City just in time for a big concert to hit town. The kids were excited and wanted to get out and be part of the action. Winthrop was tired of these nubiles who were too young to sexualize; they had to go. He promised we'd meet them at a gas station after we found parking, and they started walking. One of them accidentally left his skateboard behind. Oh, well – that didn't stop us. We took off, left Utah and found our way across Colorado. Some days later, we pulled into the Kansas Welcome Center to warm up and get coffee and were amazed to see the skateboard runaways. We hit the highway immediately to get away from them.

All along the way, Winthrop and I kept up the pump-and-run routine until we got pretty good at it. But in a one-road town somewhere in Mississippi, we pumped gas and ran – right into the sheriff. Winthrop took off on foot, and I did the same old dance for the thousandth time – he'll be right back with the money, blah blah blah. Winthrop eventually returned with 20 bucks, which we personally delivered to the gas-station attendant with heartfelt apologies for our absent-mindedness. Winthrop told me he'd sweated blood hawking our trusty Mace and survival knife, and this time he'd actually succeeded in selling them. That left us weaponless and more pathetic than ever. I spent many years believing I wasn't part of this cross-country crime spree, but in fact, I was the one pumping the gas. So now, for the first time, I can own my part in this dishonorable behavior.

For me, the jig was up. I'd had enough of this nefarious lifestyle, but I had no place to go. I was in deep, and I was stuck. We stopped to eat in another cow town, and I felt a fatalistic reality of this disreputable lifestyle that I'd managed to avoid my whole life, up until now. I had always been as honest and trustworthy as I could be, but this was different – something had changed. I was finally over my pneumonia enough to come out of the haze and feel all the shame and guilt that was waiting for me. I was no longer a spectator, able to be objective and separate myself with surgical precision. I was the disease. I wrote a song to go with how I felt.

You Are the Disease
You carry it on your lip
Baby, it's on your hip
You're going out to have some fun
You pass it around to everyone
You are the disease, the disease is you
It lives in your vein
Oh, baby, baby, it's in your brain
It's drivin' you insane
Baby, baby, it fits your looks

Baby, baby, it fits your style
It's running rampant, oh, it's running wild
Oh baby, baby, it's on your hip
Baby, baby, it's on your lip
You got it off a toilet seat
You are the disease. You are the disease
Baby, baby, it's on your hip
Baby, it's in your vein
It's inside your brain
Drivin' you insane

As we drove through the bayou, I recollected stories I'd heard of people being tied to trees and left for crocodiles to eat alive in the swamp. Somewhere along the causeways to New Orleans, a bit of hope and inspiration filled my veins. I'd been there before and remembered it as a party town I'd gotten very drunk in. We parked in the old, Mardi Gras part of town, where Winthrop began picking purses and backpacks. This was a dangerous ploy in an insulated neighborhood, and sure enough, Winthrop grabbed a pack from the wrong ruffians, and we were suddenly on the run from rough-looking locals.

We went incognito and stopped in a dingy, horrible-looking restaurant where everything on the menu was expensive. I refused to blow what little money we had on that. I decided to find my preferred nourishment on the street in the form of unfinished drinks that had been left on the sidewalks in the hot, noonday sun. This was a cheap high, and it didn't take much since my immune system was still compromised from my recent pneumonia. Once I had a good buzz going, Winthrop drove us off to his new destination – a large boat in the water. Unbeknownst to me, he'd discovered a new place to gamble.

"Oh, shit!" I said, going off on him. "I'm really over this! Not again! I'm over it – I've had it! I'm done with this bullshit!"

Winthrop promised he would call his father and get money for us to return safely to San Francisco. I relented and believed him one more time, and we boarded the boat. I felt hopeless and out of place in these opulent surroundings. I was drunk and smelled like the streets. People looked at me like I was an insect, and I looked back at them like I wanted to dismember them with my hands. Finally, I went to the restroom and cleaned up the best I could. I still stunk to high heaven of every beer and mixed drink I'd picked up off the street earlier that day.

Meanwhile, Winthrop was on the phone with his rich father, who had heard this story many times before. After 15 minutes, he hung up and went to the cashier's booth to get the money his father had called in with his credit card. Three hundred dollars! Eureka, I was saved! We waited … no money. Winthrop finally called his father back, and this time, he gave me the phone. I promised his father I would be responsible for the money and get us safely back home. I went on and on about how I would not mess up this chance, and how grateful Winthrop and I were. I cordially said goodbye and went to find Winthrop. I was so happy. Walking through the tables, I spotted Winthrop standing at one, with three $100 chips placed on three cards in front of him. The dealer reached out and slid them silently into the house money, and all life and hope drained out of my body.

Winthrop could not believe his bad luck. I could not believe I had just given my good word to his father, and it had turned to shit in less than one minute. As a poor person, my good word was the only thing I had of any value. This turn of events broke me down to about the lowest place I could be. In a hopeless, drunken rage, I screamed obscenities at Winthrop. We got in the van, and he really got it – I was so fucking pissed off, I had had it. I wanted out of the fucking van, and I would hitchhike from here! I was quite the spectacle of terror when I was drunk. I felt superhuman, and my threshold of pain was high. I was ready to rumble and destroy things in a catatonic rage. But of course, all I wound up doing was the same thing I'd done before. The wheels rolled, and I slowly sobered up.

We crossed into Texas and headed toward Beaumont and Houston. The day was beautiful in its own way, and the long and lazy miles drifted into the blackness of night. The alcohol I'd found on the streets of New Orleans was long gone, and I was back in my body, sort of. It was time to get gas. We filled the tank and drove off without paying. The attendant shook his fist at us. Something didn't feel right. It was 11 p.m., and there were few cars on this desolate stretch of highway. This did not bode well when patrol cars were on the lookout for a white van. Winthrop sat in the back seat, getting ready to go to sleep – and that's when all hell broke loose.

Seemingly from out of nowhere, troopers pulled in front of the van, forcing me to stop. With blinding lights and blaring loud speakers, they pulled me out of the van with their guns drawn and slammed me face-down on the ground. Winthrop pretended he was asleep. Handcuffed and furious, I yelled for Winthrop to get out of the van. I tried to stand up, and a trooper trained his Glock on me and yelled, "If you don't lay down, I will shoot your dumb ass, boy!"

I was terrified, with my liquid courage mostly gone, and I shivered in the night coolness. I wore shorts, a T-shirt and flip-flops, and I really felt the coldness of the pavement when the forceful hand of an officer returned me to the ground. The other officer opened the door of the van and found Winthrop hiding under the seat. He yanked him out, and the interrogation began. I smelled of alcohol, so they did a field sobriety test on me, which I failed. I protested, saying I'd just taken the wheel at the gas station and hadn't had a drink in seven hours.

"Then we're arresting you for drunken walking, boy," said one of them, laughing while they shoved me in the squad car. The smell of cigarette smoke and the sound of country music seeped out into the countryside all the way to the county jail. I was shoved into a cold, concrete holding cell with stainless-steel benches and urine on the floor. With no ventilation system, the cigarette smoke from the previous day's inmates remained to suffocate me. I finally passed out in an upright position. The stench of smoke-'em-if-you-got-'ems woke me in the morning. I was horrified at the conditions in the cell and yelled at Winthrop to call his uncle or his rich daddy to bail our asses out of here.

Eventually, a one-armed judge came to see us. He told us he'd lost his arm in World War II, and this was his county. Anything that happened here went through him explicitly. I was a smart mouth, complaining about the conditions and blaming Winthrop entirely for our predicament. The judge gave us the option of visiting with him for six to nine months or making out a check in his name for $460, for which he would let us go, no questions asked. I was astounded and wanted to get all righteous about the illegality of his offer, but Winthrop was smart and asked the judge to please let him make a phone call.

The judge had to let Winthrop out four times to make that call – after all, the judge wanted his money! Finally, Winthrop got his father, who wired the money to the judge. The judge came back and let Winthrop out of the cage, talking to him like he was family (now that he got his money). "You got a good daddy, boy. He must love you a whole lot! I got a boy just like you; he goes out and gets in trouble all over tarnation, and I go get him out of all kinds of scrapes all over the South."

Then the judge stopped and looked at me like I was beggar scum. Slowly, in a stilted manner, he said, "Now, your friend here, I don't know about. He had a real foul mouth, and I don't like his attitude or the way he's been talking about my jail. Maybe he needs to visit down here for nine months on those charges I got him on."

The jig was up. I was stuck in a smoky jail in the Deep South in a T-shirt, short pants and flippers. There could be nothing worse. The judge said to me, "I want to see a real change, real fast, boy. Now, why don't you get on your knees and tell me real pretty why I should let you out of here?" His drawl was controlled and even.

I dropped immediately on my knees and apologized for my behavior and misgivings, promising I would never show my face in his fine county ever again. "How about apologizing to your friend now," the judge replied, "and showing some appreciation for his daddy?" This was tough to do. I swallowed hard, gave the best acting performance of my jail career and apologized. The door clanged open, and out into the morning we went, free men. We had to call Winthrop's dad again to get the van out of holding, and off we went.

Now, I was sure I didn't want to keep this game up. I would be the one to lose, doing the crimes he could get away with – and, I might add, got away with a hundred times in San Francisco. Strong-arm robbery, rippin' and runnin', stealing motorcycles, check fraud, credit-card fraud. I realized that I would be the one to be incarcerated, not him, if we got caught again. I didn't want to do time with a wife named Dick, telling me to come over here and give your wife some head with those purty little lips!

I decided this shit was finally over. I knew how to make it alone. Houston is a big, sprawling city, so I looked hard to identify landmarks. I remembered the time I came out here to visit my friend, Francisco, who built music studios in four states. There was a Civic Auditorium in Houston that looked like a creation of the artist Peter Max; it had a marine theme with aquatic features I couldn't miss. I finally spotted it in the vast flatness of the city, and I asked Winthrop to drive me there and let me out. He was sad that we were parting ways. He would be alone, and as we all know, misery loves company.

The van drove away and left me standing alone in the broiling Houston sun. I walked toward Francisco's four-story building that housed about 120 large music and artist studios. Free at last! I had built many studios for him, so with my hyper-grandiose entitlement issues fully engaged, I knocked on the door and asked for the person in charge. There I stood in my shorts, T-shirt and flip-flops, looking like a refugee with that faraway look in my eyes. That combo platter was enough to earn some beer money from the punks in one of the studios.

I tracked down the manager, a real character named Shotgun Mike – so named because of the shotgun strapped across his back like Rambo. I worked hard to impress upon him how important it was that I get ahold of Francisco so I could cash in a few favors. Unimpressed, Shotgun Mike said he wasn't calling anybody and that I should get the fuck out of his studios if I didn't want my ass kicked. His insolence infuriated me. I was drunk from the beer money and used my foul mouth to emphasize exactly who I was – and who I thought he was, carrying around a shotgun as an extension of his penis. He gave me a look of deadly disdain and said, "You remind me of a deer in the sight of my hunting rifle."

I continued to blather on incoherently, but inside, I was getting scared. I was not welcome here, and the sun was setting. I had no money and no one to call for help. I was alone. I gave up and started walking aimlessly around the industrial part of town, looking for shelter or any way to survive. It had been a long time since I found myself in a new place with no options. Walking the streets on speed was certainly familiar, but now I was exhausted from sleep deprivation and alcohol consumption. Then, it started to rain. With my scant clothing, the coolness of the night soon turned cold, and I returned to the only place I knew – the studios.

The studio doors were locked and impermeable, and a

long loading dock ran along part of the building. I looked
under the dock with trepidation. All I saw was darkness,
trash, tumbleweeds, broken glass and gravel. But it was
relatively dry. So I crawled in and lay down in the cool,
dank dirt, with water dripping all around me. There, I
passed out. The night before, I got only a few hours of sleep
in a smoky jail. I had flashbacks to my childhood runaway
days. A cry for help to God from a runaway child; these
memories I remembered well. But now, I was 39 years old.

I woke up the next day with spider bites, suffering from
exposure, and looked at the stark reality of my situation.
I carefully navigated my way out of this hellish place and
into the cool morning air. I immediately began searching
for help. I walked toward the downtown area and asked for
assistance, and I was treated like a bum – a worn-out piece
of shit. Then, I dragged my tired bones from one possibility
to another. Houston is a big city with its resources sprawled
over miles and miles of walking. Finally, I found shelter for
the night, although the safety of this dark place was dubious.
Everyone worked each other relentlessly for whatever they
could muscle out of them. I was lucky; all I had was the
merciless realization that I didn't want to stay there for long.

I was given some clothing so I could get a job at the
temporary employment agency there. The shoes were tight
and gave me blisters immediately. I got some socks, but
that just made it worse. The heat was sweltering, so no
matter what you wore, it was drenched by the time you
walked a few miles in the blinding sun. Somehow, I got
some day jobs that paid about $4 an hour. Then, I landed
a few days of work at the Houston Coliseum while the
rodeo was in town. I worked a pretzel booth next to a malt
liquor stand, right in the middle of the complex. I watched
the calf-roping, bull-riding and horse-riding competitions,
and then late at night, the music started. I didn't have
anything else to do, so I worked 12-hour shifts. I saw all the
country greats with their red, white and blue fanfare. Reba

McEntire performed with three of her country girlfriends and dazzled the crowd. I was really impressed with her show. I also saw the members of ZZ Top standing in a cordoned area, so they would not have to fight the madding crowd to get to the stage.

When it got late and the people shuffled out of this amazing structure, I would walk along the seats and pick up trash. My real goal was to get to the top of the roof and see if I could gain access to the catwalk high above the arena. I got way high, but couldn't get through the keyed doors to the top. I did find a cool camera, though, and pocketed my bootie for the day. I also found a jacket and hat, and my wardrobe, although mismatched, was looking good.

I finally got ahold of my friend Francisco, who rolled out the red carpet for me and introduced me as a quality person to his crowd of artists and musicians. This led to a real shift in my personality. I softened and enjoyed the great people I met. I stayed on as a guest, doing little things for Francisco, until I started drinking again and brought this honeymoon period to an end. I wanted to go back to San Francisco, so Francisco tried to put me on a Greyhound bus. But the police pulled me off, saying I couldn't travel in my inebriated condition and that I was a danger to myself and others. Proving them right, I babbled incoherently and then passed out cold. We tried it again the next day, but this time I was smoking crack with the locals around the Greyhound station and picking up hookers. I was pulled off the bus again and told not to return to the bus station, or I would be incarcerated.

Francisco broke down and bought me an airline ticket back to San Francisco. He was careful to give me no extra money I could use to get drunk. But, many passengers on the plane had complementary drink tickets they weren't using, so I took it upon myself to entertain the troops on this flight. By the time I got back to the city, I made a lot of temporary new friends and was extremely drunk.

– 26 –

The Last Squat

After I got back to the city, one of my first stops was the house of a dealer, an African-American man named Pierre. An HIV-positive hairdresser, Pierre did all of his dope transactions under the guise of haircutting. I loved Pierre for his carefree lifestyle and his ability to show that love crosses all boundaries. He was funny and full of life, able to see beyond my heterosexual fears. Over time, Pierre managed to help me work through all of my discomfort around being with a gay man, and we became lovers. We had an agreement: I would do household maintenance, cleaning and massages, and Pierre would deliver the drugs and the blow jobs.

It was an honest alliance that worked; he became one of four dealers I frequented during the week. This was the secret part of my life – the gay part. I am not ashamed of it, but I didn't think the rest of America had the bandwidth to understand, so I lived many other lives at once. Pierre and I shared a happy, shining, loving energy that lasted two

years. He let me stay at his pad and was my comfort in the
storm. But I was a fast-moving hurricane through the lives
of others, and eventually, I disappeared.

When I resurfaced after my cross-country trip, I was
heartbroken to find Pierre in the last stages of full-blown
AIDS. It seemed that when I left the city, he stopped taking
care of himself and just let go. Now, he had all the ominous
signs of death. He writhed in his bed, yelling insane things
that a broken, unchecked mind would say in delirium. I
tried to recapture the positive energy we had in the past,
but it just wasn't the same. He was beyond reach and didn't
want to see anyone. I had broken some deep, unspoken
code, and he decided to check out.

Pierre had a black, live-in lover – a well-endowed
"house mouse" who had serviced Pierre's hedonistic needs.
I was so lonely, still grieving for Jane and my baby. The
house mouse told me to stay. It soon became clear that he
was lonely, too, and seeking comfort. And he had drugs! I
had been clean for weeks while I was in New Orleans, and I
really wanted to get high. This now becomes a classic story
of how people can die from their mistakes when they're
grieving and unable to see clearly. I was a person who did
little maintenance shots of speed so I could maintain for
weeks on end and not burn out. I was a prime candidate for
a "hot shot," shots people mix up when they want to kill
you. I did not know this man, and I thought he might just as
well kill me while we got it on.

The mouse gave me a tantalizing look at the needles and
began to mix up the shots. We stood in a dark, smelly room
with trash piled up to our hips, computer parts everywhere,
garbage that hadn't been taken out for weeks, electrical
wires and lamp parts, food that had been left uneaten in
white plastic containers. We poured water from a tap into
a dirty glass. In the next room, I could hear Pierre shouting
crazy things. I felt so much shame; he had brought so much
joy to my life, and now I was so close, yet unavailable. I

stayed in the darkness and did the biggest hit in years.

I was paralyzed, so comfortable I couldn't move. I slid some trash over and made a place to lie down, feeling like a stunned fish. It seemed like hours went by as the house mouse gave me head, then turned his attention to my ass.

"Don't do this!" I protested weakly. "Do you have AIDS??"

"Don't worry," he said reassuringly as he mixed up another shot. "It's OK."

I looked blurrily at him, trying to hang on to some control. I asked how he knew which needle was which, wondering if he had mixed them up or if he even cared. I was confused, feeling my loss, tormented by the sound of Pierre in the next room. I did the shot and went into a euphoric state of temporary bliss. The house mouse took his opportunity and returned to the patient work of gaining entry. By the time he accomplished his goal, I could not believe I was so relaxed, after a lifetime of fears about anal sex. I also was so high, I thought I was astral-projecting this experience to Pierre in the other room. Here I was, giving another man the only thing Pierre had wanted from me. When the house mouse climaxed, I wondered what the fucking big deal had been my whole life. Do this and you're good; do that and you're bad. None of it mattered anymore. Pierre was dying in the next room, and that's all that was real at that moment. That was the last time I saw him.

I went back into the lifestyle I knew so well. I wandered in the morning sun and started digging through the trash on my endless quest. Did maintenance shots, drank, worked, and wandered. In between the craziness, I would stay with Cindy. She had been there for 14 years or more, always with a room to sleep in or space in her bed when there was no room in her apartment. I owe her my life. She always gave me a sane place to be, and she always accepted the person I was beyond the disease of addiction and my mental-health problems. I would go to her and tell her of the atrocities going on in the world; she would relate the hardships of going to work and dealing with people there. I would eat, sleep, and then it was back to the drugged-out races and the vicious cycle. I would be dead many times over without her sanctuary through the years. In a way, I was recreating my father's pattern: Disappear for 13 days, show up for two or three, and then off again. The difference between my father and me was that he was supporting a family, and I was a bum who showed up for victim relief – a shower, some warm food, and the snuggly body of someone who loved me unconditionally, to her detriment. The terror I brought with me … I usually had life and death at the tip of my tongue. And the relief she must have felt when this poor, disheveled creature went back out into the darkness of his life.

In my wanderings, a squat on South Van Ness Avenue in San Francisco caught my attention. I heard that a couple of friends of mine had died after spending time there, and I had to find out why. The friends, drugged and depressed, had gotten heavily loaded, then taken a couple of masks and a large container of nitrous oxide over to the Army Street freeway. There, they got comfortable in the bushes alongside rush-hour traffic, put on the masks, turned on the nitrous and went to sleep. Their bodies, partially decomposed with the masks still on, were found about three weeks later.

I was an exposed nerve, someone who could feel all of this and process none of it. I believed I was a clairvoyant thought sent by God to help people like this learn to love themselves. Everybody, no matter what they do for a vocation, deserves to have a chance to live a quality life spiritually. Armed with this mission, I went to the Van Ness house. The house was a large Victorian owned by a former football player who'd been hit in the head a few times too many. Now it was a squat full of an eclectic bunch of Wild West misfits. The place had three stories, a basement and an attic, and every last corner had someone living in it. It smelled to high heaven from the trash the occupants constantly dragged in. They were masters of "Put Out Night," when San Franciscans would put objects they wanted to discard out on the curb. They would arrive before the trash trucks and pick out what they could try to sell for drugs. The front door had been kicked open so many times, it had been permanently unlockable for a year and a half. Anyone could come in, but you entered at your own risk. The people there lived by their own codes of ethics, so you had to be brave and tough to hang out there. From the attic, you could peep into every room on the top floor, including the shower, if you wanted to be a voyeur. The top floor had four rooms, and every one was full of people shooting up. It was a real shooting gallery.

I discovered I knew everyone living at Van Ness, but I initially was not welcomed in any way. I definitely was not cool or hip enough to get past the hallway, so I would sit on the stairs and wait, sometimes for days, for someone to come out of a room and sell me $5 or $10 worth of speed. Denny*, one of my music-studio friends, had a room there and started to let me come in out of the hallway for short periods of time. I had no money or connections and nowhere else to go, so after I would make my rounds all over the city, I found myself returning to Van Ness with more regularity.

I began to meet the locals and the crazies, like Paco, the local crazy guy on heroin. He was for hire to do unspeakable deeds and had loose connections with the Mexican gangs and dope dealers from the Mission. He was indispensable when people wanted drugs, but otherwise, he was a liability. Paco was always angry, macho and badly in need of heroin. He was willing to do anything to get it. The night I met Paco, he was sitting on the stairs constructing three Molotov cocktails he wanted to use to burn down the house of a dude who had wronged and disrespected him in front of his posse. There we sat, two outcasts on the stairs among bicycles, trash and computer parts – Paco seething, and me trying to talk him out of his arson plan. We wound up getting very close, connected on a level of being fully outcast, even from our own people. He had just gotten out of prison and didn't want to violate his parole, so he hung in the shadows with me.

Eventually, I got to know the owner, William*. A tall, big-boned man, William had been a tackle in the NFL way back, before the padding was improved. He was like an old boxer, a little skewed in memory and mind. He lived on the second floor with his wife, and you often could hear her screaming at the top of her lungs. She was a person with mental-health issues, an abuse survivor, and she would shriek as if she were trying to shatter glass. The reasons William never really complained about the rest of the house were to cover the instability of his own life and to satisfy his religion-based desire to help others – a very nice theory, but hard to put to practical use.

William would walk through sometimes and grab anyone he could find to muscle people for rent. The people upstairs would pay a little for the privilege of living there, depending on how much dope money they had to spare, but nothing consistent. When William came through, all the doors in the house would shut and lock, as 20 or so people dodged seeing or paying him. One of the tenants went on a bogus rent strike, and that attracted the city's attention. Inspectors came in and condemned the place as uninhabitable. I happened to be there when the first orders came in for the occupants to clean it up or get out. Suddenly, I was in high demand among the tenants – fixing wiring, putting in locks, trying to patch the roof, repairing the plumbing. Everyone had been flushing their needles down the toilets, along with all kinds of newspapers and clothes they used as toilet paper, so raw sewage was coming down from the second floor and spraying the trash area below. The overflow would come up from the paved trash area and flood sewage all over the back-porch area where William's dog was tied up. The upstairs sink drained straight out the window and onto the side of the building.

People constantly came in off the streets and took showers, leaving the facilities an unsightly mess. We're talking infections; abscesses from shooting up with unclean needles; hepatitis C; HIV; chlamydia; gonorrhea; HPV; colds, viral infections and athlete's foot, to name just a few of the pestilences encountered. For some precious cleanup and quality sleep time off the streets, these people would trade drugs or give their bodies for sex. Some of them were nefarious criminals who had just gotten out of prison. They didn't last long. Everyone there was taking care of their own business. All of this added up to the red tag nailed to the front door.

For the work of making this huge, squalid squat habitable again, I was paid in drugs. But the house remained a high-traffic area, with about 60 people per week coming to buy. Most of them were so drugged out, they didn't get the implications of any legal parameters. They would piss on the carpets that covered the floors and stairs and bring more trash in with them. As I would empty debris box after debris box, the tenants would fill the rooms up with new stuff. Each room was filled until there was room to sit only on top of the trash – with a little floor space left on the fringes for dogs or cats to relieve themselves. There were fleas throughout the house, and if you sat in any room too long, you had welts to show for it. Anyone who was strung out and paranoid would wind up going insane from the delusion that things were crawling all over them. In that house, the delusion was real.

I was old friends with one guy who squatted there named Baum*. He and I had similar lifestyles; he would take off for weeks at a time, come back for a bit, then take off again. Like me, Baum also drifted around the drug world, moving from dealer to dealer to keep his highs up, so he had to process the dangers of that tumultuous lifestyle, too. He had a hot, young girlfriend with blond dreads, but the life of speed and heroin had taken its toll on her. Much worse, Baum had two German shepherds who had pissed and shit on the floor so much, it had become a smooth surface of nothing but scraped shit. The uncleaned-kennel smell permeated the air.

Faced with all this, I finally had to pour gallons of bleach on the floors to work on the stench. Trash bags were a total novelty in the house, so I began handing them out liberally. I figured it could only help me to get them into the habit of at least putting their garbage into bags. I spent hours upon hours crushing everything into its smallest size, then cramming as much as I could into the limited waste cans I had available. I would fill William's car to bursting every day and pack as much as I could into friends' vehicles, and then we would go on massive excursions to distribute our waste around the city in big commercial trash receptacles.

I quickly proved to William that I could do anything he needed. I would go out at night and keep people on the lookout for the materials I required to fix the toilets, sinks and kicked-in walls. After fixing the kicked-in front door a few more times, I installed a lock and then handed out many, many keys to anyone I deemed likely to break it in. The house would have to decide who they didn't want. After that, the way to get into the house was to wait outside – or, if you came for drugs, to call before you showed up so someone would let you in. The other, more hazardous way to gain entry was to use the side door, which led to the dealer's place in the basement. Then you took your chances going up the side stairs through all the trash and clutter. This system was an improvement, as the front door got kicked in only every few months from that point on.

To get to the kitchen, you had to go through Pacman's*
room and risk running into his crazy psycho girlfriend. If
you made it, you found a 6-by-8-foot room with a stove,
a refrigerator, and piles of trash and dirty dishes. There
was just enough space to stand in front of the sink, which
looked like a place where Jeffrey Dahmer would do his
business. It was heavy with the stench of rotting meat
and putrid fluids, with molds growing on everything. The
small space that was meant to be a dining area always
housed five or six heroin addicts, nodding off while they
waited to score. Any closet space in the halls was saved for
transients' belongings. Of course, the joke was that once the
stuff went in there, no one would ever see it again.

I managed to get into people's rooms or into the attic
once in a while to sleep. The attic was a massive room with
rugs from the neighborhood covering its floor. It was dark
and musty, and you could feel around and quickly come up
with some shiny trinket in the blackness. I, naturally, was
always looking for some dope.

Now that the city was involved, the race was on between
the inspectors and me. Concerned citizens couldn't help
but notice the people sleeping out in front of the building
or under the front steps, waiting to score. The neighbors
wanted this pestilence out of their neighborhood. The
police couldn't empty a house that big with that many
tenants on their own. Inspectors would stream in, citing
the plumbing, the wiring, the non-compliant construction,
load-bearing walls that had been removed, trash and filth.
Nuisance properties like this often wound up being burned
down by "someone." When the front door was wide open,
the police would come right in, but the raids just wound up
ruffling feathers. Everyone barricaded themselves in their
rooms, and the police would have had to tear down the
walls to get to them. I just kept working as fast as I could.

William kept his badly neglected, old hound dog tied
up by the stairs. The dog was covered with sores and had

infected ears and pus oozing from his eyes. He had such a horrid case of fleas, he smelled like rotten flesh. Unable to stand seeing the dog neglected this way, I began to take him for walks. He really started to come alive when it was time for a walk. Old, sick and confused, the sound of the side gate opening would make him bolt and take off. William would drive around looking for him, and I would spend time looking for this wonderful dog, too. He was one of the dearest friends I made during this time.

– 27 –

Loose Cannon

The area of South Van Ness between 20th and 21st streets where I lived was overrun with gangs, drugs and prostitution. Two Mexican gangs fought for its turf in block-by-block warfare. Once when I was sitting on the front steps on a beautiful, sunny day, kids across the street from one gang started jeering at kids from another gang on my side of the street. Without warning, the threats and name-calling turned into guns blazing. It was just as natural as the sun coming out to shine. You could tell they had no experience with aim as the bullets sprayed all over the place. Now I could understand why innocent women and children were always in the paper as victims of gang warfare. I just sat there, not wanting to draw attention to myself as a witness, and they kept shooting as they ran up the block, trying to hit each other. I thought I had it under control; I was real cool and laughed out loud at how natural this event seemed to be. It wasn't until I stood up that I realized I was in shock and my knees were knocking. I guess I was temporarily stunned by how quickly a sunny day turned into a shooting match.

At night, women patrolled our blocks, looking for tricks. They hung out under the cover of the trees in front of our house. Sometimes they would come in, score some heroin and hang out for a few hours. William had a thing for young blondes in distress, and he would continually fall for any unbelievable ruse as he tried to help them. He always stuck to his spiritual path, but his wish to help these women made him vulnerable. William and his wife wanted to adopt, and he was relying on me to fix the house, get the disreputable tenants out, and turn the Victorian into a respectable place.

By now, the neighborhood had coalesced, and the city had a point person coordinating all of the charges against the house's legal right to exist. I was getting $50 a day to buy speed and work on the house. I took it as my last chance to do something good, to fill the hole in my soul and redeem myself as a good person. I had to kick out, one by one, all of the tenants, while making sure the Mexican gangs and the Hell's Angels were on board, or I would be killed just walking down the street. After all, the house's occupants bought major amounts of heroin from the Mexican dealers and speed from the Hell's Angels. It was a battle to get anyone to move out, at first. The first tenant to go was Greg, and he was not going without a fight. He grabbed a metal rod used for barbell-lifting and went into a psychotic rage, putting the bar through the wall into the bathroom, through the floor and into the dining room ceiling. He just trashed the whole room and then stood there like a matador with the rod, gesturing, posturing his insanity, and welcoming me to fuck with him. I let him tear up whatever he had to, but once he was done, he had to go. Greg left, threatening the whole house with his destruction, ostracized by everyone. Finally, a room was vacant. The inspectors had a field day proving what a disaster the house was. After that, I would often see Greg at flea markets; he was still sore at me, but at least he wasn't threatening to kill me anymore. With that kind of beginning, I knew this was going to be a rough road to go down.

By now, I had an entourage of my own drug-taking community of friends, showing up and wanting to hang out. I used this as my first opportunity to show my work. The deal was, I would get just enough money for us to get high, and they would work for a hit of speed and a place to sleep. But it was hard to sleep on a hit of speed. I left to take care of some business for a few hours, and while I was gone, my friends decided to do some painting. To match the texture on the walls, they concluded they needed to add some sand to the paint. The only sand they could find was in a litter box. This was typical of the insanity of working with crazy, drugged-out people. When I came back, the wall matched perfectly, but the smell of urine and used cat litter lasted for weeks.

Every room in the house was still full up to the waist with heavy, unmovable objects and metal pieces that had been dragged into the house through the years. Room by room, I had to find ways to disperse what I could not take to that night's "Put Out" location. I would take load after load to debris boxes all over the Mission, rearranging the trash that was already there and filling the bins up to the top. Objects that were too large for that would be taken to the Goodwill or the Salvation Army. I would leave bags of putrid clothes, mattresses and broken objects. I am ashamed of this part of my experience, but there it is – the truth once again. I would take trash to all these places, then bring each night's collection of found construction materials back to the house.

At the Goodwill and the Salvation Army, it was common practice for people to pilfer through donations that were left overnight. With the new goal of fixing up Van Ness to rent to college students room by room, I needed to furnish the whole house with found objects. I collected clean mattresses; dressers I glued back together and fixed up; rugs; silverware; dishes; pots and pans; light fixtures; tables and chairs; bookshelves – room by room, I amassed enough articles to furnish the Victorian and start renting rooms while I rehabbed the rest of the building. This whole process took a total of two years.

Our first real tenant was Wendell*, a structural engineer who had fallen from grace and was trying to get back on his feet. Wendell got to know a prostitute from the area who was chipping down, trying to wean herself off of heroin and change her life. Her face and character had been broken by the harsh lifestyle of being around abusive, ruinous men who violated her in every way. I helped her wean off of heroin with speed, and she and Wendell kind of became bedfellows. They turned his room into a love nest. She worked during the day doing construction and was Wendell's lovebird at night. It was quite a sight to see this beer-drinking, cigarette-smoking woman with broken front teeth, talking like a raspy construction worker by day, then dressing up for her boyfriend at night. It was the opposite of seeing a flawless movie star make herself up to look worse than she really did; this woman looked better in my eyes because of the great journey she was on. She worked out great for several months and became quite an assertive, demonstrative person, capable of deliberating for her needs. She was very impressive.

One day, she decided to go visit some of her old clients to show them how much she had changed. They happened to be some of the notorious, macho men of the Mexican heroin trade. Apparently, they didn't like her new ways of living or communicating, because they killed her, cut her body up into several pieces, and stuffed her into trash bags. Trash collectors discovered parts of her when the bags broke in their truck's compactor. I found out what happened to her when the coroner's van showed up outside the house,

and the worker started asking me all kinds of questions
about her. I never knew her real name; I only knew the
street name she used as a hooker. When I found out that
they had killed someone who was trying to get out of this
hellish, vicious, nightmarish world of shadows we lived in,
I fell apart.

It really hit me that I was alone – and not only that,
I was being monitored and watched more closely than I
ever realized. How could she have been traced back to
me so quickly? Now all the ominous death threats and
warnings I'd been receiving lately started to make sense.
I had ignored all of it. I had been threatened by so many
angry people and by friends of friends who wanted to do an
anonymous favor by just twisting my shit up and leaving
me dying in a pool of blood. After she was killed, I started
hearing Mexican gang members all around, in the back
yards and out front, using Bic lighters in their click system
of communication. I would hear the clicks late at night, at
times when there was usually silence and an occasional car.
At first, I tried to protect myself by nailing shut all of the
windows and screwing the front door shut. The house had
about nine points of entry.

I was so paranoid, and it started to show. I started
hearing noises and freaking out. I saw the six or seven
bums across the street talking to the henchmen. I saw
the actions of all, and I knew I was next. I was really
ready to die. After about two weeks of crazed paranoia, I
surrendered. Moaning and crying, I opened up all of the
doors and windows and just welcomed death to come
sweetly knocking. I was always up until 4:30 in the
morning, so familiar with the night. I would have to be
foolish not to know what was up. I had lived with death
all of my life, and I usually had a spirit that replaced the
stillness of death with movement and life. This time, I
curled up and relaxed with the ominous specter that was all
around me.

Then, the clicks stopped. The endless exaggeration
of danger ceased, and my constant attempts to thwart
impending doom came to a halt. I walked calmly into
the streets that were so comfortable all my life at 4 in the
morning, without a weapon, with tears in my eyes. You
see, there is nothing you can take from a person who has
nothing to lose. What are you gonna do, kill a walking dead
man? Kill me now before I die! I had been ready for a long,
long time. I was calm and had a certain freedom again,
a certain inner strength. My talisman became a stuffed
animal, a "boneless cocktail moose" I carried everywhere
I went. It may sound crazy, but this little furry thing saved
my tormented mind. I would cuddle it and tell people of the
amazing, magical powers it had to make me feel good. I
finally got the value of having something to love that would
not leave you and wouldn't talk back. Yeah, I was crazy
lost.

I met a man named Colin* who owned a shop on
Valencia. He had every unique and strange oddity a person
could want, with things stacked precariously on shelves all
the way up to the 20-foot-high ceiling. Colin helped me
complete the massive undertaking on Van Ness by working
with me to transport and unload truckload after truckload of
outgoing objects to "Put Out Night" locations, and helping
to load up new acquisitions and bring them back to use
or sell later. I also needed a sponsor to assist me with the
drugs I needed to complete this project.

It became an exchange of sorts. Colin sort of looked like
my dad, and I felt that God sent him into my life to heal
the rift of seething anger I had carried all these years. Colin
was gay, but not in the classic sense; he was more like a
hardworking lumberjack kind of guy. I began to rely on
him for his talents, and I helped him out with things he was
doing. He got me high and took care of a lot of my needs.
I felt mature around him, and with the drugs, I enjoyed our
times together. We comforted each other in the world of

Dog Eat Dog.

Colin came to stay with me in the Van Ness house, and we cleared a little space for a bed under the eve of the house where there used to be a bookshelf. Someone had made a little window there so you could see if the cops were coming. We hung precariously over the front of the house, and the bed was like a sounding board: You could hear every sound in the whole house. You could hear people walking up the stairs. I was living with dealer after dealer after dealer, and whether a man or a woman, I tried to have real clarity about what was going on. I tried to figure out how we could manage this strange environment with some honesty and integrity. It required a lot of eye contact with a dealer who might have 50 clients warning him. It was not my first time around the block, and they were all trying to protect their interests as well.

Then, a local newspaper called the Potrero Times published an article citing the goings-on at a particular Victorian squat on South Van Ness. The article was four columns long. Someone succinctly put into print what an abomination this place was and how it was the scourge of the neighborhood. It described the house, its occupants, and the clientele the house served. The writer had deep knowledge of the inner workings of the house and amplified the lifestyle in a very unflattering way. The writer said prostitutes worked right out in front of the house, but neglected to mention that they really were working up and down the whole block. Our house really was no worse than any other place on the street, but collectively we had our fingers in all the action going on in the area. It was the pulse of what people wanted to change about our society. But as proven so many times, if you close one down, a new one sprouts up somewhere else. The idea of change is to educate the people and give them opportunities to change their lifestyle and address their behaviors, not attack them as human beings.

Our block was a fertile environment – the untamed Wild West at its best. This was the street where everyone had problems; where the screams of sirens and ambulances would sear the silence in the dead of night, and the next day you would hear about gangland shootings or drive-by's that killed innocent bystanders. As for prostitution, these women did more for the neighborhood than any community policing could do. They knew everything that went on in the 'hood, and they knew everyone worth knowing, including some high-profile customers who would drive by to pick them up.

The Times went on to write that dangerous criminal types frequented the house and threatened innocent passers-by. In scorching words, it illuminated the drugs, the people who came to get them, the larger subculture that got the drugs to others, the crimes and stolen vehicles and motorcycles and bicycles. It wrote about the innocent young people who became cannon fodder and grist in this vicious cycle of destruction. In truth, these children had been thrown away by society long before they showed up on Van Ness, and they were much older than their actual ages would indicate. The article cited the constant amount of trash, health violations, gun-running, animal abuse, under-age kids, and on and on. It went on to cite the city's crusade to close down the house for all the city code violations.

After that, I was meeting with city officials, inspectors and police on a regular basis. I was a tenacious force to be dealt with, trying to give this house back to the community, not have it condemned or taken away from the owner. I received many other visitors, too – representatives the Hell's Angels sent incognito to threaten me. I laid out all the great effort everyone was putting into this, and how this would be one way we could improve our images with the government and the community.

When these shadowy figures would come and go, there

was never much said other than the ominous danger I was
in. I would know the answer by not being killed that day,
they said. I never knew if I would be killed when I left
the house. Many disgruntled past and current tenants had
friends in the shadiest and deadliest art of retribution. These
people would arrive, show me their guns, and give me the
cold, impersonal, detached report of their latest acts. They
didn't want to hurt me, they would say, but they would do
the deed if I wasn't listening. I would entertain them, and
we would throw knives at a board and get drunk or high.
I would then proceed to find out as much as I could about
them – who they were, if they were on parole, if I really
had a problem here. I would talk to whoever sent them and
try to negotiate for my life. They usually went right back
to prison on a parole violation, and I was momentarily safe
again.

I stashed my drugs and needles in walls with fresh mud
over them, so no one could find them. I always was without
a shirt and kept paint on the need tracks on my arms. After
I shot up the speed, I would put a dash of white paint on
the spot. It was hard to keep needles clean; I used bleach
to kill the hep C and hydrogen peroxide to kill the HIV. I
would send a tenant to the Needle Exchange to get us new
points. It was a laborious process just to shoot up with
a dull piece of metal that pierced my skin with stubborn
determination. Often, I would get Cotton Fever from
sucking up cotton fibers into the needle that would race
through my bloodstream. This would raise my temperature
to 104 degrees as my body tried to burn the fiber out of
my system. I would sit with dope sickness, hungry, tired,
worn out, and under so much pressure to finish the job. The
mental illness was now pervasive. I walked around like a
crazy man, rhythmically screaming, "Double-psychotic
paranoid schizophrenia!" over and over again.

It was about this time, in the spring of 1997, that the
Comet Hale-Bopp came into view in the night skies. I

bought a 6-inch reflector telescope from an undercover cop at a flea market. We joked about surveillance and the ways our lives had such confluence. I got a cheap camera stand and dropped the telescope immediately, cracking the front glass piece, drunk and high as usual. But I was amazed at the clarity of the telescope. The comet moved as a celestial body so fast that you could watch it for a minute; then, you would have to find it again in the night sky. We were live cavemen with a new tool. This comet was the one thing the house could enjoy as a family. We would get together and watch it out the window. It would shine, and all the talk for a few minutes would be of wonder and what-if's. There also was a partial lunar eclipse at that time, and we all went into the street and howled like wolves, to the alarm and dismay of the neighbors.

Pacman, the stone-cold lifer junkie, was still one of our tenants then. A heroin man, he also had great talents. He was a real craftsman and capable of deep compassion. Pacman was a breath of fresh air. We started to work together. He still had the girlfriend who was going stark-raving mad, and finally we arranged for her to go to her parents for a drug detox. He now had time to work for his heroin. As for the people who came over to score heroin from him and get high, they now had limits. We instituted the "Five Minutes to Shoot Up" rule. If anyone was in the bathroom for longer than five minutes, we would beat the door down to get them out of the fucking bathroom. If you couldn't find a vein, you weren't invited back to the house. We needed junkies who could do their business and free up the bathroom. This was one of the most vivid lifestyle improvements ever made at Van Ness.

The cops started coming around looking for people on parole and probation. I would greet them at the door and say, "The doors are always open for you. Come on in." Then, I would casually scream up the stairs at the top of my lungs, "The cops are here and they're coming upstairs

– hide the dope!" The cops would look at me, shaking their heads in disbelief. "Why did you do that?" they would ask. I would reply, "You know what kind of house this is. This is just to protect the tenants. Saying 'the doors are always open for you' is for all of our comfort."

You could hear the scrambling of nervous people, moving things and barricading doors, toilets flushing dope and needles – and then, an eerie silence. The cops would enter and try to talk to anyone they found in the hallways. Whatever tenants were calm enough to engage with the police without paranoia would tell them that whomever they wanted wasn't there. I would then give them a tour of the house and describe my plans for improvements. They would leave, and I would say, "Goodbye – the doors are always open for you."

By now, the building inspectors were working with me as I replaced any load-bearing walls that had been wrongfully removed. They would ask for permits, and I would tell William to get the ones I needed. We only got permits that we were forced to get. The plumbing inspectors were the most invasive. They had to get into every room, so I had to get tenants to open doors and let the inspectors see the bastardized plumbing and the makeshift sinks, toilets and bathtubs that people had put in their rooms or in the basement, as this was an old boardinghouse at the turn of the century. I would unhook all of the plumbing to the tubs and the illegal water lines to make it look like no one was using them. Eventually, I had to remove all of the fixtures, water lines and drains that were installed illegally and get the main ones up to code to keep the city from condemning the house.

We had to hire a professional electrician who tore the house up from bottom to top, installing all of the code electrical servicing for a four-story building. I then had to re-sheetrock the entire house where they cut into the walls to run the new wiring. I got help, and we filled all of the walls with trash and sheetrock waste from tearing the walls down. It soundproofed the house, as well as insulating it against the cold San Francisco weather. I had great experiences handling crews of people who were high on drugs and alcohol. I would get the materials for free wherever I could, and William would buy sheetrock, lumber, doors and windows whenever I couldn't find them at the recycling places. With all of this construction going on, the tenants trickled out one by one, and we emptied their rooms one by one, filled from top to bottom with trash.

I was now passing my weekly inspections by every department in the city, and one by one, they grew more comfortable that I was a man of my word and I would be able to complete the tasks before me. But I was wearing thin from working too much. My workaholism wasn't working anymore, and my obsessive-compulsive need to finish at any cost was wavering. I still had three obstinate, entitled tenants to move out. I started offering incentives, obliging, compromising and kissing ass to get them to move on. We got U-Hauls and offered to load them up and get them gone. This was a massive undertaking, as the amount of trash accumulated in these rooms was incredible. Donny and Tristan* were next in the eviction parade. They were a couple, and as we started to move things out, they took what they wanted and then feigned that the rest was precious and we would have to move it for them. Tristan claimed that a $10,000 ruby from a major heist in the city was lost somewhere in their room. She was a thief, the type who would steal your watch and stand there wearing it while you looked for it. She would ask helpful questions – did it have Roman numerals or marks for the hours? A metal or leather wristband? Wind-up or battery-powered? – while she laughed and turned away to check the time on her new watch. She knew how to play any fool. She had hustle and game.

I believe Tristan took the ruby, but at least it really got people interested in helping to clean the room. Everybody wanted to help. Things really got interesting when one helper after another began to discover their own stolen belongings among the trash-filled heap in Donny and Tristan's room. It became apparent that she had ripped off just about everybody for one thing or another. This came as no surprise to me. As we cleaned out the closet, we discovered two kittens at the bottom that had been crushed by heavy bags months earlier. When we lifted the heavy plywood configuration of a bed, we found the partially disintegrated corpse of an adult cat. The smell was horrible, and we just kept cleaning layer after layer of mess. We were all homeless, and I felt bad that this was what happened to people who lived for free off the system. Eventually, the system catches up with you and you feel the pain of your loss – you feel like an entitled victim. I paid the price for helping these friends move along in their lives.

The next person to go was Vissiel*. He was hard-core and would not budge – a hard case to crack. Finally, we came to a slow and dogged agreement to move him out. One day, he changed his mind about moving and wouldn't open the door. He yelled from the other side, "Matt I bought you a present!" I laughed. "Oh, yeah? What is it?" He told me to stand close to the door so he could show it to me – and then he fired a double-barrel shotgun into the door. He had a solid-core door with a 1-inch plywood board attached, and the force of the blast shook the door. In shock, I laughed, but I was shaken to my bones. I told him to open the fucking door and get his ass in gear, and thanks for the present. Nothing was going to stop me from finishing the job, at this point.

As I moved out his stuff, I saw the carnage of the blast and was reminded of my near miss. We filled the U-Haul with his belongings and were going to give him a ride to the destination of his choice, but as is often the case with homeless people squatting for free, they have no place to go. Full of angry-young-man syndrome and "the world owes me a living" entitlement issues, Vissiel grabbed the keys and took off with the U-Haul. William had to report it as stolen. We never learned what happened to that truck, but it never showed up back at the U-Haul place.

The last to go was the dealer in the basement. He was a great friend of mine, if you could call it that. He had helped out immensely with all of the tenants, and now it was his turn to go. We got him as together as we could, and out he went. I moved into the basement, and it was the last frontier to clean up and get up to code for the city. They dogged me every inch of the way. The inspectors kept coming and changing faces, new unbelievers who doubted that I could singlehandedly pull this off. It had been a year and a half of solid work, trying to make this squat into a fully furnished house of bedroom apartments for college students who would share the kitchen and bathrooms.

Slowly, we moved the students in. We had a Spanish student who was studying engineering, along with three Russian students who were fun to have conversations with. More and more people moved in, and I was suddenly the last junkie standing. I did not make the place look good with my disheveled appearance and sucked-up face. I didn't fit in with the new, demure collegiate feel of the house. There was still a lot of work to be done, but I didn't have the drive or inspiration anymore.

William and his wife finally had a stable enough home to pass the preliminary tests to become adoptive parents. Soon, they achieved their dream and adopted a brother and sister who were 5 and 9 years old. The kids had lived down the street with gangbangers; their birth mother was a prostitute. Even at their ages, they already knew every hustle and game to be played on suckers. The boy was already holding people up with knives and real-looking plastic guns. The cops warned him of the dangers of this type of behavior. He would steal William's wallet and take out money; if William begged him to tell where the wallet was, he just might get it back. As the years went on, the kids had a much better life than they would have, although they still dabbled in the nearby gang life.

As for me, I was no longer a benefit to the house. But how could I leave and hand it over to this man with no conditions? I now felt that William owed me his life, and I was at least part-owner of the house! Well, wasn't I?? Shouldn't I be compensated in some way? He still owed me money – how would I ever get that back? How could I trust him? William now had what he wanted, and I was of no use to him anymore. I had kicked his lazy ass all the way through the process, and his loyalty had worn thin. Besides, once he got rid of me, he was free and clear from this debacle. He could go about his business with a clean slate.

But I realized I had done all this hard work just to try to make up for the loss of Jane and my son. It was time for me to go. I was worn out, in bad health, tore up from the floor up. All this hard work had brought me nothing but self-will and maintenance of my drug habit. I now felt sneaky when I moved around the house, like I was unwanted, and none of the new tenants believed a word of what I had done. They looked at me with pity and disdain and wanted me removed from the premises for their own safety. I was not a pretty sight. I still got high and drank daily and was in frail health. I had young girls over who needed a place to stay for a few hours, but I trusted no one. I was a loose cannon. I used to hide my needles all over the house, and now I had a limited space in which to hide things.

The basement was very dark, and you could hear every noise from upstairs. William's wife would do her high-pitched screaming routine. I was not going to let this nut case ruin all the work I had done. As far as I was concerned, she had to shut up or get out. She was now the last thing that might scare the tenants away from making this thing work. William had to protect his wife's insane bantering, so I took it upon myself to make her stop. I screamed at her at the top of my lungs. I threw and broke almost everything I owned in the basement, trying to outdo her screams. The result of this was that the whole house concluded that I was the enemy, and word was that I had to go.

– 28 –

Salvation

My life in August 1998 was much the same as it had been for many years. I was in frail health, squatting in the basement of the Van Ness house I had rehabbed but where I was no longer welcome. A couple of former tenants, Karen and Trina*, stopped by to visit and do some drugs. I left them to do their business while I went out for a few hours. When I returned, I found some of my dull needles in one of the few hiding spots I had left, jammed one mercilessly into my vein, got high and thought no more of it.

A few days later, I felt even sicker. In my compromised state, I wondered if I had finally gotten AIDS. After lying sick in the dark, dank basement for a while, too sick to even shoot speed, I got up to use the bathroom. It was mid-day, but only a hint of light came in from the front window. I had mounted a light on a string right above my hammock in the middle of the room, which was filled with my treasure trove of junk and broken things. The trash was waist-high. I pulled the string and heard the switch click as electricity surged through the inadequate, dangerous wiring. Under the buzzing light, I made my way to the door, which was held shut by a spring. Ever striving to move undetected, even when I was ill, I gently, quietly opened and closed it.

I waded through more trash until I reached the outdoor toilet – a lean-to that had been tacked onto the exterior of the house. I closed the door and sat down to do my business. Winged insects danced around my head as I meted out my jurisdiction. "I am Lord of the Flies," I thought, laughing harshly to myself. Getting up, I pushed the lean-to's door open and turned to inspect my work. The stool in the water was whitish.

I was thunderstruck. I knew from my days as a nurse's aide that white stool was a symptom of hepatitis. I also knew that hepatitis and HIV tended to travel together. I had dodged both for decades, always believing I was special. I was the "good one," the indestructible "gutter layman" who was strong and good-looking and always made sure my part of the street was clean. Had I contracted HIV, too? I kicked, cursed and screamed. This couldn't be happening to me. I went back to the basement and got very drunk and very high on speed and marijuana. Then I decided to hunt down the perpetrators.

I went from one SRO to the next, looking for Karen and Trina. At the fourth place I checked, I found them. They were in a rented room, drinking beer, smoking cigarettes, and doing drugs with several other people. This SRO was like all the rest, furnished with a bed, a chair, a sink, and a dim light. Clothes and trash were all over the place, and it reeked not only of drugs, but of exhaust from the buses passing by outside. Everyone was coyly clamoring to win the dealer's favor and thereby receive his coveted dope. Trina sat across the room, smoking and talking.

"Can I talk to you for a minute?" I called out, striving not to draw the others' attention. Trina stepped over clothes, junk and people until she stood in front of me. I tried to start out cool and reassuring. If I gave her any reason to think I was angry, she might not give me the information I so desperately wanted.

"When you guys were over at the squat, did you happen to use my needles?"

"Nooooo," she said, looking as shocked as if I'd accused her of stomping on a box of kittens. "No, no, no. No way."

I struggled to remain calm. "Did you happen to – find my needles in the kitchen?"

"No, Matt – no," she said resolutely.

"You didn't find my needles above the water heater? Behind the wall?" I said, my words faster, louder and more desperate. "I really need to know!"

"No, I didn't – I didn't," she said.

"Just tell me," I said, my voice cracking now. "I need to know. I need to know so I can take care of myself. I've been kind to you, and this is serious. Just tell me – did you find my fucking needles or not??"

Trina stared at me blankly, as if waiting for me to give up. Tears now filled my eyes, and she seemed to take pity on me.

"All right," she said flatly. "We used your needles. Yes. It was us. Sorry."

In truth, Trina and her friend probably had nothing to do with my hep C. More likely I was infected much earlier. It could have happened as far back as when I was 13 years old in Dover, shooting heroin for the first time with the Pagans, or hundreds of times through the years after that. But I didn't know that until much later. So, I went back to Van Ness and crawled into my cellar hammock. I felt angry. I felt betrayed, hurt. I experienced pure desolation, and I wanted to die. I was disgusted that I had finally been compromised. I got as high as I could, but not even the drugs could prevent me from realizing that, after 30 years of abusing substances, it was time to stop. And not just because I was out of money. This time, I would have to quit for good.

With no guidance or support, I went about it the only way I knew how. I quit drugs first, using malt liquor as a substitute for methadone so I wouldn't go mad. I lay in that hammock in the basement for the next 12 days, drinking King Cobra, microwaving Ramen noodles, and trying to stay asleep. No speed, no weed, no heroin. No drugs. I was so weak, I couldn't move except to go to the bathroom or stumble to the corner store for more beer. I was totally dehydrated. Rosacea consumed my face, and the area around my nostrils and hairline were flaming red with irritation, as were the spots where I'd burned myself with tars years earlier. My right ear, which had been partially torn off in a long-ago bicycle accident, looked blue. With all this, I looked to myself like an AIDS patient covered with Kaposi's sarcoma.

The speed crawled out of my skin like acid. I was driven crazy with formication, or the sensation of bugs crawling all over my body and biting me. This phenomenon, also called Delusional Parasitosis, can be caused by drug addiction and mental delusions. The speed sweats out all the healthy body oils, and then the poisons from the speed leach out of the skin. I couldn't tell which were the fake fleas and which were the real ones. I had paranoia about this most of my adult life from being homeless and staying in bug-infested environments, but I always stayed so medicated, I could detach from it and just assume I was crazy on drugs. Now, I was a raw, exposed nerve ending, feeling everything with maddening acuteness, with no coping mechanisms or survival strategies.

I would wake up frightened about my son, and now I could feel this painful reality with no drugs to dull the grief. I didn't think I could get help from government services because I'd been tearing up notices from the IRS and drinking my worries away for so many years, I was sure they were hunting me down by now. I was panicked about my hepatitis C, but I could never go to San Francisco General Hospital and wait for seven hours in line to be seen. I could not hang out for fear of getting lice or scabies from sitting on the chairs in the waiting room. I was obsessive, compulsive and paranoid, and I ran through the whole scenario in my head. If I went to the hospital, I would lie boldly to the nurses about my perceived mental problems, but my euphemisms, incoherent parables and tangential speech would give me away. I would think I was holding a conversation with the staff, but they would see through the cryptic illusion of my banter. They would shove me to the side, move me through their overwhelmed system as fast as possible, and give me four or five medications for my perceived illness that I would not take because of my paranoia and fears of the American Medical Association.

After all that, I would realize that I was devastatingly lonely, and I had used up all of the options that would have been healthy. The only options I had left were drug-seeking behavior, and those now would destroy my hep-C-compromised liver and kill me.

My sleep patterns had been so abnormal for 20 years that I didn't have a normal sleep pattern to return to. I would squirm at night for five or six hours, and then be the walking dead during the day, yawning loudly for five or six hours until I needed a nap. I cried at the drop of a pin, and then rage and want to kill someone if they didn't listen. Still feeling perpetually tired and as if my body had completely shut down, I walked to the fruit stands in the Mission. I would find the fresh fruit that had been thrown away because it was too ripe to sell, gorge and fill up on that, and then go back home to sleep. I ate raw ginger and raw garlic to build up my immune system. After eating two or three whole, raw cloves, I would sweat it out, and people would give me plenty of room.

I started to feel like I needed something to replace the emptiness. I had accessed a vulnerable and sensitive part of myself, and I didn't know what to do with that. I would try to jerk off to magazines to feel like I was worth something. I became aware that I was grunting and muttering under my breath, living inside a world where others were not welcome. I didn't trust anyone, and my old drug-taking friends just kept saying all I needed was a hit of speed or some liquid courage, and I'd be back to my old self again.

Someone suggested that I go to an Alcoholics Anonymous meeting. I didn't really know what these were, so I showed up at one in the neighborhood. I recognized the people in the meeting as men and women I'd seen standing outside, smoking and talking, during my aimless wanderings through the city. I always thought these people were part of some strange organization. I thought Narcotics Anonymous was an organization where people met to snitch out dealers and bust people. I couldn't believe these people could really be this happy. I hated the meetings, the smelly cigarette-smoking and coffee-drinking, and the bullshit I perceived. I took everyone's inventory and judged each one as they spoke. I thought I could go to meetings and meet a nice woman, and I'd be all right.

I went back to the Van Ness house, feeling unbearably raw and sensitive, and I tried to get into a detox. The person who answered the phone said I had to stop taking drugs AND stop drinking to get into these places. I was so pissed off that I had to stop on my own. "Why do I need these people?" I thought. "If I could stop on my own, that's all I need besides a job, right??" I couldn't cope, and I reacted to every little thing with anger and animosity. I would return to sexualizing my anger, stress, frustration and resentment by jerking off to pornography.

While all that was happening, I did somehow manage to stop drinking, and I finally got a date to show up at the Salvation Army Detox. They wanted me to call every day and demonstrate for my place. I was stunned that I had to do so much work just to get some help. While I waited, I began my endless night wanderings around the city again, occasionally staying at my friend Cindy's.

The day finally arrived for me to report to the detox. On my way, I was so excited that I thought I better have one more beer, if it was going to be my last. I bought a 40-ounce King Cobra malt liquor and drank it right before I went in. I hadn't drunk in weeks, and it got me drunk fast. I went to toss the bottle in the debris box right outside of the Salvation Army Detox, and I noticed a little microphone sticking out of the papers in the trash. In my delusional belief that I was being watched, I started looking around for surveillance cameras. The voices I was so used to hearing in my head were telling me firmly, "Don't do this," as I walked unsteadily toward the door, with all the adrenaline of a crime in progress. Scared and vulnerable, I walked in and sat down.

The Salvation Army staff asked me if I'd had anything to drink, and they laughed when I said I hadn't. Then, they put me in a room with 11 other men detoxing off drugs and alcohol. I think I was there for about 10 days, but I couldn't judge time very well. Right from the start, I felt perceived threats from just about every single thing that happened. Someone stole my slippers; someone else stole my bedspread. I was ready to kill anyone for anything. I should have tattooed, "Matt Doesn't Play Well with Others!" on my forehead. I was worse there than anyplace else in my life. I felt like a caged animal. I was dealing with brain-dead junkies and street winos who didn't even know where they were or how they got there. I would get so angry, I would want to beat their senseless, babbling asses into the ground. It was like a zoo in the back when no counselors were watching us.

They really needed to know how angry and frustrated I was. I threatened them, and they laughed in my face. I hit a wall so hard with my knuckles right by their heads, and they laughed as I writhed in pain. The punch tore my skin, revealing the flesh on my knuckles. I was in real pain, without drink or drug. I had to feel this pain and not get caught, or I would be thrown into the streets again. I finally had to mentally shut down completely and go into a zombie-like state, or I would not make it. I was given some sedatives to calm me down and help me sleep. I would have a few blissful hours of sleep, and then I would awake to the nightmare again.

We were made to wear flip-flops, a liberation from socks that I normally would have enjoyed. But in this place, my roomies had fungus, Athlete's Foot, rotting flesh, purplish splotches on their lower extremities from bad circulation, and gout-like features on their legs from exposure to the elements. One guy shared with me that he would eat, sleep and shit just a few inches from his cardboard box, and he did not like the idea that he had to walk to the bathroom instead of soiling his pants. He was in the last stages of cirrhosis, and he just didn't care about living anymore. He had dementia and was one of the walking dead.

I was in a dorm-like room with men who farted constantly and had sores, scabies, lice and fungus. They were toothless, and pyorrhea and gingivitis flowed freely through the air when they would yell and scream incoherently. The smell of abscesses from infections oozed throughout the room, and one wino in a wheelchair had infections that would not heal on the stub where his leg used to be. Some men had the DTs from alcohol, and some were coming down off heroin. I was just a mental nutcase who didn't think I belonged in this place. There was a general lack of social skills, with guttural utterances, theft of anything that wasn't nailed down, and guys sleeping wherever they fell. After soiling one bed, they would just move and fall asleep in another.

I was ready to yell, scream and violate these nasty, grossed-out, stinky-ass motherfuckers. These bums had been rippin' and runnin', lyin' and stealin', sleeping on the streets as winos, beggin' for money, and they didn't really know or care where they were. After five days when the drugs and alcohol wore off, then the nasty personality disorders came out into the light, and we had ourselves a real problem with these entitled assholes, of whom I was one. I was a paranoid sleeper and woke at the slightest noise. These guys not only talked in their sleep, they burped, farted, moaned and groaned, pissing in their beds or being incontinent. Some would be in real alcoholic withdrawal, and they would go into convulsions. I learned that I was very quiet and protective of my space, and when I perceived the ominous threat of someone crossing my safety boundaries, I would react like a crazy person with Turret's. I would yell, scream, threaten and call for help – Wolf! Wolf! Wolf! The staff treated me like a caged animal. They had seen it all before.

I entered the detox weighing 140 pounds, and in 10 days, I gained 15 pounds. I ate anything they put before me, and I ate between meals and snacked. I didn't realize how hungry I was. I had gotten used to just shooting speed, and food didn't matter. I would drink to cover the hunger, 'cause I had to have my buzz on before I ate.

The staff started holding AA and NA meetings in our detox area, and I finally started to get a glimmer of hope. These people talked about their lives – how they started where we were and made successful lives from the wreckage of their pasts. Now they put before me an opportunity. If my behavior improved, I could become a client at a place called Harbor Lights, a program in another building on these grounds. I started to "act as if" and tried to show sincerity and stop reacting to every little thing that happened. I had a little taste of sobriety, and I had nothing to lose. The alternative to what they offered was becoming homeless again, walking the streets right outside these walls that I had walked like a zombie for years and years.

After several days of detox, I was allowed to go outside

to a fenced-in area and breathe the fresh air. It felt great. I
looked up and was actually able to see the blue sky with
azure colors and the intensity of the sunlight beaming
through the fog as it drifted by. I felt the chilled, fresh air as
it filled my lungs to capacity. I was alive, and I had hope.
The others were smoking and doing what they did on all
those street corners to survive – those bullshit stories and
machinations to keep the stolid belief systems alive. But
I had found my own freedom – it was outside. It was real,
and I really loved it. It was brand-new and bright. I felt that
my freedom of walking more than 20 feet in a fenced-in
area was close at hand.

This is where I began, crawling through my wreckage,
and into my recovery.

Epilogue

As I sit here today, I have 15 years clean and sober. How I got that way and have stayed that way is a story in itself, one which I might write down someday. I can't say it was easy. In fact, in many ways, it was harder than many of the life-threatening adventures I share in this book. But I did it, and continue to do it, one day at a time.

In my new life, I have a loving, brilliant, beautiful wife to share my days with. I own a home with fruit trees, a hot tub, an art studio, and a spectacular view. I display and sell my artwork all over the San Francisco Bay Area. I hold a certificate in Drug and Alcohol Counseling, and work with addicts and alcoholics as a Recovery Coach to help them stay clean and sober. I cleared the Hep C virus from my system with a challenging year on interferon/ribavirin treatment. People no longer run away when they see me coming; instead, I am welcomed by friends and colleagues who like and respect me. And I wrote this book.

I tell you about my life today not so that you will envy me, or because I think I am somehow better than those who are still suffering out there, but so that you will understand what I know to be true. Every human being has value. Every human being has promise. There is hope for even the lowest of the low, as I once was. Don't give up on anyone, and especially not on yourself.

Matthew Kowalski
August 2013

Acknowledgements

First, I would like to thank my father, Lester Kowalski. I know he did everything the best way he could, and he still lives his life with the driving force that I have been blessed with. Today, he is my best friend, and I love him very much.

Thank you also to my stepmother, Alice, for being a solid, loving influence in my father's life and mine, and to my brother Mark and sister Kat for never giving up on me.

I thank my loving wife, Kat, for every day and every second we cherish together, for every precious breath we consume with loving kindness and radical acceptance of the world as it is right now.

I thank C.J. Hayden for her incredible friendship, guidance, business coaching, perseverance, belief in me, and support and help with this book. I am now in business as a Recovery Coach, helping others to thrive, succeed and be abundant with life on life's terms.

Thanks to my extended family – Dwight and Linda Ost; James Kimba Anderson, Symon Michael and Larry Heaton; Dino Santamaria; Francisco Gamez; Debra Tremain; David Kroziere, and Scott Martin. There are many more people to whom I owe thanks for saving my life. I remember you all.

I would like to thank Walden House in its entirety for all the behavioral modification I received to be the incredible man I have become. "Each One Teach One."

Thanks to Tamara Tucker for being my therapist in those raw early years.

Thanks to Georgeana Roussos and Adam Kobos, the SSI lawyers who got me on the road to recovery.

Thanks to "Friendly Dave" Herninko for getting me straight with the IRS.

Thanks to the countless masses who have helped me in my recovery in the 12-Step community with alcohol, drugs, and sex and love issues.

Thanks to Dee-Dee Stout for her devotion to Harm Reduction and Motivational Conversations. Without her, I would not be the skillful addiction specialist I am today.

I would love to honor Pema Chodron's teachings and loving voice, guiding me over and over again with the lasting tenets of peace within and how to honor and free this world from suffering and the root of suffering.

I am grateful for the disciplines of Non-Violent Communication, which taught me that if I speak in a way that others can hear, I am more likely to get my needs met.

About the Author

Matthew Kowalski is a recovery coach, certified addiction counselor and motivational speaker who has worked with recovering addicts in both clinical and 12-step settings for the past 14 years. He is an abstract artist who creates multi-media works in his own Radical Relief style. A professional multi-instrument musician, Matt played drums and guitar and sang with dozens of bands in San Francisco in the 1980s. He continues to play in the East Bay.

He and his wife, Kathryn Sterbenc, reside in Oakland, Calif., where they actively participate in building a healthier community. In accordance with their motto – "Oakland: It's a hometown, not a crime scene" – they invest considerable time and energy in Oakland's violence prevention and public library programs.